100
Safest
Investments
for Retirement

By
Kevin Pilot

CAREER PRESS
180 Fifth Avenue
P.O. Box 34
Hawthorne, NJ 07507
1-800-CAREER-1
201-427-0229 (outside U.S.)
FAX: 201-427-2037

100 SAFEST INVESTMENTS FOR RETIREMENT
ISBN 1-56414-071-7, $14.95
Cover design by A Good Thing, Inc.
Printed in the U.S.A by Book-mart Press

To order this title by mail, please include price as noted above, $2.50 handling per order, and $1.00 for each book ordered. Send to: Career Press, Inc., 180 Fifth Ave., P.O. Box 34, Hawthorne, NJ 07507

Or call toll-free 1-800-CAREER-1 (Canada: 201-427-0229) to order using VISA or MasterCard, or for further information on books from Career Press.

Important: While much careful thought and depth of research have been devoted to the writing of this book, all content is to be viewed as general information only and should not be construed as actual legal, accounting or financial advice of a personal nature. The ideas, suggestions and general concepts are subject to federal, state and local laws and statutes. The ever-changing economic, political and international environment may well demand reinterpretation of some or all of the concepts presented herein. The reader is urged to consult competent legal, accounting and tax advisors regarding all legal and personal financial decisions. This book is not meant to be utilized as a substitute for their advice. The information in this book has been obtained from what is believed to be reliable sources. The author does not, however, warranty their accurateness.

Library of Congress Cataloging-in-Publication Data

Pilot, Kevin, 1964-
    100 safest investments for retirement / by Kevin Pilot.
        p. cm.
    Includes index.
    ISBN 1-56414-071-7 : $14.95
    1. Retirement income--United States--Planning. 2. Investments--United States.
3. Retirement--United States--Planning. 4. Retirees--United States--Finance, Personal.
I. Title. II. Title: One hundred safest investments for retirement.
HG179.P553 1993
332.024'01--dc20
                                                                    93-22391
                                                                        CIP

Acknowledgments

To Lois and Dylan,
whose patience made this large undertaking possible.

Contents

Chapter 1

Overcoming Retirement's "Catch-22"

In 1955 Joseph Heller wrote the book *Catch-22* and coined an expression that denotes a no-win situation. Everyone faces a financial "catch-22" at retirement. Conventional wisdom demands that all savings be put into risk-free liquid investments, since there is little chance of recouping a lifetime's savings.

For the past decade, it's been easy to earn a good return on a liquid investment. Thanks to the government-subsidized savings and loan business, both CDs and Treasury bills have offered returns of 8 percent or better, without any risk to principal. As the savings and loan debacle comes to a close and the Federal Reserve Bank cuts interest rates to prop up a slumping economy, the decision becomes more difficult.

And therein lies retirement's "catch-22." Although preservation of principal is important, few can afford to live on a 4-percent investment return. And what about purchasing power? If the earnings of the average short-term investment were reinvested, the income would barely keep up with inflation, let alone provide a comfortable return. Investments that preserve principal and provide liquidity do not pay much or protect purchasing power. Investments that protect purchasing power or provide higher rates of return, on the other hand, do not provide liquidity.

To better illustrate, take the following examples. A mythical investor, Mr. Smith, retires in 1959 and invests $100,000 in a Certificate of Deposit (CD). In 1988, he's earning 7.5 percent. Inflation, however, has averaged approximately 2 percent per year since 1959. Every dollar of income he receives is now only worth 59 cents (in 1959 dollars). His principal remains intact but he has to spend twice as much to maintain his lifestyle. On top of the decline in purchasing power, when he renews his CD in 1991, the rate is only 4 percent, a 50-percent cut in income.

Hedging against inflation requires an investor to forego preservation of principal. An investment needs to rise in value in order to keep up with inflation. Income also needs to increase. Unfortunately, what goes up...

Mr. Smith decides to invest his $100,000 in a conservative stock mutual fund. The income is initially $3,400 a year but then grows to more than $40,000. The principal grows to more than $1 million. A good investment? Maybe. If Mr. Smith invested his $100,000 in 1973, his investment would have been worth $92,330 in 1982. The income would have been $4,200 per year. A CD paid 14 percent in 1982 or $14,000 per year. Preserving principal means risking a deterioration of purchasing power. Preserving purchasing power means taking a lot of risk. Or does it?

The many faces of risk

Most investors associate risk with fluctuation in principal. Risk can take many other forms. If interest rates fall, investment income will drop drastically. Inflation always looms, threatening to eat away at purchasing power. An accident or illness can wipe out a retirement nest egg. Risk generally takes four forms:

1. Risk to principal or investment risk
2. Interest-rate risk
3. Inflation risk
4. Catastrophic risk

1. Risk to principal. Risk to principal takes two forms, *systematic risk* and *nonsystematic risk*. Systematic risk is market risk. If the stock market drops drastically, and an investment falls, the loss is associated with systematic risk. Market risk also applies to bond markets, real estate markets and any other type of market "system." Nonsystematic risk comes from individual choices of investments. A bank account has greater security than a junk bond. The backing of the U.S. government secures the bank account. The junk bond, on the other hand, is basically an IOU from a company that is already financially strapped.

The term *credit risk*, a form of systematic risk, usually implies the risk of default or of a company not paying its obligations. Even the strongest companies can be whipsawed by another type of nonsystematic risk, market risk. AT&T may be an extremely solid company but that doesn't prevent the stock's price from changing if the company has a bad quarter. Market risk applies to the fluctuation in the price that people are willing to pay to purchase a specific investment on the open market.

2. Interest-rate risk. A government bond is purchased at 8 percent and interest rates rise to 12 percent. The investor is earning 4 percent less than the going rate but...it's still a government bond, right? The market value of bonds moves in the opposite direction of interest rates. If the investor sold the bond, it would be worth less than what he or she paid. Why? The bond exchange is like any other marketplace: supply and demand determine price.

Interest rates also affect short-term investments. If our investor decided not to invest in long-term bonds but in a short-term CD, interest-rate risk would take another form. An investor may put his nest egg into six-month CDs at the local bank, yielding 8 percent. This would seem to be a safe investment, since the principal is guaranteed and the money is relatively liquid. In six months the CD rates drop to 4 percent. The investor's income is cut in half. Short-term investments can be just as volatile as long-term investments. These two types of volatility comprise interest-rate risk.

3. Inflation risk. Rising prices are guaranteed to undermine any fixed-income investment. As inflation grows, so should retirement income. Few fixed-income investments do grow. For example, if a couple retired in 1970 with $24,000, they could have lived quite comfortably. A typical house in Southern California sold for just $40,000, a new Cadillac

$10,000, and dinner would run about $8 for two at a modestly priced restaurant. In 1980, the same house cost $140,000, the Cadillac $18,000, and the meal $15. By 1990, the house cost a whopping $250,000, the Cadillac $28,000, and the dinner $22. The pension check, if un-adjusted for inflation (as many private pensions are) would remain at $24,000 per year. As time went on, this once happily retired couple would have to cut back more and more.

Social Security and some pensions are adjusted for inflation. Personal sav-ings are not. Inflation has averaged a little over 4 percent in the past 20 years. Some costs have risen even more. Med-ical care has soared by 20 percent per year in the past 10 years. Inflation may be down, as many claim, but it's cer-tainly not out. A low inflation rate of 2 to 3 percent can still whittle away at a fixed income. At a 3-percent inflation rate, for example, $1 in purchasing power declines to 55 cents in 20 years.

4. Catastrophic risk. Catastrophic risk is usually associated with sickness, such as Alzheimer's disease. Medical science enables us to live longer, but at the cost of having to provide for spe-cialized care for a longer time. The aver-age stay in a nursing home is over two years, often at costs of $3,000 a month or more. The most difficult type of risk to foresee, catastrophic risk usually has devastating effects. A couple's life sav-ings can easily be exhausted in a few months as a result of medical costs, which the surviving spouse or family is often forced to pay. A large (very, very large) cash reserve can help, but the risk remains. Insurance often provides the only solution to this dilemma and other types of catastrophic risk such as law-

suits and accidents. Chapter 17 covers this in more detail.

At one time in our history, risk was a foreign word to the average retiree. Inflation was low, banks paid relatively high rates of interest, and bonds paid back their principal when they came due. The world has changed. Interest rates are no longer controlled, the U.S. dollar is no longer necessarily the safest currency in the world and the United States doesn't account for 60 percent of the world's economic activity. Being con-servative no longer means buying only bank CDs and bonds.

As the nature of the economy con-tinues to change, so do our investment options. There are over 10,000 mutual funds available today, compared to fewer than 1,000 in 1960. Government bonds are no longer only Treasury bonds but GNMAs, FNMAs, FHLMCs. Acro-nyms such as LYONs, TIGRs, CATs and COGRs add to the selection of govern-ment bonds. Junk bonds are no longer junk but "high-yielding, nonrated cor-porate obligations." And bankruptcy is no longer a corporate disgrace but a ploy to lower costs by breaking unions.

Nothing is as it appears. For a re-tired investor, it is not enough just to de-fine risk, or even to understand it. A strategy is needed to *defeat* it.

Prospering in today's economic en-vironment isn't as difficult as it first appears. Investing money may be more complicated than ever before, but there are four basic rules that can help pre-serve principal and yet hedge against inflation.

Rule 1: Diversify

Anyone who has ever invested in stocks knows this rule. Don't put all your eggs in one basket. Spreading investments among different issues and industries limits the risk of any particular event wiping out a retirement nest egg. Studies on stock market performance have shown that holding seven or more individual stocks in separate industries provides the optimal amount of protection against individual stock declines. But what about other investments?

The diversification rule also applies to different types of investments or investment classes. A portfolio made up entirely of six-month CDs, for example, would not fluctuate in value but would not lock in a high rate of return if interest rates should drop. Long-term bonds provide a guarantee of income, but don't hedge against inflation. Utility stocks provide a good hedge against inflation but can be affected by changes in the stock market. Each class of investment, by itself, has a specific risk, but when combined together, these investments create a portfolio that would protect the overall investment in a variety of different economic circumstances. When one class does poorly, another should compensate. Here are some of the investment classes to choose from:

- Short-term fixed (T-bills, bank CDs, money markets)
- Long-term fixed (government bonds, corporate bonds, municipal bonds, annuities)
- Domestic stocks (U.S. companies)
- Foreign stocks
- Foreign bonds
- Real estate
- Precious metals

A mixture of three or more of these investment classes drastically reduces the amount of risk taken when investing. Take an example from history, the period from 1973 to 1983. In 1973 and 1974, the performance of the stock market was abysmal, yet "hard" investments such as gold and real estate did quite well. In the late 1970s, interest rates rose, causing long-term bonds to plummet, but short-term investments and gold did very well. In the early '80s, short-term rates began to fall, as did gold, but long-term bonds and stocks took off.

Investing in a variety of investment types does not eliminate risk entirely, but it should drastically reduce risk. When one market performs badly, another almost always does well.

Rule 2: Look for safety

A wise broker once told me, "If it sounds too good to be true, it probably is." The fact that this advice isn't especially original doesn't take away from its truth. Higher returns come about in only two ways in any market: by taking more risk or by extending maturity (which also takes more risk). If government bonds are paying 9 percent and someone calls with a bond that is paying 12 percent, it probably isn't a government bond (or at least not the same kind you are comparing it to).

You need to fully understand the risks before making any investment. Then, you can decide whether the return warrants the risk. Take the example of bonds. If a government bond is yielding 9 percent and a high-risk corporate bond is yielding 9.5 percent, the extra half-percent probably isn't worth the risk. If a five-year government bond, on the other hand, yields 9 percent and a five-year bank CD yields 10.5 percent, the bank CD is a better buy. Since the

CD has only slightly more risk than the government bond, the added uncertainty is more than compensated for by the higher return.

Risk and reward are measured only on the most subjective basis. Different people have different risk tolerances. Individual junk bonds and penny stocks are best suited to only the wealthiest and most experienced retired investors. Although safety and risk management consume a great deal of thought when constructing a retirement plan, this is by no means the end of the planning process. After all, it's not what you earn or preserve that counts, but how much income you get to keep.

Rule 3: Avoid taxes

The 1986 Tax Reform Act lowered tax rates but it did not lower the amount of tax paid by retired citizens. Since few retired Americans have large mortgages or any dependents, they usually can't take advantage of the two largest deductions available. Fortunately, investments such as tax-free bonds, annuities and life insurance still provide tax-sheltered income for those who take advantage of them.

Just because an investment is tax-advantaged, however, doesn't mean that everyone should buy it. If two investments are available, one yielding 6.5 percent tax-free and the other 9 percent taxable, all factors being equal, which is better? It depends. Someone in a 40-percent tax bracket would have to earn 10.8 percent in a taxable investment to put as much money in his or her pocket as the tax-free investment would. A person in the 15-percent tax bracket would only have a 7.64-percent taxable equivalent yield. In other words, a taxable investment earning 7.64 percent would put as much money into his or her pocket as a tax-free investment bringing in 6.5 percent..

Obviously, those in the lower tax bracket benefit from the *taxable* investment, those in the higher tax bracket benefit from the tax-free investment. Tax-advantaged investments are purchased every day without consideration to tax bracket. In spite of the displeasure of paying taxes, which comes over most of us around April 15, tax-advantaged investments are not for everyone.

Purchasing stocks and real estate that appreciate can also offer tax-deferred growth, at least until profits are taken. A growing federal deficit and ballooning state deficits insure that the problem of taxation will probably get worse before it gets better. Careful tax planning can be essential to a successful retirement plan.

Rule 4: Insure against catastrophic risk

Even the best-laid investment plans can be destroyed by an unexpected event. An illness, a lawsuit or an accident can force the liquidation of assets that would have otherwise provided retirement income. An adequate cash reserve provides one safeguard against unexpected catastrophes. Even though cash reserves tend to rise after retirement, certain events, such as hospitalization, can wipe out all but the largest passbook savings accounts. Liquidity also costs an investor lost income, making it undesirable to be overly liquid.

Insurance provides the best protection against this type of risk, even medical risk. Long-term health care insurance, a relatively new entrant into the large number of insurance products, is an increasingly necessary part of every retiree's portfolio. Along with standard liability insurance, and health insurance, long-term health care coverage allows an investor to free up more money from low-paying liquid accounts and put it to work producing income or growth. Medigap and other Medicare supplements can also help reduce medical costs after retirement.

Putting it all together: The investment pyramid

While some of the pyramids of Egypt took almost 100 years to complete, building an investment pyramid is hardly an arduous task—30 minutes and a pencil and paper will easily accomplish the job. A pyramid, as you know, is wide on the bottom and narrow at the top. Imagine your investment portfolio as a pyramid. All of the money you have to invest has to fit within the pyramid. The pyramid is divided into sections (see the illustration below). The largest section of the pyramid, the bottom, is where an investor places his or her safest investments, such as bank CDs, government bonds and bank accounts. Each section above the bottom becomes progressively smaller and includes investments with greater risk.

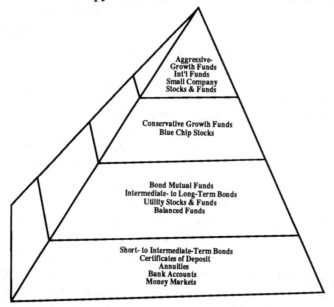

Everyone's pyramid is different because everyone has a different risk tolerance. An older investor's pyramid is generally wider and flatter than a younger investor's, meaning that the portfolio entails less risk.

Yet, even the widest and flattest of pyramids should have room on the top for some type of inflation hedge—stocks or real estate, for example.

Using this simple concept, you not only have a blueprint for diversification, but you've built in a planned limit for risk, which increases the relative safety of your portfolio. Take the time to draw an investment pyramid, using the concepts in this chapter, before you go on to Chapter 2. Having a basic blueprint is the first step in establishing your goals and creating a financial plan after retirement.

Chapter 2

Setting Goals

Imagine trying to take a vacation without an itinerary, airline tickets or hotel reservations. Or planning a wedding without reserving a church, making a guest list or ordering a wedding gown. While few of us would ever neglect to carefully plan for even the smallest dinner party, thousands of people invest their life savings without any plan in mind.

Take the example of retired aerospace worker George Thompson. George is retiring from a major aerospace firm after 20 years. He's been planning his retirement for the past year, and allocating his days between golf, sailing and an occasional trip in his newly acquired motor home with his wife, Jane. As an engineer, George has always been meticulous about managing his time. Every week for the next year is planned out almost to the hour.

About four weeks into his new routine, a check arrives in the mail. The proceeds of his retirement plan arrives right when he expects it to. "$340,000!" exclaims Jane. "What should we do with this?" "I don't know," says George. "My broker called yesterday with some kind of new thing that sounded pretty good. Let's put it in that."

As exaggerated as this example may seem, most investors act like George, especially when they suddenly come into an unusually large sum of money like a pension plan disbursement. Most people don't know what to do with a large sum of money. They feel uncomfortable even writing a check with more than four zeros. Financial decisions are made in haste, often with little regard to value and lifestyle decisions. The old adage describes it as "the cart pulling the horse." A successful investor will evaluate his or her needs first, and then look at the resources, choosing the course of action accordingly.

What exactly are "lifestyle" and "value" decisions? In a nutshell, lifestyle decisions involve how you want to live your life after retirement. What do you want to do with your time? Where do you want to live? Value decisions determine how you prioritize each of these lifestyle wants, based on your available resources. Since very few of us are able to have everything we want, prioritizing allows us to choose what's most important to us.

Lifestyle decisions

Where to live. Selling the homestead and moving to Arizona may be attractive to some, while staying close to home the only choice for others. Other considerations are income taxes (some states are income-tax free), housing costs, quality of life (weather, crime,

11

culture), health care facilities and proximity to friends and relatives. While many retirees flee to the so-called "sunshine states," an equal number choose to be close to what they've become familiar and comfortable with. Staying in your home town, however, doesn't always mean living in the same house. A four-bedroom Cape Cod with a half-acre front lawn and apple orchard may not be everyone's idea of a restful retirement. Downsizing to a smaller dwelling or hiring extra help is another choice to consider. Whether to live in a retirement community and selecting that retirement community are yet other decisions best made well in advance of retirement.

Live it up? Yesterday's Norman Rockwell image of a gray-haired lady rocking on the porch and knitting socks for her grandson couldn't be further from the picture of today's active, healthy retiree. Tennis, golf or even parasailing are just as likely to occupy a typical day at some retirement communities as bridge or lawn bowling. While some retirees like to see a show and have dinner, others are content to work in their gardens and watch a little television. Different lifestyles require different resources, both physical and financial. Understanding how you would best enjoy your retirement allows appropriate planning.

Retirement or semi-retirement. Part-time employment is increasingly popular after retirement, regardless of financial status. More and more men and women continue working past retirement age, for personal fulfillment as well as for economic reasons. Self-employment, especially consulting in a field of expertise, has become especially popular. But individuals who are planning

to semi-retire, or work part-time after retirement, should be aware that this can have several consequences, including reduction of Social Security benefits and taxes.

Travel. If you've ever sat at work in the middle of a particularly difficult day, dreaming about standing in front of the Great Pyramid, or lying on a beach in Bora Bora, you may equate retirement with travel. Maybe your dream is to ride across America on a motorcycle, or travel leisurely in a motor home. Whether planning a world cruise or a trip to another state, you should consider your travel desires when you're setting retirement goals.

Children and family. Aside from spending time with family, parents and grandparents may wish to offer assistance in financial ways as well. Helping a child buy a first home, supporting a grandson in college, or supplying a little cash from time to time to an impoverished niece are just a few examples of goals that should be planned for.

Contingencies. In spite of how well we've planned, something unforeseen always emerges that frustrates the best-laid plans. An unexpected illness, a family emergency or an exceptionally poorly performing investment can all drastically alter a well-conceived retirement plan. Back-up plans should be a part of any goal-setting process. Emergency funds for rainy days, alternative choices in lifestyle, and investment diversification and flexibility are examples of contingencies that can counteract unexpected events.

Since few emergencies are unexpected, but rather the apex of a series of events leading up to a conclusion, some common sense can save a lot of future trouble. For example, if you have a heart condition that has gotten progressively worse, you may change your retirement spot from a secluded cabin in Montana to a more populated area where you have access to better health care. Planning for the worst will eliminate most negative surprises.

Value decisions

Value decisions prioritize lifestyle choices. Which is more important—living in an upscale home on the beach or being able to take the two-year world cruise that you've always dreamed of? Perhaps you'll have the resources to accomplish both goals. But if not, making choices will be necessary. Ranking each lifestyle goal before reviewing resources allows you to choose what you value most, and accomplish those things that are most important first.

Evaluating your resources

Most dreams of retirement are far removed from the reality that sets in after the last day on the job. Some people say they've never been busier, others complain that they've nothing to do. Whether a retirement goal becomes a reality often depends upon resources available and if they're effectively used. Taking a look at your assets and matching up your desires might produce some surprising results. Some things to look at are:

- **Investments.** Bank accounts, certificates, stocks, bonds, real estate, collectibles and anything else that can be readily sold.
- **Retirement income.** Annuities, pensions and any other retirement income.
- **Earned income.** Includes salaries earned for consulting or part-time work.
- **Future inheritance.** Money you may receive during your lifetime.

From these categories, you will draw your financial resources. This total should be calculated in terms of income so that it can be matched against the expenses you incur. If you're already retired, determining your income or potential income is relatively easy. Simply take what you have coming in, or *could* have coming in if all reinvestment was discontinued, and add it up.

If retirement is several years away, a little more complex formula might be needed. Consult your investment advisor or a financial planner for an in-depth analysis.

Retirement planning can never begin too early. Developing a realistic strategy early is the best way of insuring a comfortable retirement. If you're already retired, planning is crucial to assure that you don't outlive your resources. Whatever stage you might be at, setting or evaluating goals is the first step toward a successful retirement.

Chapter 3

Choosing Advisors

A recent poll in *The Wall Street Journal* revealed which professionals are trusted most—and least. The top three were doctors, ministers and bankers. The bottom three were lawyers, stockbrokers and insurance agents. None of the members of this group could diagnose a clogged artery or give a shred of spiritual consolation, but the role they play in your happiness and financial well-being after retirement could be indispensable.

Choosing an investment or other financial advisor may be one of the most important decisions of your life. Such a decision warrants some research. If you're willing to read back issues of *Consumer Reports* before buying a new car or find out about resale values and school districts before buying a house, reading this chapter should be a prerequisite to choosing your advisors.

Thousands of individuals give investment advice every year. The array of titles is amazing: Financial Consultant. Investment Advisor. Certified Financial Planner. The list goes on. The CFP designation (Certified Financial Planner) is the best-known title. While requiring coursework on financial planning, the CFP designation, as with any title, does not guarantee competent or ethical advice.

Advice can be found in newsletters, magazines and syndicated newspaper columns across the country. An investment advisor may even moonlight, writing a newspaper column but also offering investment services. The easiest way to classify investment advisors is by how they get paid. Using that criteria, there are four types of investment advisors.

Nonprofessional advisors

This includes everyone from your Uncle Harry to an economics professor often quoted in your favorite business magazine. The value of advice from these sources varies widely. For example, Uncle Harry may boast of having watched the market for 30 years but has he ever made a dime? Why does he still drive the same VW bus he bought when he graduated from college? Perhaps your Uncle Harry is one of the "children of the Depression." The sum of his advice is "Never buy a stock, never buy a bond, only bank accounts and only if all of it is insured."

An offshoot of the children of the Depression are the doomsayers. They see another market crash just around the corner, every year. While stocks have averaged 12 percent a year, and bonds just a little less than that, these advisors are saying "Sell everything, buy some gold, get a gun and get ready, 'cause this time it's really going to happen."

Not all financial writers are predicting the end of the world as we know it. Some, albeit only a few, offer solid advice for the do-it-yourself investor. "Hulbert's Financial Digest," a newsletter about newsletters, gives an objective rating of most major investment newsletters' actual track records. Since almost every newsletter writer claims to have predicted the crash of 1987 and every other major financial event before and since, this can be valuable.

The claims of other financial writers, such as magazine writers and newspaper columnists, are often much harder to trace. Their advice varies greatly in quality, depending upon their experience and knowledge. I've read ridiculous investment advice in major magazines although often it's the non-committing nature of the advice that is most distressing. One major magazine, for example, printed an article on collateralized mortgage obligations filled with misleading facts. Another touted the benefits of real estate limited partnerships a few years before "limited partnership" came to mean "investor rip-off."

Many magazines, newspapers, private investors, friends and relatives can offer some helpful tips. Much of the advice from private sources, however, is worth the price paid. Nothing. Always check out ideas like this with a second or a third source. Educate yourself before blindly taking advice from any source.

Stockbrokers and other commission-paid advisors

Increasingly, stockbrokers suffer from a negative image, often unjustly. At one time, not very long ago, a broker was a trusted advisor to many families, akin to the family lawyer and doctor.

People dealt with the same person for years and even from generation to generation. All the personalized service and customer loyalty seemed to disappear when the brokerage industry was deregulated in the 1970s. Discount brokerage firms cropped up, interest in investments began to rise dramatically, and brokers began to move from firm to firm, trying to generate the highest percentage of commissions they could. As both the stock and bond markets began to take off in the early 1980s, brokerage firms began to hire more brokers and offer a greater selection of products. Sales ability began to supplant investment knowledge as a desirable characteristic in hiring.

The results that followed were inevitable. Overzealous brokers began marketing products based on sales commission rather than on investment merit. Management rewarded brokers who successfully moved a stunning array of new "special products" designed to maximize profit to the company rather than returns to investors.

In many cases, the bad reputation that tarnishes brokers is justified. But those brokers who have stayed on a more conservative course often suffer from guilt by association. The majority of stockbrokers, commission-based financial planners, insurance agents and independent investment representatives do commendable jobs for their clients.

Financial planners: Percentage of assets

Choosing a financial planner rather than a stockbroker is often positioned as the intelligent choice of the informed investor. After all, why pay all those fees to someone who only makes money when your investments are bought or sold? A financial planner who charges a percentage of your assets, the logic goes, makes money when you make money. In other words, the more your assets grow, the greater the financial planner's profit.

Virtually anyone can call themselves a financial planner. The licensing requirements are even less than those for a commission-based broker or insurance agent. However, in spite of the abuse in the asset management business, there are many financial planners who offer good, solid investment advice and more than earn any fee that they may charge. The title of financial planner alone, however, does not necessarily make for more valuable advice.

Financial advisors: Fee-based

These advisors charge a fee for advice, similar to a lawyer or accountant. Some charge a fee and commission. Others charge the higher of commissions or a fee, which is much different. A third group charges a fee only. They argue that theirs is the fairest compensation system since they neither charge commission nor a percentage of assets but only for the work they do. It sounds reasonable. After all, why pay a percentage of assets? Again, it depends on the value of the advice received. Although it's important to know how your investment advisors are compensated, it's more important to know how well-qualified they are and what they can do for you.

Five crucial questions

The most important things you need to know about choosing an advisor can be covered with five questions.

1. How are you compensated? Which one of the four categories does the advisor fit into? How is the money earned from the client and on what terms is he or she paid?

2. Are you an investor yourself? What do you invest in? The number of financial advisors who fail to take their own advice is shocking. Granted, sometimes it isn't possible, since many investment advisors are younger than their clients and, therefore, have entirely different investment objectives. Regardless, financial professionals ought to have enough faith in their own advice to put their money where their mouth is.

Personal investment is also a sign of individual interest in the markets. Advisors who invest will think like an investor, and manage client assets with the care as if investing for themselves. Their level of knowledge will generally be higher and their attention to client accounts greater. Open-ended questions like "What are you doing for retirement?" or "Do you have a savings plan for your kid's college?" work well. Whatever the advice to you is, ask what the advisor is doing in his or her own situation.

3. What do you do to keep track of the markets and the economy? A salesman sells. He or she uses whatever material available that supports the product. He or she chooses a product (sometimes based on a client's needs) and *sells* it. A true investment advisor goes a step further. He or she is aware of what is going on, understands the financial climate first and chooses an individual investment based on his or her assessment of the environment and the needs of an individual client. He or she can give solid, logical answers to generic questions like "Where do you think interests rates are going?" and "Don't you think the market is a little high right now?" Asking a prospective advisor what magazines and newspapers he or she reads to keep track of financial trends can also be revealing.

4. How many different investments do you offer? Are you given a higher compensation to sell your own company's products? Many mutual fund and insurance salespeople masquerade as financial advisors when, in fact, their investment selection is actually limited to a few selections. This may not always be bad. Some bank and insurance company mutual funds have enviable track records. Many more do not. How can an investment advisor give objective, valuable advice when his or her selection is severely limited? An advisor's greatest asset is his or her ability to select good investments. If the investments are already chosen, what value is the advice?

5. How often can I expect to hear from you? How do you keep track of my holdings and what do you do to keep me informed? Whatever form your payment takes, you are purchasing a service. The advice given should not be limited to the initial investment, but should be ongoing. Is there a regular newsletter? Will you receive a call annually? How often will your holdings be evaluated? Most investors seeking a financial advisor are not shopping for a product but for a relationship. The level of service received is an important consideration when choosing an investment advisor.

Asking these five questions won't guarantee financial success—but should help in the selection process. Remember not to put too much emphasis on title or supposed accomplishments. Get to know the person before choosing to work with him or her. Use your instinct. Spend the time it takes to get to know him or her. Focus on the value of the investment advice rather than title, method of compensation or other secondary factors.

Insurance agents

Walk into any major life insurance sales office and you won't find any insurance agents. On everyone's desk or office will be a title like "Certified Life Underwriter" or "Chartered Financial Consultant." No one is willing to admit that they sell life insurance for a living—life insurance agents suffer a reputation so bad that nobody wants to talk to them. If you doubt it, the next time you're at a social gathering and someone asks you what you do, reply that you sell life insurance. The whole room will clear.

As a result of public animosity, insurance agents have begun to represent themselves as financial advisors. This may or may not be true. The lines between investments and life insurance have never been more clouded. For example, a stockbroker, financial planner or bank investment representative may be able to sell life insurance. On the other side of the coin, an insurance agent may be able to sell mutual funds.

Knowing what your insurance representative can offer you is important in understanding his or her motivation for choosing a particular investment. An agent who can *only* sell insurance is likely to recommend insurance. Even when alternatives to life insurance can be offered, agents usually use them as a last resort, focusing on their core product, life insurance.

An insurance specialist can be useful in many instances, however—such as in cases of estate planning, business insurance and certain types of retirement planning. If your insurance advisor isn't experienced in other types of investments or isn't a full-service financial advisor or planner, it's wise to limit your purchases to basic life coverage. Otherwise, consult another financial advisor who has a wider breadth of knowledge before taking an agent's recommendations regarding estate planning and business insurance. After determining a need, here's what to ask:

1. Do you specialize in any particular type of insurance funding? Is his or her expertise in estate planning, retirement plans, business insurance or is he or she a generalist?

2. Do you represent more than one company? How did he or she choose these companies? Obviously, an agent that represents only one company may not give the best selection in price or features. (More on rating insurance companies in Chapter 16.)

Do the companies represented have strong financial ratings? How closely has the representative researched the companies he or she has chosen to deal with?

3. What is the insurance company's rating? The four major rating services are A.M. Best, Standard & Poor's, Duff & Phelps, and Weiss. Best is the most lenient, Weiss the strictest. Standard & Poor's and Duff & Phelps offer good middle ground. The highest rating from both Standard & Poor's and Duff & Phelps is AAA and goes down to AA, A, BBB and so on. Choose only companies that have A ratings or better.

4. What does the company invest in? Ask to see a copy of the portfolio. Avoid companies with large holdings in real estate (30 percent or more), junk bonds (15 percent or more) and stocks (15 percent or more). The bulk of a portfolio managed for safety should be in U.S. government or agency bonds and high-grade corporate bonds (BBB or better).

5. How long has the company been in business? Where can you call to get service besides the agent's office? Agents come and go and if you should need to contact someone, there should be a customer service department at the insurance company.

Insurance is an integral part of any portfolio, but shop around. The service, expertise and cost will vary widely. A good insurance advisor is often worth a slightly higher cost in premium or a lower rate since they could save you several thousands of dollars over the long haul. (More detailed information on choosing insurance can be found in Chapter 7.)

Attorneys

A popular joke asks, "How many attorneys does it take to screw in a light bulb?" The answer is, "How many can you afford?" Lawyers have borne the brunt of jokes since Shakespeare's day, often for good reason. In our litigious society, it's likely that most of you reading this book have had an encounter with an attorney, and probably not a pleasant one. Perhaps your neighbor sued you over a fallen fence, or your attorney settled too quickly over an auto accident, leaving you less than you could have gotten on your own after he takes his percentage. However, given the complexity of today's tax and estate laws, it would seem that a good lawyer might be an indispensable part of your financial planning team.

For example, in a large estate, a good attorney's advice could save tens of thousands of dollars, or more. There are four times when you definitely should talk to an attorney regarding your estate or finances.

- If your estate is larger than $600,000. Estate taxes begin on estates with assets over $600,000. An attorney can help reduce this tax liability. (See Chapter 16.)
- If you hold any real estate or other appreciated assets in your estate, especially if you're married. How you hold your real estate can affect how much you pay in taxes. Appreciation on stocks can be sheltered from taxes upon death in a variety of ways.
- If you have a lot of life insurance. Life insurance is considered a taxable asset for estate tax purposes.
- If you have small children or beneficiaries whom you do not wish to receive your estate in a lump sum. An attorney can set up a trust, guardianship or any other similar document.

Most lawyers either work independently or as part of a law firm. Depending on where you live, law firms vary greatly in size and speciality. A very large, complex estate might best be served by a large firm. The sheer number of attorneys and the availability of multiple specialists in areas such as tax, estate planning and family law create a one-stop legal firm for all of your needs.

Costs will rise accordingly, of course, and the personalized service found at a smaller firm may be lacking. First- or second-year associates, fresh out of law school, will probably be assigned to all but the biggest cases.

The specialization of your attorney should also be carefully considered. Does he or she only do estate planning? How much of the business comes from tax planning? Depending on your need, seek out someone who does more than half of his or her work in an area of specialization. With the popularity of living trusts, almost any attorney can claim to specialize in estate planning. Find out how long he or she has been doing trusts, among other types of estate planning.

Customer service is the principal reason you deal with a local attorney. If your phone calls go unreturned and your messages ignored, think about shopping for someone else. The business of law is very competitive and many small practices welcome new clients. After deciding whether you want to go with a big firm or a small one, ask friends and business associates for some recommendations. Other advisors, such as stockbrokers, financial planners and accountants, also have extensive contacts with the legal profession. Stay away from lawyer referral services (attorneys pay to have their name listed) and store-front law offices. Once you've chosen someone, ask for a free consultation and explain your needs.

Accountants

Unlike attorneys, stockbrokers and insurance agents, accountants enjoy a high level of trust from the general public. Certified Public Accountants (CPAs), especially are revered by their clients.

An accountant may field just as many questions about investments and life insurance as about taxes. While most accountants are not qualified to answer investment and insurance questions, their advice can be invaluable in tax and estate planning. Not all, however, have the same level of expertise. Types of accountants most commonly used by individuals are tax preparers, bookkeepers, enrolled agents, and CPAs. Each has a varying degree of education and experience.

A tax preparer or bookkeeper is not required to have any formal education beyond a two- to three-week course that some tax preparation firms require. H.R. Block, for example, trains people who come from a variety of other professions. The tax preparer could be an unemployed aerospace worker, a housewife or just about anyone else in need of a seasonal job. The training may suffice for filling out a basic tax form, but for more complex tax planning, you're better off with someone with a little more experience.

An enrolled agent has either worked for the IRS or has completed a battery of tests on tax code. Although having IRS training doesn't inspire confidence in most people (especially those who've tried to get tax advice on the IRS tax line), most enrolled agents are well-informed and fairly well-trained. Their expertise usually lies in specific tax matters and what is allowed. When dealing with an IRS problem, an enrolled agent may do an even better job than a CPA.

For tax planning and estate matters, CPAs are usually the best source of advice. Their knowledge on a wide range of subjects outside the tax code enables CPAs to offer more comprehensive advice and to better relate to other advisors. CPAs will usually have a four-year business degree and two years of "apprenticeship" before taking an extremely comprehensive exam. Upon passing, they're awarded a Certified Public Accountant designation.

As with an attorney, try to get a referral when choosing an accountant. Ask for an initial interview to determine whether you're compatible as well as to evaluate the accountant's knowledge of tax code. Remember not to shop from January to April—an accountant's busiest time of the year. But, rather, wait until after August.

Watch out for accountants and tax preparers who double as investment salesmen. While some financial advisors are qualified to give both kinds of advice, investments are usually a sideline for accountants, if they sell them. As a result, your account may not receive the kind of attention it would from someone who gives investment advice full-time.

All your advisors should interact with you as a team, yet provide specific answers for specific needs. A network of financial advisors creates a system of checks and balances, a way of double-checking the advice you get. For example, your broker tells you that your IBM isn't a very good investment and recommends that you sell it. Before selling, you consult a CPA who tells you not to do it because of the tax consequences. After passing this information to the broker, he modifies his advice. Each advisor has a place and offers a valuable service.

Chapter 4

Managing Risk

"There are two times in a man's life when he should not speculate; when he can't afford it and when he can." —Mark Twain

The difference between a speculator and an investor is in the way he or she views risk. A speculator tries to take advantage of risk and outguess the markets. An investor tries to preserve what he or she has by hedging against risk.

The trick in understanding the category you fall into depends on your understanding of risk. Most investors view risk as the potential to lose principal. As long as they can't lose principal, they're not taking any risk. Risks such as inflation, interest-rate risk, and catastrophic risk are ignored. By focusing only on the return of principal, and ignoring other factors, risk-adverse savers try to outguess the markets and, without knowing it, become speculators. They speculate that inflation won't rise, interest rates will remain the same and no unexpected catastrophes will befall them.

An investor, on the other hand, hedges against each type of risk by diversifying his or her portfolio among several different types of investments, each offering protection against certain types of risk. Before designing an individual investment plan, you must understand the types of risk to hedge against and the nature of each.

Risk to principal

Most people equate safety with stability of principal. If you invest $1, you will be able to take out $1 at the end of a given term. The principal is guaranteed. But who guarantees the principal? What if the principal is guaranteed to be returned in 10 years and you have to cash it in right now? Can the terms of the security or account be changed in certain circumstances? The perceived safety of an investment that "guarantees" the principal can be very different from its true safety.

Take a look at credit union accounts. For years, investors in Rhode Island put money into credit unions with government guarantees—or so they thought. Some of these credit unions held state-sponsored, private deposit insurance rather than federal insurance. When the insurance fund went broke, the credit unions defaulted, resulting in losses for thousands of investors. Who would have thought to check the insurance?

Here's another example. Mutual Benefit Life of New Jersey was not known as a high-risk insurer. In fact, its agents touted it as an old, stable company with a solid investment base. Annuities purchased through the company were guaranteed to return their principal after a given period. "No one has ever lost a dime in an insurance company," agents would say. Negative news reports panicked some policyholders, causing a run on the insurance company not very different from the runs that many banks experienced during the Great Depression. Mutual Benefit declared its own bank holiday and a few weeks later, it was taken over by regulators.

Not everything is as it appears. Regardless of how safe something seems to be, a little bit of research can go a long way in determining exactly how safe your principal is. Here are a few things to look for:

1. Who is issuing the guarantee and what does the guarantee cover? If it's a bank account, is it *federally* guaranteed or insured by a state or private agency. FDIC or the Federal Deposit Insurance Corporation insures most bank accounts and has the full backing of the U.S. government. U.S. government bonds may be direct obligations of the U.S. government, have direct backing (GNMA) or be issued by a U.S. government agency (FNMA or FHMLC) and have the implicit backing of the government. (See Chapters 6 and 7 for more on government bonds).

Other types of bonds, such as corporate bonds and municipal bonds, usually have a rating from a national rating agency. An AAA-rating is usually the highest and a D-rating the lowest. Three different agencies account for most of the bond ratings in the United States; Standard & Poor's, Moody's and Duff & Phelps. With all three services, a BBB rating or better is considered investment grade.

Investment grade implies a high-quality bond unlikely to default in the immediate future. Usually reserved for higher yield or junk bonds, lower grades have a much higher chance of default. The lower the rating, the higher the yield and the higher the risk from default.

Insurance companies usually back their annuities, life insurance and other investments with assets such as government bonds, corporate bonds and real estate. Insurance companies also carry credit ratings, as mentioned in Chapter 3. Check the company's rating and assets when looking at the safety of their investments. Understand exactly what backs the investment—and to what extent—before investing in it.

2. What if I need my money early? Most term accounts carry some type of penalty for early withdrawal. Liquid accounts, of course, such as passbook accounts and money markets, are accessible at any time but offer lower rates. Certificates of Deposit (CDs) charge penalties for early withdrawal, which can eat into the principal if taken out too early. For example, if your CD has a nine-month interest penalty and it's taken out after three months, the six months of interest will come from the principal originally put in.

Annuities often have a fixed-rate penalty that declines every year. A bond will have to be sold on the open market at whatever price it will bring. Know these costs and risks before buying, and plan accordingly.

3. Are the terms of the agreement guaranteed? The interest rate may sound good when you lock it in, but how long will it last? Once taken over by the FDIC, a bank's high-yielding, long-term CDs are often canceled and customers given a choice of taking a lower rate or getting their money back. Municipal and corporate bond agreements usually include *call* features, where the municipality or corporation can pay off the bond at a given price (usually a little higher than the issue price) earlier than the maturity date. Many bondholders who were patting themselves on the back for locking in high yields during the early '80s are now getting their principal back, often 20 years early.

Interest-rate risk

Short-term and long-term investors alike bear the risk of interest rate fluctuation whenever they purchase a fixed investment. Whether buying a short-term CD or a long-term bond, changes in interest rates affect either the income or the principal value of the investment. If interest rates should fall, buyers of short-term CDs or other fixed investments see their income drop substantially. A drop from 8 percent to 4 percent, for example, results in a 50-percent decrease in income.

Shell-shocked bank account holders have experienced short-term interest-rate risk first-hand in recent months. Long-term bondholders, on the other hand, see the value of their bonds rise when interest rates fall. If interest rates should rise, though, bond prices will fall. It's better to hold short-term investments when interest rates rise and long-term investments when they fall.

The difficulty is in knowing exactly how changes in interest rates will affect specific investments, because of the great variety of term, quality and tax status of the many fixed investments available. For the more advanced investor, here are some simple rules of fixed income price fluctuation.

The longer the term, the more sensitive an investment will be to interest rates. A 30-year bond will rise in price more than a 10-year bond if interest rates should fall. The opposite is also true.

Interest-paying bonds will be less sensitive to interest rates than non-interest paying bonds. Zero coupon bonds, or bonds that do not pay interest out but accumulate it, fluctuate in price more widely than bonds that pay interest every six months. A U.S. Treasury STRP (Stripped Treasury Receipt Interest Payment) with a 10-year maturity has roughly the same price fluctuation as a 30-year interest-paying Treasury bond. If interest rates fall, the STRP will rise in value about as much as a 30-year Treasury bond.

The lower the quality of a bond, the more its price will react to a change in interest rates. Lower-grade bond prices tend to rise and fall faster than higher-quality bonds as interest rates change. This conventional wisdom has come under greater scrutiny in the past decade as junk bonds seem to defy this rule quite regularly. With ratings much lower than most conventional bonds, junk bond prices are tied more to the fortunes of the company they're issued from, its industry and to equity markets.

Tax-free bond prices are also affected by changes in tax rates. When tax rates rise, tax-free yields fall in response, and their prices rise. Higher tax rates increase demand for the bonds, pushing their prices up. As a result, the tax-free market marches to a different drummer than taxable bond markets. If interest rates rise but tax rates also rise, the effect on tax-free bonds might be mixed. Higher interest puts downward pressure on tax-free prices, but higher tax rates create upward pressure on the bond. The net effect is impossible to predict.

Knowing the effect of interest rates on your investments might be valuable when the direction of interest rates is clear. But who can predict interest rates? Everyone has an opinion of where interest rates are going. Some see double-digit yields being revisited, others anticipate lower rates reminiscent of the 1950s and '60s. Most forecasts are guesses at best, but some are better informed than others. Knowing some of the underlying factors that drive rates higher or lower greatly increases the odds of your investment success. Here are some factors that influence the direction of interest rates.

1. Inflation. By far, the biggest influence on interest rates, inflation itself is caused by several factors. *Demand-pull inflation* occurs when strong economic growth creates a shortage of labor or goods used in the economy. This shortage causes a rise in prices, which is passed on as higher cost. This type of inflation usually comes in the middle of an economic boom. *Cost-push inflation* results from an unexpected cost increase in a widely used commodity or in labor. A good example of this was the Arab oil embargo in the 1970s, which quadrupled the cost of oil. This cost eventually spread through the economy, contributing to the runaway inflation of the '80s. Generally, a rise in inflation is preceded by a rise in commodity prices.

2. Money supply. More money in an economy generally pushes down interest rates. By money, I mean cash, liquid bank accounts and even loans.

The more money available, the lower the interest rate will fall. Lending institutions will compete for borrowers by offering lower interest rates on loans.

If there's too much money available, however, interest rates may eventually rise because of inflation. If banks ease lending requirements, more money enters the economy, causing upward inflationary pressure. Since more people can get loans, more people are spending money. The same effect is true of lower taxes, higher wages and any other lower living cost. The Federal Reserve Bank is constantly doing a balancing act.

3. Alternative investment returns. If real estate is returning 20 percent a year, or the stock market is booming, fewer people would be willing to buy fixed investments, creating an upward pressure on rates. The effect will probably hardly be noticed, since most alternative investments do well when inflation is high, which in itself will have a great influence on current interest rates.

The dangers of inflation erosion

Interest trend forecasting is far from an exact science, but knowing the basics can be helpful in managing your money. Since inflation is the biggest determinant of future interest rates, and one of retired investors' greatest fears, a closer inspection of its effects, might be helpful.

A penny saved is a penny earned, the old adage goes. But a penny saved 20, 15 or even 10 years ago might be worth only a fraction of a cent. The cost of living tends to rise a little every year, slowly deflating the value of savings year after year. For example, $10,000 put aside in 1977 could only buy $4,221 in goods and services in 1991.

Wait a minute, you might say. That money would earn interest and grow. How much it grows depends on your investment. Inflation has averaged a little more than 3.14 percent a year from 1926 until 1991, while Treasury bills have averaged 3.70 percent during that time. That leaves a .56 percent return a year on short-term investments since 1926. That minuscule return goes even lower when you take taxes into account. Someone in the 28-percent federal bracket would average *minus* .48 percent a year, losing money!.

The effects of inflation are especially devastating after retirement, when income tends to be fixed. That's why it's always essential to include some type of inflation hedge in your portfolio, regardless of your age. Several types of investments tend to rise in value as inflation rises.

1. Stocks. A premier inflation hedge, stocks have returned above-average yields for several decades, easily outpacing rising living costs. Buying a share of stock equates to buying a piece of a business. Businesses merely pass on any increases in cost, increasing profit and raising dividends to their investors.

2. Real estate. Since rents rise as costs rise, and real estate is valued by its rent or usage cost, prices of land rise with inflation. As an investment, property isn't always risk-free since values can fluctuate because of speculation and other factors. Most property owners also make generous use of leverage, or debt, which makes the investment even more volatile. Still, the value of real estate as an inflation hedge remains undisputed.

3. Precious metals. As with any commodity, gold, silver and platinum prices go up (and down) with inflation. Unlike stocks or real estate, a bar of gold doesn't pay rent and a silver coin won't declare a dividend. It's a wasting asset. Buying stocks in precious metal can produce better returns, but these stocks can be extremely volatile.

4. Collectibles. A fair inflation hedge—if you can bear the whims of buyers and are intimately familiar with the market—are collectibles such as art, coins and stamps. Most investors never make a lot of money, but perhaps personal satisfaction can make up for lower earnings. Barely considered an investment, buying collectibles for a profit is definitely not for the faint-of-heart.

Most inflation hedges have one distinct disadvantage: Their principal is not guaranteed. For this reason, some investors avoid inflation hedges like the plague. By their very nature, growth-oriented investments, like stocks, real estate and precious metals, will fluctuate in value. Although market risk is not unavoidable, it can be effectively managed.

Market risk

The Dow Jones off 180 points!
Market hits all time high.
Stocks mixed as market awaits employment numbers.

Headlines such as these strike fear in the heart of any reader who has money in anything remotely connected to the stock market. What does it mean? In my experience, it's headlines like these that cause average investors to lose money in the market because they panic. Most investors will buy at the top of a market and sell at the bottom because of what they read and what they fear.

Successful investors do two things:

1. They hold their investments for longer periods of time.
2. They buy when nobody else buys and avoid buying when everyone else does.

Take the example of the stock market. While short-term investors have been whipsawed over the years, long-term investors have been rewarded. Since 1926, stocks have gone up 47 years and gone down 19. Yet only one 10-year period has seen stock market declines, while 65 five-year periods have been positive. Not one 15-year holding period has seen a loss in the stock market. A long-term investor is rewarded while the short-term speculator is whipsawed. These numbers only apply to risk of the market as a whole.

Market risk is usually divided into two categories: *systematic risk* and *nonsystematic risk,* as mentioned in Chapter 1. Systematic risk is the risk of the entire market going down. A loss due to a 300-point drop in the market would be a systematic risk.

Nonsystematic risk usually refers to individual investments. If the market is rising and your stock drops by 50 percent because its new drug doesn't get FDA approval, this is a nonsystematic risk. The individual investment goes bad, but it does not reflect the general condition of the market.

Both types of risk can be avoided by diversification—investing in a variety of markets, such as domestic stock markets, overseas markets, bonds, precious metals and short-term bond markets.

Liquidity risk

Remember that limited partnership you bought? Although it sounded like a good deal at the time, things just aren't working out. It's probably best just to take the loss and get out of it. The problem is you can't. Nobody's willing to buy it. There's no market.

Often when an investment is made, there's an implicit assumption that there's a market where that investment can be bought or sold. Many people have learned otherwise in the past decade. Even if there's a market, sometimes its so small that you can lose your shirt just trying to sell.

Take the penny stock market. The stocks are cheap, usually a dollar or less, but the sell price can often be half of what the buy price is. It's called "the spread." Generally, the smaller the market the greater the spread. This is how brokerage firms, market makers and other professional are compensated for making a market in illiquid security. For example a penny stock might sell for 50 cents a share, but the bid (what the dealer is willing to pay to buy it back) might only be 25 cents. A $10,000 investment is worth $5,000 overnight.

A stock like AT&T usually only has a one-eighth-point spread because it's traded frequently on a major stock exchange. Most investments with high spreads trade in over-the-counter markets and are not found on major stock or bond exchanges such as the New York Stock Exchange or American Stock Exchange. Their lack of liquidity can cost investors dearly when they attempt to sell.

Even a highly liquid stock can become illiquid at certain times. During the crash of 1987, for example, even blue-chip stock orders went unfilled for hours, some not until the next day. Liquidity should be an important factor in choosing any type of investment.

Investments usually having high liquidity

- Stocks listed on the New York, American, and NASDAQ exchanges.
- Bonds listed on New York and American exchanges
- U.S. Treasury obligations
- GNMAs
- Large-issue, general-obligation and essential-service revenue municipal bonds
- Mutual funds

Investments with fair liquidity but higher spreads

- Nonlisted bonds
- Small-issue municipals
- "Pink sheet" or supplemental-list NASDAQ stocks
- Options (varies)

Investments with low liquidity

- Real Estate Limited Partnerships (RELPs)
- Penny stocks ("pink sheets")

Catastrophic risk

Open-heart surgery can easily cost $250,000. Medical expenses are soaring and many insurance policies limit their coverage more and more every year. Lawsuits abound for everything from auto accidents to dog bites to not installing a light bulb correctly in a rental house. Let's look at a couple of scenarios. Each is an event that actually took place.

A couple living in California had saved about $200,000, paid off their house and are comfortably enjoying retirement. The wife is diagnosed with Alzheimer's disease and goes to live in a nursing home at a cost of about $4,500 a month. Even though her husband is 10 years older than she, he's forced to pay the bills until he has only $66,000 remaining—and only then will MediCal pick up the tab. He's destitute in a few years, having only his home and a small bit of cash.

A widow caring for her orphaned grandson with multiple sclerosis lets her homeowner's insurance lapse to make ends meet. A tragic accident between a truck and a motorcycle on her street corner leaves the cyclist paralyzed. He sues the truck company and every homeowner on the block for having their hedges cut too high. Each of her neighbors' insurance companies settles. The insurance companies then sue the uninsured widow for her portion. They attempt to foreclose on her house and attach her bank accounts.

A tenant is electrocuted and left in a vegetative state when turning on a chain-switch light bulb in a damp laundry room while barefoot. The young man's parents sue the landlord and, after exhausting the insurance limits, attach property and bank accounts, then go after the light fixture's manufacturer.

There may not be a right or wrong in some of these examples, and perhaps grievous injustice in others. The point is that catastrophes can befall anyone regardless of how careful or responsible they are. Catastrophic risk can't be hedged or prevented by diversifying or by making sound investments. But the risk of damage can be spread more thinly by having adequate insurance and by protecting your assets before damage is done. Carrying adequate insurance and properly vesting your assets helps reduce much of the danger of unexpected events. There's more on this in Chapter 17.

Avoiding risk entirely is impossible. Regardless of how safe a particular investment seems, something will threaten that investment, whether market fluctuation, inflation or changing interest rates. No one investment is a perfect investment. Building a portfolio that spreads out the risk, hedging and diversifying it away, offers the only credible solution to the risk dilemma.

Chapter 5

Building an Income Machine

Anyone who has ever built anything begins with a model, similar object, picture or idea—a beginning concept. From birdhouse to bungalow, the model provides a framework on which we heap our own embellishments and satisfy special needs and desires.

Similarly, a three-point model for retirement provides a strong foundation on which an individualized investment plan can be erected. A mixture of short-term, long-term and growth investments, in proper proportions, provides what could be called a bulletproof portfolio. Come what may, such an investment mixture should provide the maximum protection from the variety of risks that retirement can bring. Runaway inflation or zero inflation, high or low interest rates, a strong economy or recession—a well-balanced investment plan takes all contingencies into account.

Bulletproofing your investments

Diversification provides the cornerstone of any good investment plan. But diversify among what? I knew a retired real estate developer who bought second trust deeds. We talked about his need to diversify and he insisted that he was diversified. He always held more than one second trust deed and they were never in the same neighborhood.

Everyone has a different idea when they hear the old saying "Don't put all your eggs in one basket." Diversification should include a balance of three groups: short-term fixed, long-term fixed and growth/inflation hedge investments. The percentage in each depends on age, financial resources, and personal preferences. A younger person saving for retirement, for example, needs more in growth investments than someone collecting Social Security, in most cases. Or a retiree who follows the stock market as a hobby might have a relatively large percentage of his or her assets in stock. Regardless of individual needs and predilection, a good basic guideline is as follows;

Age 20 - 40

Short-term fixed	20%-30%
Long-term fixed	10%-20%
Growth/inflation hedge	50%-70%

Age 40 - 60

Short-term fixed	30%-40%
Long-term fixed	30%-40%
Growth/inflation hedge	20%-40%

Age 60+

Short-term fixed	40%-45%
Long-term fixed	40%-45%
Growth/inflation hedge	10%-20%

These guidelines don't account for money that should be set aside for emergency or for specific use such as purchasing a house, college education or home renovation. Emergency funds should be set aside first, before making any other investments. Usually between three to six months' coverage should suffice.

Each of these three investment categories balances each other, complementing one another in good and bad markets. For example, when interest rates rise, short-term investments perform well while long-term investments lag. Inflation bodes well for growth investments, badly for fixed-income investments. Each portion of the portfolio offsets another, providing protection.

1. Short-term fixed investments

A short-term fixed investment is shorter than five years (usually two years or less), it doesn't fluctuate in principal and is generally available at a minimum penalty or cost on immediate notice.

Besides providing liquidity for emergencies, a short-term holding hedges against rising interest rates. For example, if rates were to rise, the investment would come due in a relatively short time and be rolled over to a higher rate. If a six-month CD is paying 4 percent, and rates go up to 8 percent in six months, the rate would increase to 8 percent at the time it rolled over.

Unfortunately, as many investors have come to learn, this rate advantage is a double-edged sword. When rates decline, the certificate rolls over at a lower rate, sometimes drastically reducing returns.

Short-term fixed investments include CDs, U.S. Treasury obligations, short-term corporate bonds and notes, and some annuities. A complete list and explanation are in Chapter 6. A short-term position is essential to a balanced portfolio, in spite of current rates. It's the only effective hedge against rising interest rates.

2. Long-term fixed investments

As interest rates have fallen in recent months, droves of savers have bought long-term bonds and mutual funds. Usually boasting higher rates than short-term assets, long-term investment rates are often locked in for 10 years or more, hedging against falling interest rates. Locking in a higher yield insures a future flow of income.

If rates should rise, however, the liquid value of a long-term holdings could fall. The principal is usually guaranteed only if the instrument is held to maturity. Market value, in the meantime, could fluctuate. If our saver in the previous example had bought a 10-year Treasury bond paying 6 percent instead of rolling over the CD, and interest rates rose to 8 percent, the principal value of the Treasury bond would fall. If the holder liquidated, he would not get as much as he had paid. On the other hand, if rates fell, the value would rise.

Long-term fixed investments are not purchased as cash holdings. Rather, they're purchased for income. You're buying a steady stream of income when you buy a bond or other long-term investment. The income is not necessarily paid out and used. It could be reinvested. But the stream of income should still be present. Early liquidation shouldn't even be a consideration until short-term funds have been exhausted.

Examples of long-term fixed investments are long-term CDs, U.S. government notes and bonds, corporate bonds, municipal bonds and fixed-income mutual funds. This portion of an investment portfolio hedges against falling interest rates.

3. Investments providing growth and inflation hedge

The dramatic fall in interest rates has also led many to try their hand at the stock market. While growth investments such as stocks should never be a substitute for fixed-rate investments, they do offer several advantages making them essential to any portfolio, regardless of an investor's age.

Younger investors looking toward future costs, such as retirement and college expenses, are best served by more aggressive growth instruments. Most of these pay little in the way of dividends and have the greatest potential for the highest rates of returns. The level of risk rises accordingly. Since longer holding periods usually equate to lower risk, these aggressive investments are best held for longer periods.

An older investor might substitute a dividend-paying security, like a utility stock or high-income industrial stock, since these produce income as well as acting as inflation hedges. Some of these inflation hedges currently pay more than even short-term CDs.

Real estate, in spite of recent declines, offers another option. As interest rates decline and property prices appear to bottom out, real estate has again become attractive in some parts of the country. Don't expect the astronomical returns of the 1970s and 1980s, but prices should keep above inflation, perhaps even adding a small profit over the next decade. Since it can produce income, real estate attracts investors willing to deal with the inevitable problems of managing rental property.

Gold, although rising in price dramatically lately, should be the last resort as an inflation hedge. As mentioned earlier, it doesn't usually produce income, and gold stocks that do can be extremely volatile in price. Unless you see the end of the world approaching rapidly, it's best to stay away from this commodity.

This part of your portfolio protects against rising prices. While short-term and long-term fixed investments guard against changing interest rates, growth investments protect your portfolio from rising inflation. Whether inflation is high or low, these investments will keep up. The younger you are, the larger the proportion of growth investments in your portfolio should be. Since the effects of inflation are felt more drastically over longer periods of time, a younger investor risks more loss from inflation than an older one. Conversely, an older investor would have a smaller percentage of his or her assets in growth investments, most of which would be in income-producing stocks or real estate.

Growth investments should also be diversified amongst various sectors. For example, some overseas investments offset any risk to the U.S. economy. Small capitalization stocks round out the growth portion. Just as the growth portion of your portfolio grows smaller with age, the overseas and small cap portion of this part of your assets should also shrink with age.

The income machine

The result of all this planning is a portfolio that resists almost every type of catastrophe imaginable. Here's how it works:

If interest rates rise...
- Short-term fixed investment rates rise.
- Long-term fixed investments fall.

- Growth and inflation hedges initially fall until inflation begins to rise.

If interest rates fall...
- Short-term fixed rates fall.
- Long-term fixed rates hold steady, while their values rise.
- Growth and inflation hedges rise in response to lower interest rates.

If inflation reappears...
- Short-term rates rise as interest rates rise.

- Long-term fixed investments fall, as interest rates rise.
- Growth and inflation hedges rise along with inflation.

Each component of the portfolio offsets a different kind of risk. The over-all diversification should protect the investor from most major types of uncertainty inherent to investing. Now that the framework is in place, specific investments can be selected for your specific needs.

Chapter 6

Understanding Short-Term Fixed Investments

During the past decade, the number of short-term investments available to the average investor has mushroomed. At one time "short-term" meant bank accounts and Treasury bills. Other options were available only to large institutions. As the types of short-term investments have grown, so has their complexity, leaving even the most experienced brokers and other professional market watchers increasingly bemused every year. A lack of understanding of these investments leads to missteps, such as the short-term global fund and prime rate trust debacles of recent years, which left many investors poorer albeit wiser.

If a broker can't understand the increasingly complex short-term market, how can the average investor have any hope of success? Avoiding hard-to-understand investments should be the first rule of thumb. The second is to gain thorough comprehension of the safer investments that are available. Most of the investments discussed in this chapter have a guarantee of principal from a reputable source, except for the mutual funds. Although the funds are quite safe, their value can fluctuate. Following is a detailed look at each of the short-term fixed investments.

Certificates of Deposit

One of the first investments any of us ever made was in a bank account.

Banks offer the safety of federal insurance and the convenience of local branches, making these financial institutions an essential part of just about everyone's lives.

CDs are term accounts, essentially a contract between you and the bank to leave a given amount of money in an account for a fixed period, in return for a guaranteed rate. If the money is taken early, a penalty is charged, usually expressed as a certain number of months' interest. The longer the term, the larger the penalty for early withdrawal. Strictly enforced guidelines usually make such penalties unnegotiable—even for the bank's best customers.

All accounts held by a bank are insured under the Federal Deposit Insurance Corporation (FDIC). In spite of negative publicity as of late, the FDIC has the full backing of the U.S. Treasury Department and, thus, the full taxing power of the U.S. government. Credit unions are also insured, but under another entity, with no degradation of safety.

The FDIC insures up to $100,000 per account holder per institution. In other words, if you have $100,000 in one bank and $100,000 in another, both are insured. In addition, retirement plans are insured separately—an IRA held at the same bank as an individual account is insured separately. At one time, even business retirement plans were insured separately from IRAs but this has recently changed.

Vesting determines insurance coverage. This makes it possible to have more than $100,000 in an institution and still be covered by insurance. Vesting refers to the names that appear on an account. A joint account including the names Harry and Ann Smith has a different vesting than an account only in Harry's or Ann's name. Plus, each vesting has separate insurance.

For example, Harry and Ann have a joint checking account at their neighborhood bank. They also have a CD in Harry's name with Ann as the beneficiary, and a savings account in Ann's name only. Both have IRA accounts and Ann recently set up a custodian account for her grandson. Which accounts are insured? All of them. As long as the vestings are separate, the $100,000 limit applies to each.

There are some exceptions. Trust accounts, with one name listed as trustee for another, have special rules. Called Totten trusts, they are only available in banks and must be for the benefit of an immediate blood descendant to be federally insured. So if Harry sets up a Totten trust for the benefit of his son or grandson, it would be insured separately, while a trust in the name of an uncle or nephew would not.

Living trusts present another challenge of interpretation. Under old savings and loan rules, accounts vested in living trusts were insured for $100,000 for each beneficiary, as long as the beneficiary was a legal descendant of the trustor or the person(s) creating the trust.

Since the FDIC has taken over the role of the old FSLIC (Federal Savings & Loan Insurance Corporation), all the rules have changed. The problem is that no one knows exactly what the rules *are* now. Ask your bank representatives and they'll refer you to the FDIC, or at least that's what they've usually been told to do. Call the FDIC, and you'll be referred to your local bank. Until somebody issues an opinion and defines the rule, it's best to assume that a trust is only insured up to $100,000.

Bank accounts are one of the safest, most liquid, and convenient ways of investing the short-term fixed portion of your holdings. Contrary to popular opinion, they're most certainly not the only way to invest short-term dollars and sometimes not even the best.

Money markets

When interest rates soared in the late 1970s and the government imposed fixed-interest rates on bank accounts, money market funds took advantage of higher short-term market rates, offering them to individuals accustomed to bank accounts. These new accounts weren't very different from traditional bank accounts. The principal didn't fluctuate, the money was completely liquid, and you could even write checks on the accounts.

Merrill Lynch's CMA (Cash Management Account) paved the way for brokerage firms to compete in an area once the exclusive domain of banks and savings and loans. Offering the same services as banks, brokerage firms enticed billions of dollars from checking and savings accounts into their new, higher-yielding product. While most people have an impression that money markets are essentially bank accounts, there are some important differences.

Money market funds are not insured. While many brokerage firms are quick to point out that no money market has ever defaulted, and that they do offer insured versions of money markets (essentially arranged through a network of banks), money markets are backed only by their securities. This does not usually present any difficulties—except when one of the securities defaults. More on this later.

Not all money markets are the same. Especially in recent years, the number and types of money markets have proliferated. Some examples are:

- **U.S. government.** All securities are government- or agency-backed. This is the safest type of money market.
- **Regular money market.** These money markets buy government and corporate short-term debt. The corporate note usually has to be investment grade. Short-term debt seldom defaults, but it is possible and actually has happened. In 1990, Integrated Resources defaulted on its short-term obligations carried by several money market funds. Rather than pass the loss to investors, the funds bought back the obligations at face value and absorbed the loss themselves. If several companies defaulted at once, however, no one really knows how individual money market funds would react.
- **Tax-free.** Investing only in short-term, tax-free notes, this type of money market avoids federal taxation and in the case of state specific funds, state taxes, too. The risk of municipal paper can vary

greatly, as can the management style of various funds. A lower average security rating signals danger.
- **Worldwide or global.** These funds buy U.S. denominated debt of foreign governments, banks and corporations. Since laws vary from country to country, and risk generally increases when dealing with foreign securities, this is the riskiest of most major money market fund types.

Money markets don't guarantee principal. A bank account is essentially a contract between a bank and a depositor, which is guaranteed by the FDIC. The contract guarantees the return of principal. A money market fund invests only in short-term securities (usually 180 days and less), but the sponsor does not guarantee the return of principal, let alone promise the backing of the government. Money market share prices have almost never fluctuated. But, as mentioned earlier, defaults are possible, especially if the fund's manager is reaching for higher yields and taking more risks.

While money markets are not risk-free, they offer an excellent alternative to bank accounts at certain times, if you're selective. For a money market investment to make sense, the rate should be at least one-half percent better than a bank alternative or, if you're in a high tax bracket, the after-tax equivalent (amount you put in your pocket after taxes) should be higher. Look at the ratings of the securities in the fund. Sticking to government or high-quality tax-free funds is usually the best bet.

Treasury bills

Like CDs, U.S. Treasury bills are backed by the "full faith and credit of the United States government." Considered the safest of short-term fixed-income investments, Treasury bills are easily bought and sold and are also state tax-free. T-bills bought at a discount later pay off at full face value. A $10,000 bill, for example, could be purchased for $9,750. When it matures, the holder gets $10,000. *Treasury bills* refer to any U.S. Treasury obligation one year or less in maturity. *Treasury notes* have maturities between one year and 10 years and *Treasury bonds* are 10 years or longer in maturity.

Buying T-bills directly from the government can be frustrating in most states. Although the Treasury does offer the bonds through the mail (along with automatic rollover features), bond buyers can also go directly to a federal reserve branch to obtain them. Since 1984, all Treasury debt is book entry, meaning that it either has to be held at the U.S. Treasury or at a brokerage firm. Certificates are no longer issued. Since a bill can't be liquidated if held at the Treasury, many investors buy through brokerage firms, usually at a nominal cost. A broker will charge a fee to enter your order for Treasuries ($50 or less, usually) at the auction or will buy from inventory or another dealer (the secondary market).

The secondary market, where previously owned Treasury obligations are bought and sold, often has lower yields than the auction. The larger the purchase, the more economical the secondary market can be.

A direct purchase, on the other hand, is made from the government with the broker acting as the agent, usually at the regular Treasury auction. For a purchase larger than $1 million, a bid can be placed at the Treasury auction. Smaller purchases made at the auction through a broker will be priced at the average.

If the purchase is small, and the term short, buying from a broker may not be the best alternative. For example, if you purchase $10,000 of a three-month T-bill from a broker, paying $50, the charge takes 2 percent off the yield, a steep price. In this case, buying direct makes sense. For larger amounts, however, a purchase through a broker can be wise. Since a bill held in a brokerage account is easily sold, the added liquidity easily makes up for the commission paid to your broker.

U.S. Treasury STRPs

These investments are similar to T-bills, but are usually issued for longer periods of time. Sometimes they even carry higher rates than comparable T-bills. STRPs are issued by the U.S. government but there are private labels, such as TIGRs (Merrill Lynch) and CATs (Saloman Brothers).

Government agency bonds

U.S. Treasury bills are not the only government obligations available to the short-term investor. Several U.S. government agencies also issue short-term notes.

1. Federal National Mortgage Association (FNMA). FNMA began as a wholly owned U.S. government agency in 1938. In 1968, it was transformed into a government-sponsored private corporation, with shareholders, a board of directors and private management.

The sponsorship of the U.S. government remains, giving it special privileges and keeping the company under the watchful eye of the Secretary of Housing and Urban Development (HUD). This implicit backing of the government gives FNMA an AAA-rating on Wall Street.

Although mortgage bonds are the mainstay of FNMA and can be purchased with shorter maturities, the company also issues 30 to 270 short-term obligations. All FNMA (also called Fannie Mae) obligations are bank-qualified and can be held by banks and considered as government obligations for reserve and accounting purposes.

2. Federal Home Loan Mortgage Corporation (FHLMC). A private corporation like FNMA, FHLMC issues only pass-through securities to the general public. The pass-through certificate is an undivided interest in a pool of home mortgages and has the same attributes as a home loan. Principal is paid every month, along with interest, and the loans can be paid off early because of lower financing, sale of the home or foreclosure.

All payments are guaranteed by FHLMC. Pass-throughs aren't ideal short-term investments because of their unpredictability. The maturity is always estimated and the closer you come to the estimated pay-off date, the less accurate it is. These are best-suited as intermediate or long-term investments, unless an FHLMC or FNMA collateralized mortgage obligation (CMO) is considered (more on that later.)

3. Government National Mortgage Association (GNMA). One of the most familiar U.S. government agencies is also the only agencies whose bonds carry the "full faith and credit" of the U.S. Treasury. Direct obligation of the U.S. government, GNMAs, or Ginnie Maes, carry the explicit backing of Uncle Sam as opposed to other previously mentioned agencies, which have "implicit" backing. Like the FHLMC, only pass-throughs are issued to the average investor, except for CMOs. Owned directly by HUD, GNMAs are ideal investments in longer maturities in many cases. For more on GNMAs, see Chapter 7.

4. Collateralized Mortgage Obligations. Based on mortgage bonds such as GNMAs, FHLMCs and FNMAs, collateralized mortgage obligations, or CMOs, separate the mortgage bonds into separate classes, called *tranches*. These tranches pay interest only at first, later paying principal back, hopefully more quickly than the average straight mortgage bond. Not all CMOs are created equally, so carefully read the section on them in Chapter 7. Short-term CMOs can offer attractive yields over other bonds, but since their maturities can change, use caution when buying for short-term investments.

5. Federal Home Loan Bank (FHLB). Similar to Treasury bills, in that they are discounted, FHLB offers notes with maturities from 30 days to 360 days, usually in denominations of $100,000 or more. Although not backed directly by the U.S. Treasury, FHLB securities carry the backing of the Federal Home Loan Bank, a conglomeration of 12 federally chartered regional banks. This backing essentially equates to the implicit backing of the U.S. government.

6. FICO and REFCORP zero bonds. This zero bond, which does not pay any interest until maturity, is like a Treasury bill. It's bought at a discount and then redeemed at a given price, accumulating interest as time goes on. Both are issued by the FHLB. While many still trade and both pay slightly higher yields than STRPs, their market doesn't have the same liquidity as the U.S. Treasury market. Both are state and local tax-free.

7. Miscellaneous federal agencies. All of the following issue short-term notes:

- Student Loan Marketing Association (SLMA)
- Tennessee Valley Authority (TVA)
- Federal Farm Credit Bank (FFCB)
- Small Business Administration (SBA)

All are available through brokers to individual investors. Their rate advantages over other government investments vary, and most are agency-guaranteed only (with implicit backing of the U.S. government).

The variety of government-backed short-term debt is astounding. While rates do not vary greatly, shopping around can pay off, especially if you're investing large amounts of money. Many retail brokers are not familiar with any government agencies beyond GNMA, FNMA and FHLMC, so be sure to ask about some of the others.

Tax-free investments

Since the United States Constitution does not allow state governments to tax the federal government (that's why U.S. Treasury interest is state tax-free) and the federal government from taxing state governments, one tax break is sure to be with us for some time to come— municipal bonds. Bonds issued by a state, city or local government are not taxed by the federal government and, in many cases, exempt from state taxes also.

The same is true for short-term municipal notes. Many municipal governments finance their short-term needs through municipal notes. The tax-free status of these obligations offers a big advantage over similar government and corporate debt. Individuals in high tax brackets, for example, would have to earn at least 6.48 percent in a taxable investment to put as much money in their pockets as with a 3-percent federally tax-free investment.

Unlike government bonds, however, credit quality varies greatly in municipal notes. While government and agency notes are usually rated AAA, municipals vary from AAA all the way to the bottom of the scale. Stick with AA or better (MIG 2 or better for short-term) well-known general obligation bonds, or revenue bonds providing essential services such as water, power or sewer.

Short-term municipal notes are bought through a dealer and marked up, similar to a retail store's mark-up. Purchased wholesale, they're resold at a higher retail price to investors. Avoiding nonrated bonds and low-grade bonds is always wise for an inexperienced investor. For more, see Chapter 7.

Short-term corporate notes

Similar to municipals, short-term corporate notes are fully taxable but often pay better yields than government debt. Ratings also vary greatly, but notes with good ratings and superior yields are easily found. Again avoid lower-grade issues and stick to well-known names.

Short-term mutual funds

Wall Street strives to have a product for every need—and short-term investments are always in demand. Mutual fund companies have been quick to provide investments geared toward short-term investors, with mixed results. These are, to borrow from a Clint Eastwood movie, the good, the bad and the ugly of short term investments.

The good: Treasury funds. A simple-enough idea; buy U.S. Treasuries and put them into a fund. Fund shareholders collect state tax-exempt monthly interest, usually at a better rate than they can get on their own since the notes are bought in larger quantity. The biggest surprise of all is that these short-term to intermediate-term funds have had 70 percent or better price increase of long-term treasuries with only 25 percent of the volatility. Not a bad deal.

The bad: Adjustable-rate U.S. government funds. It started out as a good idea—buy adjustable rate mortgage bonds, collect a higher rate of interest with almost no principal risk. Then everyone started jumping on the bandwagon. Soon, there were more dollars in adjustable-rate funds than in bonds. Funds started reaching into non-government-backed notes and, worse, fixed-rate notes and bonds for better yield. The bottom line is 4 percent to 5 percent returns with values that have defied expectations and declined in bad bond markets. No thanks.

The bad: Prime rate trusts. At the height of leveraged buyout madness and merger mania in the 1980s, someone somewhere on Wall Street began to notice that banks were making huge profits on loans to companies involved in buyouts or mergers. Why not package these loans and sell them to individual investors? But where to get the loans from? Banks, of course. Which loans were the banks most likely to sell? Probably not their best loans but, rather, the marginal ones.

To make matters worse, the funds were priced only once a quarter and, because there's no liquid market for bank loans, guess who priced them? The fund company. The value of these funds changed very little until, finally, some loans began to default and values had to be adjusted.

By this time, the creators of the leveraged buyout loan market were trying to figure out how to securitize car loans and credit-card bills, and the investors were left holding the bag.

The ugly: Short-term global funds. These will probably go down in history as the most plausible yet ridiculous idea of the decade. Here it is in a nutshell: Some European countries have higher interest rates than others. Yet all countries in the European Common Market tie their currency prices together by agreement. So, if a person could buy a bond from a country paying higher interest rates while simultaneously selling those from lower-paying countries, the result should be a sure profit.

A mysterious hedging technique, called cross-hedging, made the proposition even more plausible. Part of the problem was that many funds wandered from Europe and were investing worldwide, essentially speculating in currencies, gambling to see who could turn in the best performance numbers and gather the most assets from an unknowledgeable public.

In any event, even the pure European funds fell apart when European currencies did. It started when Italy devalued its lire. The culmination was England's devaluation of the pound. The worst of these so-called "safe investments" was down more than 8 percent in value, money that most acknowledged wouldn't be earned back.

Most people believe falsely that short-term investing, by nature, limits the choices of investments. As this chapter has shown, nothing could be further from the truth. A wide range of short-term investments exists and, while not all are equal in performance and safety, better rates can be found without compromising quality.

Chapter 7

Understanding Long-Term Fixed Investments

The telephone rings.

"Honey, it's for you. It's your broker."

You groan. Not again.

"Hello, George. A what? Collateralized what? Guaranteed, huh? Our government? The rate sounds good, but I don't know. Let me think about it. There's only $10,000 of it left? That's what I have in my account. OK, if you think it's good, go ahead."

Sound familiar? There've been more new types of long-term fixed investments introduced in the last decade than the previous 50 years before. Your broker may understand the cryptic abbreviations like GNMA, FNMA, CMO and UIT, but the average investor shrugs his or her shoulders. Most simply trust their investment advisor and look the other way.

Most of these investments aren't as complicated as they sound. A bit of reading mixed with a good dose of common sense can help you distinguish the winners from the losers.

Bank CDs

One of the easiest long-term investments to understand, these CDs are identical to their short-term cousins discussed in Chapter 6, but with maturities of five years or more. Few banks offer accounts longer than five years, but

when you can find them, they can be attractive alternatives to bonds. The interest rate is fixed, the principal insured by the U.S. government and the amount of risk limited to an interest rate penalty. Bonds, as we'll see later, cannot guarantee a limit to the amount lost, in theory at least.

Unfortunately, CDs offer no tax advantages and usually have yields significantly lower than comparable bonds.

Treasury notes and bonds

Treasury notes, varying in maturity from one year to 10 years, are sold at one-month or three-month intervals to finance the ever-increasing needs of our government. Thirty-year bonds are auctioned quarterly. Treasury notes and bonds enjoy steady popularity among investors for a variety of reasons.

Safety. All Treasury obligations have the backing of the "full faith and credit" of the U.S. government. While many worry about the financial soundness of our government, bond interest could always be paid by raising taxes, robbing Peter to pay Paul in a sense, since individuals are the largest holders of Treasuries.

Liquidity. The market for these bonds is the biggest in the world. A larger dollar volume results in lower spreads, or the difference dealers charge between the price they're willing to buy and sell at.

Tax advantage. Treasuries are exempt from state and local taxes. For someone in a high tax bracket, this adds a considerable advantage to buying T-notes over taxable bonds.

Noncallable. Unlike many municipal and corporate bonds, most Treasuries are not callable, allowing considerable price appreciation when interest rates fall.

Treasury notes and bonds are ideal for anyone looking for safety and relative liquidity. They pay interest every six months and the rate is fixed during the life of the bond. For those interested in monthly income, the bonds and notes can be "laddered," with staggered maturities and interest payment dates that result in monthly income.

U.S. government agency bonds

Many of the U.S. government agencies mentioned in Chapter 6 also issue long-term bonds. Unlike short-term instruments, long-term obligations usually consist of what are called pass-through securities. Rather than borrowing money from the public and lending it out, agencies put the loans into packages called pools and pass on the interest and principal payments, taking a fee to pay for services and defaults. An 8-percent mortgage, for example, might yield 6 percent to investors, the 2 percent remaining with the agency. A bondholder would receive principal and interest each month from the mortgage borrower, and principal payments when borrowers paid off loans or refinanced.

Maturities of mortgage bonds are estimates only, since no one really knows when mortgages will be paid off. An estimate is made based on previous prepayment periods but can vary from region to region. For example, in Texas, where real estate prices dropped dramatically, mortgage bonds paid off much more slowly during the late '80s than bonds from California, where the real estate market was hot.

When property prices drop like this, home owners often owe more on a home than its market value. It becomes difficult to sell when the seller is "upside-down." On the other hand, when real estate is rising rapidly, homes tend to change ownership more as speculators buy and sell and residents "trade up."

Interest rate changes also affect mortgage bond prices. When interest rates fall, owners refinance, paying off their old higher-interest loans and getting new ones with lower rates. This principal repayment "passes through" to bondholders. If interest rates rise, home owner refinancing slows down.

A slowdown in refinancing and sale of homes extends the life of a mortgage security, a pickup shortens its life. The maturity of mortgage bonds is expressed as an "average life" or the average amount of time similar bonds have taken to pay off in an environment similar to today's and assuming no change in interest rates. If rates change, or the housing market varies, the average life could change. Technically a mortgage bond could mature on the stated maturity date (usually the length of each mortgage) assuming no one ever refinanced, moved or lost their house.

Most mortgage bonds are based on 30-year mortgage loans, but it's highly unlikely every mortgage holder would take 30 years to pay off their loan.

The variety of long-term government bonds and variations can be overwhelming. Here's a sampling:

1. Government National Mortgage Association (GNMA). GNMAs or Ginnie Maes, the most familiar of mortgage bonds, provides one of the most liquid. Usually issued with a 12-year average life, Ginnie Maes carry the *explicit* backing of the U.S. Treasury. They're based on 30-year home mortgages, purchased from lenders.

2. Federal National Mortgage Association (FNMA). FNMAs, or Fannie Maes, boast a variety of maturities and underlying mortgages. Some FNMAs, for example, are based on 15-year mortgages and others on mortgages with balloon payments. A 15-year mortgage bond has a shorter average life than a 30-year mortgage bond. A bond based on mortgages with balloon payments may have a seven-year stated maturity, with the balance due in seven years in a lump sum, giving it an even shorter average life than a 15-year mortgage bond. FNMA has the *implicit* backing of the U.S. government.

3. Federal Home Loan Mortgage Corporation (FHLMC or Freddie Mac). Similar to FNMA, these securities finance home loans. A variety of bond types are available.

4. Zero coupon government bonds. These bonds pay no interest until maturity and offer an excellent alternative to regular government obligations, especially for those saving for retirement, college or any other long-term goal. A bond purchased at a deep discount matures at a future date at a predetermined value. A $550 investment, for example, might mature at $1,000.

Interest rates tend to be higher on zero coupon bonds. One disadvantage is that taxes are paid along the way on the accumulation, even though no income is received.

The U.S. Treasury issues zero coupon bonds called STRPs. Private issuers also issue zeros. Merrill Lynch's are called TIGRs and Saloman Bros., CATs. Some agencies also issue these bonds. FICO and REFCORP, discussed in Chapter 6, are two examples with higher yields yet than Treasury-based zeros. Municipal zeros and corporate zeros will be discussed in later sections.

Collateralized mortgage obligations (CMOs)

"7 percent, 10 year, government bond" reads the ad in the business section of a major metropolitan newspaper. Sound too good to be true? Maybe. The SEC has recently cracked down on a relatively new form of government bond investment called the CMO. Newspaper and magazine articles are decrying this new investment, which thousands have invested in. In blanket denunciations, writers and investment advisors alike have swept aside the investment as ill-advised and deceptive.

Some of the criticism is deserved, but, overall, a properly selected CMO offers a superior yield and greater stability of maturity than most other mortgage investments.

Why the scandal? Before I get into that, let's take a close look at exactly what a CMO is. When the mortgage bond market mushroomed in the early '80s, one objection to buying these securities was the changing maturities. It seemed to be the worst of both interest-rate scenarios. If rates rose, the bonds dropped in value. But if rates dropped, the bonds prepaid.

At first, the bonds offered a much higher yield than Treasuries, compensating the investor for uncertainties in maturity. Eventually, the yields dropped and the advantage vanished.

Brokerage firms responded by creating CMOs. The idea was to smooth out the principal repayment and to stablize maturities. Mortgage bonds, usually FNMAs and FHLMCs, were pooled and separated into groups called tranches. The tranches had a priority in principal payment. The interest rate of each also corresponded to its estimated maturity and the stability of that maturity.

For example, a CMO made up of 8 percent Fannie Maes might have five tranches. The first tranche earns 4 percent and all principal payments are directed to this tranche until it is paid off. The second might earn 6 percent, the third 8 percent, the fourth 10 percent, and the fifth 12 percent. When the first tranche pays off, principal payments are directed to the second, then the third, and so on. Accordingly, each will have a different average life. The underlying bonds might have a 12-year average life but tranche one might have its own average life of only four years, since it's being paid off first.

The later bonds receive interest only until the previous tranche is paid off, and then the principal repayment is accelerated. Each tranche is issued as a bond or bonds of a particular class. The type of class purchased determines how volatile the changes in the maturity will be. These classes are: VADMs, PACs, PACIIs and PACIIIs.

VADMs and PACs are considered the safest of CMOs, the type of bonds most often purchased by institutions. Accordingly their yields are the lowest of most CMOs. Yet, these rates are usually higher than comparable Treasury bonds and they provide monthly interest.

Vanilla bonds

The next safest tranche type is the standard bond or "vanilla" CMO. Although the maturity can vary, these CMOs still have several advantages over regular mortgage bonds. At first, they pay interest only, and then principal over a shorter time than a straight mortgage bond. The yields are usually slightly higher than PACs and quite a bit higher than regular mortgage bonds.

Support or companion bonds

This tranche is the first to be paid off when interest rates fall and the last when they rise. This most volatile of interest-paying CMOs is the type advertised in your local paper, because it carries the highest rate. A 10-year support CMO can easily extend to 24 years or contract to two years, picking up the slack for the more stable tranches within a CMO offering. While most often sold to the public rather than institutions, other more conservative bonds are just as easily found.

X or Z bonds

The last tranche in some CMO offerings is the most interesting. Z bonds act as zero coupon bonds, with some very interesting differences. First, interest accumulates by adding face value to a bond sold at par or the value it will mature at. The bond isn't sold at a deep discount but rather at par—or a slight discount. The value of the bond grows. After a given period of time, the bond converts to an interest-paying CMO, usually a vanilla or support bond.

The Z bond is well-suited to an investor who's 10 to 15 years from retirement. The bond accumulates during that time and then pays interest monthly after 10 to 15 years. The most interesting feature of the bonds, though, is the yield, usually a point or more higher than a support bond. Z bonds often sell at a discount, making them even more attractive. Even when paid off early (the bonds are a little more volatile in maturity than support bonds), a huge profit can be realized since the bonds pay off at par.

CMO investment strategies

Certain strategies can maximize your return in the CMO market, while minimizing the risk.

1. Never buy at a premium. If a bond should pay off early, that premium (or price paid above maturity price) is lost earlier than planned and the rate of return drastically reduced. Buying at a deep discount, on the other hand, lowers income. Par or slightly lower is the ideal price for most CMO purchases.

2. Stick with VADM, PACs or vanilla bonds for income. Varying maturity is the biggest risk CMO holders face. Taking a slightly lower yield in return for stability is a wise choice.

3. When buying Z bonds or X bonds, buy at a deep discount. As discussed earlier, if the bond should pay off early, a nice return is locked in.

4. Stay with government-issued CMOs as opposed to private-label CMOs. Especially avoid private-label bonds not connected with any government agency.

Remember that CMOs don't have the liquidity of other government bonds, such as Treasuries and GNMAs, making them less than ideal trading vehicles. Although dealer spreads have been coming down, there can be 1 percent to 2 percent differences between buy and sell prices, not counting your broker's mark-up. Most CMOs should be bought with the intention to hold them until maturity.

Corporate bonds

Most corporations issue debt in one form or another. Larger companies offer their notes and bonds to the public. Corporate bonds vary widely in quality, as well as in maturity and rate. The lower the quality of a bond, and the longer the maturity, the higher the rate. While a bond rated AAA might fetch a fraction of a percentage higher yield than government bonds, lower-grade bonds, commonly called junk bonds, can pay 3 to 10 percentage points higher than a similar Treasury. Of course, the risk of default rises as the rating falls. While a high-grade corporate bond reacts mostly to interest rates, a high-yield or junk bond also responds to changes in its underlying company's or industry's financial position. Here are some of the things to look for when buying a corporate bond.

Call features. Many of these bonds are callable after a certain period of time. If interest rates fall, this can limit their upward price movement. Most are callable 10 years or more after being issued and usually at a higher price.

Zero coupon bonds with call features can be extremely difficult to understand. Look carefully at all call features and try to find noncallable bonds whenever possible.

Liquidity. Are the bonds traded frequently? Where? As mentioned in Chapter 6, exchange-traded bonds are preferable, although higher yields are found in less liquid bonds.

Bond types. Junk bonds are particularly notorious for unusual bond issues. For example, PIK or Payment in Kind bonds pay no interest for several years. Some act as zero coupon bonds and others accumulate value like the CMO Z bonds.

Underlying business. A declining industry or company might soon be subject to downgrades. Usually, bonds about to be downgraded have a higher-than-normal yield. A detailed analysis of the issuing company should be mandatory before buying junk bonds, since these bonds perform more like stocks.

Corporate bond purchases require more research than government issues. Extra diligence is always recommended when dealing with lower-grade debt.

Municipal bonds

Tax-free municipals have become especially popular, as Americans brace for higher taxes and search for tax breaks. The Tax Reform Act of 1986 essentially stripped most investment tax breaks away, leaving municipals as one of the few truly tax-free investments still available. The bonds are issued by city, county, state and other local governments to finance operations or special projects.

While always exempt from federal taxes, many bonds are also exempt from state taxes in their own state. Bonds issued by territories such as Puerto Rico, Guam and the American Virgin Islands are exempt from federal and state taxes in every state. Popular with investors in high tax brackets, tax-free municipals can be bought as individual bonds, unit investment trusts and mutual funds. Since municipals vary in quality, careful analysis is essential to investment success. Here are some considerations:

Rating. Three major bond rating agencies, Moody's, Standard & Poor's and Duff & Phelps, rate municipal bonds. AAA ratings are usually the highest and D lowest. A higher-rated bond is superior to a lower-rated one in safety, but yields usually rise as rating goes down. Finding the best balance is part of the art of picking bonds. In practice, most investors should stay with AA or better.

Nonrated bonds have become more common in recent years. A bond may not carry a rating for several reasons. Perhaps the issue is too small and they didn't want to pay a bond rating agency the $100,000-plus it costs to get a rating. Mutual funds purchase some bonds as an entire issue and forgo ratings. These mutual funds may have their own in-house rating service. Or the bond could be part of a special group of tax-backed bonds used to finance community improvement. Most of these are backed by the taxing power of the community through property taxes.

Insurance is available on bonds, usually raising the rating to AAA. For example, a bond that would rate AAA on its own merits would not need insurance, while a bond with a BBB or A rating could benefit greatly. A bond with an AAA rating without insurance is, therefore, more desirable than an AAA rating with insurance.

Type. Two types of municipals are most common in individual accounts—general obligation and revenue bonds. A general obligation implies that the city, county or state issuing the bond will be responsible for paying its interest directly. The full taxing power of the issuer can be used to pay back bondholders.

A revenue bond pays its interest and principal from money received from a specific project or company being financed—a power plant, water pipeline or sewer system, for example. General obligations municipals, once considered superior in the days before budget shortfalls and state fiscal crises, now face increased scrutiny. Revenue bonds now have the limelight because the debt is backed by a specific revenue source, and not subject to the whims of state legislators. Essential service bonds, such as water, power and sewer are even safer, because these services are always needed.

A third type of municipal has become popular in the past few years—not among individual buyers but among institutions—called *derivative bonds*. Some investment bankers have created new classes of tax-free bonds by pooling bonds and issuing new securities.

The most infamous is the *inverse floater*, in which brokers pooled long-term bonds and issue long-term and short-term securities. The short-term securities were actually the same maturity as the bonds, but their interest rates adjusted every so often to reflect current rates. So if short term rates fell, the short-term securities rate adjusted

down. If they rose, the securities rate rose. The long term counterparts, as we'll call them, became inverse floaters. Since the bonds in the pool paid a fixed rate, every time the rate on the short-term bonds fell, the long-term rate rose. When rates rose, however, the rate on the long-term securities (inverse floaters) fell. The bottom line on derivatives for the average investor is to avoid them.

State of issue. The economies of states ebb and flow. While Texas seems depressed along with oil prices, the Midwest might be booming because of strong capital goods sales. Industries also move from states to state, moving to those with the lowest taxes, least regulation and most affordable cost of living.

A municipal bond investor should not only analyze individual issues of bonds but also the states from which they are issued. While many bonds, such as essential-service revenue bonds, are not affected greatly by the vicissitudes of state economics, most other tax-free bonds feel the effects of the fortunes of their state.

Other factors, however, need to be considered. Take California, for example. The weakness of the economy scares many municipal bonds buyers away. But a *California* investor is exempt from state taxes when purchasing a state bond. Since state tax can run as high as 11 percent, an out-of-state bond would have to yield considerably more—at least 11 percent more—to make it worthwhile.

Economic problems are usually overcome by careful individual selection. Even the worst state economies have shining stars. When the state of Massachusetts was downgraded to BBB, the lowest rating a state has ever received, there was no shortage of AAA and AA bonds from its city and county entities. Look carefully at fiscal conditions in the issuing state, but weigh the information carefully against other factors, like state taxability.

Tax-free bonds will continue to be popular investments as long as there are taxes. As tax rates increase, the demand for the bonds will probably increase also. Buyers of municipals should be willing to diversify among at least four different bonds. Since bonds are often sold in "round lots" of $25,000 (some firms even have $50,000 round lots), smaller investors might think the municipal market is a little too rich for their blood. Buying odd lots is one option. The other is investing in pooled accounts, such as mutual funds and unit investment trusts.

Mutual funds

At some future date, if someone was to summarize the financial history of the past 10 years, it would probably read "The Decade of the Mutual Fund." Unknown to most in 1980, mutual funds have become a household word during the past 10 years. Their growth has been astounding. Investors are flocking to funds in record numbers, helping to drive up the prices of both the stock and bond markets.

As popular as they are, it's surprising to discover how little most people know about an investment that more than 50 percent have some money in.

A mutual fund is an investment pool in which investors purchase shares. Their money is invested in securities for the benefit of the shareholders. An investment company manages the money,

taking a fee for management, and holds the securities in trust at a large bank or trust company. The fund's manager(s) chooses investments and watches the fund on a day-to-day basis. The investment advisor or broker that recommends the fund may also receive a fee.

That is where the similarity in all mutual funds ends. As sales have mushroomed, so have the variety in fund types. Funds are separated into several different categories:

Open-end and closed-end funds

A closed-end fund will sell a certain number of shares to the general public and, rather than offering to redeem them from the investor, the fund trades the shares like stock on the open market. The fund's price will vary according to the demand in the market and the number of people willing to part with their shares.

An open-end fund buys the shares back from the investor at the close of business each day. In other words, the fund keeps enough cash to buy back its own shares and takes in new cash when investors purchase new shares. The number of shares is never fixed—it varies from day to day.

This creates some interesting differences between closed-end and open-end funds. Closed end funds can trade at a discount or premium to their underlying value per share. So if a closed-end fund has $10 of assets per share, it doesn't necessarily trade at $10 per share on the stock exchange. If it sells for less than $10, it sells at a discount and could be an attractive buy. A price greater than $10 means the fund sells at a premium, making it less attractive to most investors.

An open-end fund always redeems the shares at the ending day's value. But its liquidity comes with a price. Since it can never be predicted how much will be sold on a given day, some cash must always be kept on hand to redeem shares, money that could be earning higher returns if invested. In an extremely bad market, securities may have to be liquidated at fire-sale prices.

Take 1987, for example. Many mutual funds were forced to liquidate securities to settle the mass of redemption requests received, even though most managers knew it was a terrible time to be selling.

When government bond rates are high, everyone buys into government bond funds, unleashing a flood of new cash on fund managers. The cash is reinvested, but usually at lower rates, diluting the yields from the older, higher-yielding bonds previous investors were receiving interest from. Closed-end funds, on the other hand, can be fully invested and never dilute the share-holder's value, because they are traded on the open market.

In spite of this disadvantage, open-end funds are still better for most amateur investors. The ability to exchange one fund for another is a big advantage. If you're in a stock fund, for example, and decide you'd rather be in a bond fund, most funds allow switching by phone for a small transfer fee in some cases (usually never more than $10).

While closed-end funds are purchased on stock exchanges, usually in round lots of 100 shares or more, many open-end mutual funds offer small initial payments and allow more purchases in small amounts, $50 or $100 minimums for example. Some even allow investment directly from a bank account over the phone or through a systematic deduction.

Additional purchases of closed-end funds made on the exchange require a minimum purchase and charge a commission. Flexibility and convenience are two reasons open-end funds are so popular.

Fund investments. The word mutual fund conjures up thoughts of high-flying, high-yielding investments that buy stocks and follow market fluctuations. At one time, most funds fit this description. But in recent years, they've evolved into a diverse group offering something for just about every investment need and desire. Even the variety of fixed-income mutual funds can be overwhelming. Some examples are:

U.S. government funds

Not always as secure as the name implies, the growth of U.S. government funds has taken off in the past few years. In Chapter 6, short-term and intermediate-term funds and adjustable-rate funds were covered. In addition, three major types of funds currently account for the bulk of government sales: *"plain vanilla," special strategy,* and *derivative funds.*

Plain vanilla connotes exactly what it delivers, a mutual fund that purchases regular government securities with none of the frills that enhance the yield or raise the level of risk. These tend to be the least volatile government funds in bad markets, but also lag in yield in good markets. Most of the bonds in these funds will be Treasuries, GNMAs and FNMAs. Check the portfolio to see if a fund is truly plain vanilla.

The next time you look at the top-performing mutual funds in a financial

49

magazine, chances are the top-performing government funds will be *special strategy funds*. Odds are the same funds will occupy the bottom-performing category at some future date also. These volatile instruments invest in a very small sector of the U.S. government bond market. *Zero coupon bond funds*, for example, buy only STRPs and similar bonds maturing during a particular period. Rather than buying individual bonds, investors can add varying amounts at different times, knowing the money will mature at a given date.

Although useful for retirement and college planning, zero coupon bonds can be extremely volatile, turning spectacular returns one quarter and disastrous results the next. For an average investor, the ride can be disquieting. Most zero coupon funds also don't pay interest, making them unsuitable for many government fund buyers.

Option income funds is another type of government specialty fund that peaked in popularity about five years ago. The basic idea was to buy government bonds and write options against them, collecting the extra income and paying it to the shareholders. With promises of returns 2 percent to 3 percent higher than plain vanilla funds, investors flock to government-enhanced funds, pushing some individual fund assets above $1 billion.

The strategy may have worked, if interest rates had stayed stable. But the interest-rate market changed dramatically in 1987, becoming more volatile than in previous years. Option income fund returns were decimated as the best bonds in the funds were called at below-market prices. Funds began to pay interest out of principal to maintain high dividend level, and eventually fell into

infamy as investors and their advisors began to realize what had happened.

Specialty funds come and go, depending on trends and what new types of strategies are dreamed up on Wall Street. Some, like the zero coupon funds, work well for certain special needs. Others, like the now-infamous government-option income funds, are utter failures.

The jury is still out on the newest member of the government fund family: *Derivative funds* have only recently appeared on brokers' and advisors' product lists, as mutual fund companies have sought out ways to maintain or increase falling government-fund interest rates. Most derivative securities, similar to the CMOs discussed earlier, offer a 1 percent to 2 percent yield advantage over plain vanilla funds. The problem is, many of these derivatives differ drastically from other government and government-agency bonds and can be much more volatile.

Take the reverse floaters, for example. Similar to municipal reverse floaters, the securities rise in price drastically when rates are falling and fall just as dramatically when rates rise. Since rates have been rising, the added yields and total returns have made these derivatives very appealing.

Another dubious strategy is the use of forward contracts. Fund managers sell them on existing bonds to boost income. The strategy might work wonderfully, provided interest rates and the bond market don't act unpredictably. Funds using this strategy risk the sting of falling value at some point in the future. Generally, if the yield is much higher than the market, tread carefully and invest only if you're comfortable with every aspect.

Tax-free bond funds

With higher taxes looming, billions of dollars have been flowing into tax-free investments, especially tax-free municipal bond funds. Hundreds of funds promise tax-free income.

But differences in fund structure and holdings translate into different advantages and disadvantages, depending mostly on where you reside. Some are taxable by your state, for example. Some invest for total return, which can produce taxable capital gains. A few claim to be "insured." Here's what to look for when choosing a tax-free fund:

1. National tax-free or state tax-free. National tax-free funds buy a variety of tax-free bonds from different states. These bonds are always federally tax-free, but only a portion of the interest can be state tax-free, depending in which state the owner resides. If you live in a state with no income tax, a national tax-free fund might be a good choice. For a resident of a state with high income taxes, like California or New York, a fund investing only in those state's bonds is probably a better choice. Even if the yield is lower than a national fund's, the added advantage of exemption from state taxes can put more money in your pocket.

2. Total return vs. income. Increased returns from total return funds are often negated by the taxes paid on capital gains. For example, if a tax-free fund pays 5½ percent interest and 1 percent in capital gains, the shareholders would have to pay taxes on the capital gains. Another fund paying 6 percent in interest and nothing in capital gains would be a better buy since you pay no taxes on any of the dividends. Most people invest in tax-free funds for income and tax advantages, not capital growth. A better total return doesn't necessarily put more money in your pocket.

3. Insurance. Most insurance for municipal bonds and funds comes from private insurance companies or through bond insurance companies backed by different insurers. As mentioned earlier, most insured bonds are lower-quality bonds that provide the insurance to get a lower yield. While fundholders might feel more comfortable with an insured fund, since all bonds in that fund carry an AAA rating, a few uninsured funds have a large portion of their portfolios in high-quality bonds, mostly AAA, offering comparable safety and a higher yield.

Don't be mesmerized by the word "insured." Choosing a high-quality, non-insured fund might be a better choice. Look carefully at the bond ratings in the fund and make a decision from there.

Junk bond funds

Alternatively fashionable and forgotten, junk bonds have been on the investment scene for about a decade. Although the conviction and jailing of several key junk bond promoters sent prices reeling for a time, junk came back with a vengeance in 1992 and 1993, posting double-digit returns. With yields holding at 9 percent and better, investors tempted must ask themselves, "Is it really junk or diamonds in the rough?" One school of thought says junk is junk and the price appreciation is due to speculation and a manipulated market. With Mike Milken out of the picture, the conspiracy theory becomes a little harder to swallow.

The other side of the argument likens junk to overlooked gold, and claims that diversification will solve all the problems of credit risk. That's hard to believe, too, especially when so many bonds have defaulted or have been renegotiated as of late.

I think the truth lies somewhere in the middle. Properly selected high-yield bonds can yield better-than-average returns, but at the price of increased risk. Treating the bonds as stock, analyzing the merits of the individual company closely as you would a stock is essential to being successful in this market. This is where a fund can be useful. Since selection of good bonds is important and most individuals lack the resources to select bonds and follow this complex market, a good-quality mutual fund might serve as the best vehicle for investing in this market. Municipal junk funds are also available for those looking for high yields and tax advantages.

Specialty bond funds

Several hybrids have emerged over the last decade that defy classification. Two, long-term global bond funds and strategic-income funds, warrant attention because of their popularity.

Global bond funds invest in overseas bonds, often issued by the governments of foreign countries in their currency. Along with interest-rate risk and credit risk, investors also have to cope with currency risk. If the foreign currency rises, U.S. investors' profits rise. The opposite is true when the country's currency falls. Since the U.S. dollar is hitting record lows, this type of fund has fared fairly well in the past few years. Also, interest rates remain relatively high in other countries, perhaps posed to fall.

Strategic-income funds combine junk bonds, overseas bonds and U.S. government bonds all in one fund. The idea is that when one type is doing poorly, the others are usually doing well. By balancing out the risk, the principal stays fairly stable. And the yield, right now, is considerably higher than a regular government fund.

Sound too good to be true? Maybe. But it's hard to argue with success. Strategic income funds have performed very well in the past three years. Perhaps credit for the above-average returns belongs with the junk bond portion, which has performed exceptionally well since 1990. Government bonds and foreign bonds have also performed well. According to the fund's own premise, the returns shouldn't have been as high as they have been. The best advice is to tread with caution. The safety of strategic-income funds has been, in my opinion, greatly exaggerated.

Load vs. no-load

The controversy continues. Magazines continually assault load funds, blindly exalting the virtues of no-loads. All funds are in the business of making a profit. Hopefully, along the way investors profit also. The focus of fund selection should always be on performance first and charges second. It's better to have a top-performing fund with a sales fee than a money-losing fund with no fee.

A load fund charges a front-end fee, usually paid to the broker or advisor the fund is purchased through. Many back-end funds are also sold by advisors, where a fee isn't paid initially but a smaller charge deducted every year from the fund. If sold early, a penalty is also assessed. This yearly charge, called a 12b-1 fee, was named after the SEC (Securities and Exchange Commission) rule that defines it.

No-load funds charge no sales fees at all, but levy management and operational charges, just like load funds. So if you do your own research, why not buy a no-load fund? After all, there's no sales charge.

Maybe. As so-called no-loads have sought greater market share, and traditional investment advisors have sought to be more competitive, the lines between load and no-load funds have been blurred. Some load funds, for example, have become so large that their management fees are half of comparable no-load fund charges, since it's less expense to manage a large fund.

Certain no-load funds now charge 12b-1 fees to pay for advertising, which has increased dramatically to compete with broker-sold load funds.

It's become difficult to classify any fund solely on the basis of load. What should be most important to you is how much you will net and how much downside risk there is. Whether you select your own funds, or use an investment advisor, don't be penny-wise and dollar-poor. Look at performance, volatility, management ability and expenses before making a decision.

Unit investment trusts

Often maligned as an unmanaged mutual fund, UITs offer distinct advantages over mutual funds. Although structured much like a fund (shareholders own a piece of a portfolio of bonds), their number of shares is fixed and the bonds are neither bought nor sold. The interest rate remains the same during the life of the fund or until bonds are called away.

This is different from a mutual fund, which constantly adds new money, diluting rates of return and causing dividend rates to change. A UIT interest rate remains constant and the dividend cut only when principal has been returned. Unlike a fund, a UIT also has a fixed life and pays a fixed amount of principal at the end of the term. Mutual funds constantly change price, most never really maturing.

Before you rush off and cash in your mutual funds, remember that UIT fees can be high (up to 5 percent) and they are not managed. Investors concerned with stable income over active management and capital gains should look at UITs as an alternative. Just about any type of fixed-income mutual fund will have a UIT counterpart.

Annuities

Mention insurance company annuities to most retired investors, and two words come to mind: First Executive. The now-infamous company damaged the reputation of insurance companies more in one year than it was damaged throughout the entire Great Depression. Even though investors with les than $100,000 in First Executive's junk bond annuity investments didn't lose a dime—and those over collected a large percentage of their money—most people feel that an annuity issued by an insurance company is a risky investment. Yet, annuities continue to be an attractive long-term investment.

Deferred annuities work much like CDs from a bank, except they're not insured by the FDIC, their terms are generally longer and they're tax-deferred. Money is deposited with the insurance company and, in return, the buyer receives an annuity contract. The contract states the term of the annuity, the early withdrawal penalties, the withdrawal features and the initial rate guarantee.

Money earns interest until the annuity is surrendered (cashed in), paid out (in the event of death) or annuitized. All interest is tax-deferred until the owner takes it out. The proceeds also pass directly to heirs without probate, another important feature, even though the estate would be responsible for income tax on the accumulated interest.

Since an annuity is one of the few investments that issues no 1099 and reports no taxes to the government, it also has several tax advantages.

Annuitization provides monthly income in exchange for the value of the annuity. For example, if a deferred annuity bought for $10,000, grows to $20,000 and is then annuitized (paid out monthly), the owner exchanges that $20,000 in value for an income—for a fixed period or for a lifetime—giving up all rights to access his or her principal. In other words, the owner would receive income but would no longer have the cash in the annuity.

Annuitizing usually assumes a very low interest rate, and is usually a poor investment. An *immediate* annuity begins annuitization immediately, while a *deferred* annuity delays it, sometimes indefinitely. When looking for a deferred annuity, certain features warrant close examination.

Fixed or variable. Fixed annuities guarantee principal and pay a fixed rate of return. Variables invest the proceeds in mutual funds, which remain tax-deferred while held within an annuity. Funds are bought and sold within the annuity fund family, and no taxes are paid as long as the funds are held in the annuity.

Free withdrawals. Almost all annuities offer a free withdrawal feature, usually 10 percent of the value per year. Some offer this from the moment of purchase, others after the first year. Most allow the 10 percent to come out once a year. Others allow it to accumulate so that if nothing is taken out for three years, for example, the contract allows a 30-percent withdrawal.

Tax advantages. Annuity investments are tax-deferred. No taxes are paid on interest until after funds are withdrawn. The interest isn't reported on a 1099, a useful tip covered in more detail in Chapter 9.

Penalties. Penalties for early withdrawal vary. Some companies impose high penalties during the first years only. Others keep penalties intact for several years. Some have no penalties at all, but offer low rates. Penalties should never be charged for withdrawal after seven years, and the first-year charge shouldn't be more than 7 percent. Typically, if you withdraw more than the free withdrawal the first year, the penalty will be 6 percent, the second year 5 percent, the third year 4 percent, etc.

Company ratings. Ever since the First Executive and Mutual Benefit debacles, investors have been increasingly conscious of insurance company ratings. Three major agencies rate insurance companies: A.M. Best, Standard & Poor's and Duff & Phelps.

A.M. Best is the largest of the three. However, Best has come under fire for lax rating criteria and should be used in conjunction with another rating service. Best rates companies from A++ (highest) downward. Both Standard & Poor's and Duff & Phelps use ratings similar to their bond rating systems, starting at AAA (highest) and moving down to D.

Even if an insurance product has a high rating, investors need to look a little more closely. All the major rating agencies gave both First Executive and Mutual Benefit fairly high grades, up until months before their insolvency. Checking ratings on a regular basis is one step. The other is to look at what the company invests its policyholders' money in.

Portfolio. When money goes into an annuity, the insurance company sponsoring it invests the money in a portfolio of investments. While ratings can be a good place to start when choosing an insurance company, the portfolio is what really backs the annuity. The more secure and liquid the investments, the safer the annuity. Here's what to look for:

- **Government bonds.** The safest of all bonds are popular investments with higher-quality insurance companies.

- **Investment grade corporate bonds.** Second only to government bonds, these high-quality corporate bonds usually have better yields than government bonds.

- **Junk bonds.** Ever since First Executive, most companies avoid these types of investments. A company that has a large percentage of junk bonds, over 15 percent, should be avoided. Most companies will have some bonds rated below BBB (considered junk) because of

previously high-graded bonds slipping in ratings. These fallen angels don't present as much of a risk.

- **Real estate.** Insurance companies are one of the largest holders of commercial real estate. With office vacancy rates at record high levels and prices collapsing, commercial real estate may not be the safest investment. Ask for a geographical listing of holdings and occupancy rates before investing. If a company has more than 15 percent in real estate, buy with caution, Make sure the properties are performing well, and look at how long they've held each property. Real estate could present the same problems to annuity holders in the next decade as the junk bonds presented in the last.

- **Real estate mortgages.** Treat these as if they were real estate, since a mortgage holder, in effect, owns a property if the owner defaults. The combined percentage of real estate and mortgages should not exceed 25 percent.

Look for insurance companies with the bulk of their assets in relatively liquid government and high-grade corporate bonds.

Rate history. An insurance company usualy guarantees annuity rates for a specific time and, after that, renews yearly or at some other specified interval. Some companies, unfortunately, offer high rates initially, only to drop them dramatically later. Thus, checking a company's renewal rate history is important. Not all insurance companies use bait-and-switch techniques.

Some changes in interest rates reflect a changing portfolio. That's why it's important to know how interest is allocated to individual annuity holders.

There are two ways companies allocate interest: by *segregated* portfolio or *pooled* portfolio. A segregated portfolio separates the investments purchased for all annuity holders during a particular time. When interest falls, annuities purchased earlier have higher rates, since they're invested in bonds that locked in higher yields. In a pooled account, all investments are pooled together so that when rates fall, new investments with lower rates are added,

lowering the rate more drastically for old annuity holders.

While rates in a pooled account should be more likely to rise, in practice, few annuity companies raise their rates. Only two companies that I know of have raised their rates at any time and that was during the early 1980s.

While most people are rushing to long-term fixed investments as short-term rates tumble, you should keep in mind the strategy of diversification. Long-term fixed investments, along with short-term and growth investments, are essential to a complete retirement plan.

Chapter 8

Growth Investments and Inflation Hedges

"Hindsight is 20/20." So goes the old aphorism. But if you were given the chance to invest 25 years ago knowing what you know today, what would you buy? How about 60 years ago? Bonds? Probably not. They've averaged a little under 4 percent a year since 1926, compared to inflation, which has grown about 3 percent a year. Real estate? Maybe. Nationwide, it's returned a little over 6 percent per year.

What about stocks? "Stop right there," you say. "I know about 1929 and the Great Depression." Yet, in spite of the Depression, a half-dozen recessions, a world war, another dozen or so regional conflicts and hyper-inflation never witnessed before in this country, stocks returned a little over 9 percent per year since 1926. Smaller company stocks did even better, averaging just over 11 percent per year. And over the last 10 years, the Dow Jones Index has grown 16.62 percent per year.

Few investors can afford to ignore this type of investment. Yet until recently, stocks have been an enigma to most investors. In this chapter, we'll examine some of the different strategies of buying stock and how these investments can fit into your overall portfolio.

While stocks perform as both inflation hedges and growth vehicles, we'll examine two other investments that serve as inflation hedges: precious metals and real estate. First, a closer look at building a stock portfolio.

Selecting individual stocks

Most investors think that the market is stacked against them. Buying a stock is like betting red or black in Las Vegas. You may win from time to time, but over the long haul—just like the casinos—Wall Street and those who control it will come out on top.

Most people think of stock investments as a zero-sum game. In other words, whenever someone wins, someone else has to lose. What they aren't appreciating is that stocks are pieces of businesses, and businesses grow and expand, producing more earnings that can be shared among all shareholders. Unlike a speculator, who takes a quick profit at the expense of someone else ("theory of the greater fool," it's often called), an investor holds an investment as if he or she were buying or selling a business.

Another assumption is that the professionals on Wall Street are all-knowing, and that they have access to information no one else has. Nothing could be further from the truth. Take IBM, for example. If analysts are all-knowing, how come a majority of them were recommending "buys" and holding it in numerous portfolios just before Big Blue's precipitous fall?

Most professionals buy the same stocks and sell the same stocks, whipsawing prices with the huge amounts of cash they manage. Peter Lynch, one of the brightest and best to emerge from the professional money managers ranks, calls it the herd mentality. He even insists that individual investors have an advantage over Wall Street professionals, since they are closer to popular trends and have a better understanding of what is going on in the consumer markets and in their own businesses.

The advent of mutual funds has made individual stock-picking a dying art, but here are some basics.

Technical or fundamental?

At one time, rigid lines separated these two schools of investment thought. The traditional technical belief is that the market is driven by the psychology of investors. A person buys because a stock is rising or sells because it is falling. Fear and greed are the motivating factors. It is investor response that causes stock prices to go up and down, as well as whole markets. As a result, the theory goes, rises and falls can be predicted by charting stock prices and watching for a variety of indicators that show whether buyers are excessively optimistic or pessimistic.

Fundamental investors, on the other hand, traditionally believe that stock prices are merely a reflection of the company's position, and as a company grows or declines in fortunes, so will the stock. They try to predict a company's future performance, thus, predicting its stock price.

Fundamentalists once held disdain for technicians, valuing their work much

as a medical doctor would value the amulets of a native witch doctor. "Why is it," they would ask, "that when a company's earnings rise, the stock also rises?" Technicians would counter by asking how a stock could fall even when its earnings were rising.

Most modern stock watchers understand the value of both techniques. Because of my own bias, most of the stock-picking advice to follow will lean toward fundamental analysis.

Three strategies dominate the investment scene currently, each falling in and out of favor periodically.

1. Undervalued assets. Using the oldest of all stock-picking strategies, investors try to find stocks whose assets or earnings are high relative to their price. These cheap stocks are usually in depressed industries or in companies emerging from financial woes. Here are some scenarios to look for:

- An exceptionally good company in a bad industry might have its price pushed down in sympathy with other stocks in that industry.
- A financially weak company in a good industry might pull itself out to participate in the industry's growth.
- The perception of a problem could be worse than the reality, causing the stock to be priced cheaply.
- Hidden assets the market has ignored make a stock worth more than its market price.

Undervalued stock-pickers tend to examine financial information closely. They look for low P/E ratios (price divided by earnings per share), high dividends and low debt. By finding stocks that are strong financially and paying dividends, they anticipate the company will be able to weather any problems and recover.

Undervalued stock-pickers are bargain hunters. They're constantly looking for sales on assets, just like a consumer would shop for a good deal in a department store. But they're savvy shoppers. They don't just buy stocks that have gone down, but seek out stocks that shouldn't have gone down or shouldn't stay down.

2. Earnings growth. Buyers of high flyers such as Walt Disney and PepsiCo are followers of the earnings growth philosophy. Basically, these investors look for stocks whose business is growing at such a clip, that increased earnings will drive the stock prices ever higher in years to come. Classic growth stocks include Coca-Cola, WalMart and Microsoft. None would be considered cheap by value investors, but each has handily outperformed the market in the past five years. Companies that command their market and have high profit margins are especially good earnings growth stocks.

3. Special situations. Usually including everything that doesn't fit into the previous two categories, special situations have an eclectic flavor. Stocks that could be subject to takeover, unknowns about to launch a new product, or old-line companies spinning off businesses are all examples of special situations. They don't fit any particular category, but are still good buys.

Contrarians are investors who often follow the special situations strategy. They buy investments when no one else wants them. In other words, when the worst news is out, and things look bleakest, these brave souls step right in.

Contrarians don't necessarily look at assets or at earnings. A pending sale or takeover, exaggerated bad news or a number of other factors usually come together in helping them make a decision. It's now in vogue to be a contrarian. But if *everyone* is following contrarian strategies, then the very definition of contrarian is negated.

While most investors follow one of these strategies, some blend two or more together to produce a new strategy. For example, several mutual funds look for earnings growth at a discount, combining the first two strategies mentioned here. Regardless of modifications, undervalued assets, emerging growth and special situations strategies are basic to any portfolio plan.

Brokerage recommendations

Full-service brokerage firms produce a staggering amount of research every year. The larger the firm, the more reams of paper available to its brokers and, through them, the firm's clients. Whether it's the firm's advice or an individual broker's, thousands of investors rely on advice from major brokerage firms. The results are mixed. For every person whose broker has him or her a fortune, there are probably five who haven't a good thing to say about either their broker or firm.

Deciding when to take a broker's advice is a difficult decision. For one thing, brokers are compensated not by your profits but by the number and types of transactions they make. Even if they are long-term oriented and don't overtrade your account, they have to rely on their firm's research. They have been accused by critics of treating the firm's client companies' more leniently because of investment banking and other corporate relationships.

Another problem is that brokerage firms haven't any incentive to issue sell opinions. There isn't much money to be made when a stock has a sell rating and the firm may upset a potential client. How many times has a brokerage firm had a negative opinion on the stock or bond market? Unless the company is teetering on bankruptcy or the president has disappeared on a Brazilian cruise with most of the corporate bank account, the worst you'll see, in general, is a neutral opinion.

To find a broker who will work for *you*, start by finding out who the top-performing analysts are. Get a copy of the *Institutional Investor* All Star Issue. In it the top analysts on Wall Street, as determined by institutional investors, are named. Then ask your prospective broker for recommendations and performance history.

Then, test the broker. Give him or her a small amount of money. Follow the recommendations. Look for a broker who is also an investor and has a love of the market but doesn't constantly recommend buys and sells. Even if you make money at first, an actively traded account is likely to lose the gains in short order.

Newsletters

There's a newsletter for almost every investment topic—agricultural biotechnology to over-the-counter European stocks and everything in between. But be careful. Just about anybody can start a newsletter and claim to be the decade's next financial guru.

There are very good newsletters, though, offered by serious and perhaps brilliant stock watchers. "Hulbert's

Financial Digest" is a newsletter that rates the newsletters. There's also a book, *The Hulbert Guide to Financial Newsletters*, which tracks the performance of most major market newsletters. Once you've selected one or more newsletters, ask for a trial subscription, just to make sure its exactly what you want.

Following your hunches

Many people buy a stock because their friends have bought it or because the stock has been in the news. These are probably two of the worst reasons to buy. A wiser strategy is to stick to stocks of companies that you know.

Think back to some of the best stocks of the 1980s. Were those companies riding trends that could have been recognized? Look at Walt Disney. When its amusement parks started opening around the world, and its Touchstone pictures enjoying a string of hits, it was obvious that Disney would start growing. But you didn't have to see an annual report to know that Disney was a good prospect. You could determine that by what you read, the number of people you knew who'd enjoyed vacations at Disney parks and the amount of activity you witnessed in Disney stores at the malls.

The same is true of WalMart. If you walk into a store, you can see that it's clean, well-stocked, the lowest price is always guaranteed—and the customers keep on coming.

How about Price Club? Or Microsoft? As a consumer, none of us should have missed out on those stocks. A good investor looks for additions to his or her portfolio every day. Not in the library or at a broker's office, but in the shopping mall, supermarket and place of employment. Invest in what you understand

and use the other sources we've discussed to back up your choices. There's no such thing as a successful passive investor. Use your knowledge and special interest to choose stock investments

For some, investing in individual stocks is not only to create a nest egg for their future but also to have a bit of fun along the way. Most people who buy individual stock make picking the stocks a hobby of sorts. Many investors have neither the time nor the inclination to be involved with the market. They turn to mutual funds for simplicity and ease of investment.

Stock mutual funds

Mutual funds have truly come of age in the last decade. Few investments have experienced the kind of growth that mutual funds have in the past few years. Thanks to the media, and persistent advertising, nearly everyone is at least aware that mutual funds exist.

Falling bank rates are driving more and more investors away from traditional bank accounts and CDs, creating a new class of investors. In spite of this mass immigration into fund families, few people understand exactly what a fund is. A basic description was offered in Chapter 7, but stock funds have some unique characteristics.

First a review of fund basics: A mutual fund is a pool of money managed by a professional money manager, usually employed by a mutual fund company or brokerage firm. Investors own a share and benefit accordingly.

There are several types of funds. Here's a brief overview.

1. General funds. General funds invest in a variety of stocks and sometimes bonds, usually not limiting the manager to specific securities. The investment strategy is what separates funds with a general orientation. Some strategies include:

Balanced, equity income, or growth and income. While each of these types of funds at one time defined a specific strategy, they now overlap to such an extent that most investors would have difficulty separating them. All three strive to balance their portfolios and minimize risk by having a percentage of the portfolio in bonds or focusing on dividend-paying stocks. Most portfolio managers will have value-oriented stock-picking philosophies. While underperforming the market, the funds in this class also tend to do better in down markets. Stability and conservative investment philosophies attract investors to balanced, growth and income and equity income funds.

Growth and aggressive growth funds. These mutual funds look for capital gains over income to propel their total returns. Since they tend not to diversify into bonds or even conservative dividend-paying stocks, growth funds also fluctuate more than many of their more conservative counterparts. As the name implies, aggressive growth funds pursue this strategy even more forcefully. Most growth managers follow an earnings growth investment philosophy. While fluctuations in price can be greater, long-term holders of growth funds usually receive better returns than growth and income shareholders.

2. Specialty funds. Investors wanting to focus their investments more closely can turn to a variety of specialty funds that concentrate on a specific industry or area while maintaining the diversification of a mutual fund. Here are a few:

Small company growth funds. Similar to growth funds, small cap managers limit their investments to lesser-known stocks with a greater growth potential.

Sector funds. Convinced that the oil industry is going to rebound? That gold is ready to soar. Now offered are specific funds for specific industries. Fidelity is best-known for sector funds. Not all are speculative, either. Utility funds are among the most conservative and best-paying funds available.

Overseas funds. Global funds offer diversification on a worldwide basis. Many overseas markets have greatly outperformed our own in past years. Specialized global funds allow investors to focus in on specific areas like Asia or Europe, or even specific countries.

Specialized strategies. Fidelity offers the Contra fund for contrarians. Other funds use margin to increase (or decrease returns). Some use strategies devised by market gurus such as Martin Zweig or Al Frank, with varying degrees of success. The focus is on *strategy* rather than holdings.

Regardless of the type of fund you choose, it's important to select carefully. Out of thousands of funds available, only a few have outperformed the market indexes over the past decade. How can you tell the good from the bad? Most investors don't know where to begin when choosing a mutual fund investment. The selection process doesn't have to be difficult. The mutual funds selected in the center portion of this book were all chosen by unique criteria you can use as an individual investor.

Five criteria to selecting a good mutual fund

1. Track record. How well has the fund performed? Some of the biggest funds in the country have mediocre track records at best. Look at three-year, five-year and 10-year performances and compare them to the market averages and other funds. Also, look year by year. An especially good one-year return can make a mediocre fund *look* like a superstar.

2. The fund manager. How long has he or she been there? If a fund has an excellent track record for 10 years, but the manager recently went to another fund, perhaps you'd be better off following the manager. The manager's tenure should match the track record. If your fund has a new manager, ask for his or her performance record from the previous position. When you buy a fund, you are buying the management. Some funds have multiple managers and yet have good performance.

3. Does the management style fit your personal investing style? If you're an aggressive investor and look for high returns in spite of volatility, perhaps a balanced fund isn't the best choice. The same is true of conservative investors. Don't be mesmerized by astronomical returns. Stick with a fund that invests the way you would invest.

4. Portfolio turnover. This measures the amount of trading that the manager does. A fund with a high portfolio turnover usually buys and sells a lot, trading stocks to get higher gains. There are two reasons most conservative investors want to avoid this. First, the more times a person buys and sells, the greater the odds of making a bad trade. A frequently traded portfolio, may do well for even a long period of time. But what are the odds of the manager always timing the market correctly?

In addition, a less frequently traded fund should generate fewer and smaller capital gains distributions. While in tax-deferred accounts, such as IRAs, this isn't very important, for taxable investments capital gains distributions have a big impact on total earnings. The fewer profits taken, the lower the gains on average.

5. The fund family. Bigger is better, just in case your choices turns out to be bad or your investment objectives change. Since most funds allow switching into other funds in the same family at little or no cost, look for a large selection of good-quality funds.

Following these rules doesn't guarantee investment success, but it certainly increases the odds of finding a fund that will meet your expectations. All mutual fund selections in the center section of the book were chosen based on these and other criteria. While mutual funds can be excellent investments, the benefits are not without disadvantages. For example:

Advantages of mutual funds
- Diversification allows an investor to buy a diversified portfolio of securities without high initial cost.
- Investments are in dollar amounts rather than even numbers of shares. This way, you can invest money in smaller increments, and get money in dollar increments.
- With mutual funds, you can move from fund to fund in same family with a low cost.

- To reduce the income tax obligation to shareholders, the fund manager can balance the losses against gains or maintain a low turnover.
- A good manager can add value by outperforming the market—and the returns most small investors could get on their own.

Disadvantages of mutual funds
- Diversified holdings can underperform other more concentrated investments.
- There are the costs of money management, sales and operations not tacked on to individual stock purchases.
- Capital gains is passed on each year to the investor and taxed. Individual stock and bondholders don't pay gains until they sell.
- A bad manager can make less than a fixed account or index fund would pay.

Good and bad considered, mutual funds offer the average investor a lot more benefits than handicaps. While not an end in itself, this type of investment has a place in most portfolios. Select carefully but don't stop evaluating the fund's performance after you've bought it. Managers change, as do strategies and objectives, and careful monitoring is prudent.

While stocks have been premier inflation hedges and growth investments over the past decade, other investments merit consideration also. These are true inflation hedges because they carry real value, regardless of economic conditions.

Real estate

It used to amaze me how many people considered real estate a very safe investment, at least when they were talking about their own individual homes. The same people also believed that real estate prices were always going to go up. Things change. While a few die-hards persist, for most of us, our views of real estate investment have been colored by the last recession, especially those who live in California, Texas or Massachusetts.

Buying an investment with 20 percent down and borrowing 80 percent has never been considered a conservative strategy by any measure. Granted, a primary residence is different: Since you're going to have to make the payment anyway, and there are many tax breaks associated with owning a home, buying makes sense.

While real estate might go up and down, and fortunes made and lost, one thing is certain: As an inflation hedge, a real estate investment can serve a useful purpose. As real property, its price will always adjust with inflation. Since prices have risen dramatically on factors other than inflation, and have subsequently fallen, many people are again looking into real estate investments. If you're one of those people, here are some types of real estate investments to consider.

Limited partnerships. Popular in the 1970s, limited partnerships saw the bulk of investors who jumped in during the 1980s lose their shirts. I've yet to see a real estate partnership put together after 1985 that performed up to expectations. Most have yet to return the principal to investors. Highly illiquid, these investments are difficult to sell even to take a tax loss in many cases. Initial fees as high as 25 percent to 30 percent would have destined many limited partnerships to mediocre returns at best, even if expectations were met.

This is one real estate investment you want to avoid, unless it involves a small partnership with people you are thoroughly acquainted with. These private deals can work in cases of joint ownership of large property. Another recent tax strategy is the family limited partnership, used to transfer assets to children and grandchildren. Other than that, avoid these deals entirely.

Real Estate Investment Trusts (REITs). Similar to real estate partnerships, REITs have two important differences. They're liquid, usually traded on an exchange, and the fees charged are not nearly as outrageous. REITs invest in shopping malls, apartment buildings and commercial buildings, and are generally managed by well-known real estate companies. Their liquidity makes them attractive, as do the typically high dividends.

Real estate stocks and mutual funds. Sometimes, buying the stocks of real estate-related companies can be more profitable than owning the property itself. Some stocks to consider are home builders, savings and loans, construction companies, real estate brokerages and insurance companies. While some have fortunes tied to new construction, others, as big real estate owners, benefit from any price appreciation.

Mutual funds also offer real estate portfolios, usually mixing real estate-related stocks with REITs.

Individual property. By far the most common real estate investment, individual ownership is a cornerstone of the American way of life. The United States has a higher percentage of home owners than any other industrialized country in the world. We create institutions that encourage home ownership, offer tax incentives for home ownership and staunchly limit the government's ability to take ownership away.

Individual property ownership has several advantages over other real estate investments but also several disadvantages. First, the leverage that's involved. If you were to buy a stock by borrowing 80 percent of the purchase price and putting in only 20 percent of your own money, you'd be called a speculator. Do it with a house and you're a real estate investor. Real estate investments are not suitable for the average conservative investor. The only exception, is of course, your primary residence.

Still, it's hard to argue with success, and real estate investors have done well in the past 30 years. The key to buying properties as an investment is in good selection, good pricing and sound management. It's definitely not a place for the faint-of-heart.

Precious metals

An old-time favorite of doomsayers, gold has recently made a comeback, jumping in price drastically. Gold is difficult to class as an investment because it doesn't really produce anything. The only way to make money is if its price rises. The same is true of silver, platinum or any other precious metal. It's a wasting asset—it doesn't earn anything.

Gold *companies*, on the other hand, produce something. They earn profits, grow and expand, and sometimes even pay dividends. Although usually volatile in nature, these stocks are tied to the price of gold and tend to perform better than bullion when prices rise. Many mutual funds also offer gold funds, made up exclusively of gold stocks.

In spite of strong performance recently, gold is usually a mediocre investment at best. Stocks, money markets and even bonds outperform gold stocks over long periods of time. If there must be a portion in your portfolio, it's wise to keep it under 10 percent.

The most ignored portion of a portfolio plan, an inflation hedge, is probably the most important. We've heard for several years that inflation is dead and that it's no longer a threat to our financial health as it once was. The truth is that 3 percent to 4 percent inflation is enough to cause a serious decline in living standards even over a relatively short period.. Regardless of what inflation hedges or growth investments you favor, always keep a portion of savings invested in something to protect your assets from rising prices.

Chapter 9

1994 Outlook
and Beyond

I heard a well-known analyst, a contrarian, speaking at a conference a few years back. One of his comments has stayed in my mind. "When your cab driver start telling you about a stock you've investing in recently, it's time to get out."

I don't believe he has anything against cab drivers or any other profession, for that matter. The point is that when everyone is talking the price up in a particular investment, and it finally reaches the people furthest removed from the investment business, there's no one left to buy. And unless it's really a better investment than everyone thinks (and it almost never is), the price is going to fall.

What always amazes me about this is that people never learn. And the small investor, who's the last to get into the latest sure thing, usually predicts the end of its rise.

Take a doctor I once knew. He was the best contrary indicator I ever met. If he was thinking about buying something, you knew it was just about to collapse in price. Stocks in 1973, bonds in 1979, silver in 1980, farmland in 1982—and the list goes on. He had a great deal of faith in his own judgment and, since he mistrusted most brokers and financial advisors, he gathered most of his information from tips from colleagues and newspapers. Since information usually reached him after the investment had become "hot," it never failed to decline right after his purchase.

Like that doctor, many people buy a fund because it was the top performer the year before. Or they invest in a stock because it's run up a lot and the evening news anchor is talking about how much money people have made. Investors tend to overreact on good news, driving up even the best of stocks well past the point of fair value.

Being a professional doesn't guarantee any more success. Most money managers can't even match the stock market indexes in performance. Peter Lynch, the now-famous manager of the Fidelity Magellan fund, likens them to sheep, buying the same stocks from the same institutional brokers every manager deals with.

Fortunately the door of public opinion swings both ways. While a "hot" stock may be ready to take a dive, the latest "dog" might be ripe for turnaround. Take Chrysler, for example. In 1990, nobody had anything good to say about it. Analysts shunned the stock, citing impending disasters, ranging from unrelenting Japanese competition to an underfunded pension fund. The stock price was driven down to 10, the yield rose to over 10 percent. Only a single

66

analyst had a buy opinion on the stock and everyone else was recommending a sell. The stock at the time of this writing is selling for 46. It's now a favorite on Wall Street.

But just because a stock is down and out doesn't make it a good buy. Most stocks drop in price for a reason, but it's the ones that are beginning to turn around that deserve attention. The first signs of Chrysler's recovery were the positive reviews of its new LH series of cars in automobile magazines. The second, in its successful cost-cutting and asset sales program. The final hint before the stock began its inexorable rise was when a famous investor bought over 9 percent of the company after a private preview of the new LH cars and a meeting with Lee Iaccoca.

Safe investments are usually out of favor. You won't read about them in *USA Today* or hear about them from most brokers. They don't have stories explaining why they'll differ from every other high-priced investment. Rather, they've been the subject of negative comments or news, often exaggerated claims of their imminent insolvency, or they're simply ignored by the financial community in general because of their lack of "sizzle," or because the putative wisdom of the day says they will not be attractive investments.

Boom or bust...
Where do we go from here?

Most people make the same mistake with the market that they do with the roulette wheel in Las Vegas. They assume that if the ball falls on black several times that they should bet on red. After all, the odds are in red's favor, right? The market that has run up a lot, they assume, is due to crash soon. The higher it goes, the more likely it will crash. Some analysts base their entire career on this fuzzy logic.

Just like the roulette wheel, however, movement in the market really has little to do with what it's done in the past. Its future performance is based on factors other than its past performance. If stocks have doubled in the past two years but are still cheap compared to other investments, they could continue to rise. If bonds have seen their yields halved but still pay twice as much as short-term accounts, the yields could go down even further.

Expectations drive prices in the short-term; long-term price movements are driven by emerging trends. For example, people might expect inflation to revive and push down bond prices, but if the true trend in inflation is down, the prices will rise in the long-term.

Sometimes expectations are the same as reality. Other times expectations have little to do with fact. The trick in investing is to know one from the other and take a long-term view in line with the trend. It's not as hard as it sounds. Usually the writing is on the wall, but greed and emotion blind us to its meaning. Here are some of the long-term trends that will be propelling and sinking different investments during the next decade.

Aging America. People are getting older and are using more products and services geared toward older consumers. But getting old isn't the same as it used to be. Retirees have swapped lawn bowling and bingo for backpacking and jet-skiing. People are living longer than at any time in our history. Despite market jitters, drug companies and other health care related stocks could perform much better than expected. The same is true of leisure-oriented companies such as casinos and entertainment companies.

Baby boom two. The baby boomers we read so much about are producing a second baby boom. Look around at all the children you see in the shopping mall or park. And these parents have an entirely different lifestyle and a larger pocketbook than their own parents did. More and more, stay-at-home parents (moms *and* dads) are telecommuting from home offices in a quest to make family a priority. Both Mom and Dad will be busy trying to juggle kids, work, home responsibilities and leisure activities. Companies that produce time-saving devices and work-at-home technology will boom. Toy makers, private education providers, interactive video and computer providers will also benefit.

No more company men and women. Once content—and able—to work at the same company until retirement, today's workers are forced to better manage their careers and become vocational "renaissance" men and women. Movement between companies, industries and geographical locations will all accelerate as we near the end of the decade.

More new businesses will spring up as once-burned corporate types decide to go it alone. The average age for students will rise as ex-grads return to campus for new skills. A better educated, more flexible work force will soften future effects from changes in the economy, and increase the quality of corporate America's work force. The bottom line will be more profitable, competitive American companies

Lower public spending. This translates to increases in privately provided services, such as security, education, arbitration and other locally funded services. As federal and state subsidies to local governments die out, cities and counties will respond by trying to increase revenue by enforcing ordinances, cutting spending and raising taxes. Private security, education and waste disposal will be a few industries that will benefit. Anything that can be privatized, resulting in cost savings and greater efficiency, will produce a private industry alternative and pressure will fall on local governments to convert.

Low interest rates. They won't be climbing anytime soon, barring a sudden increase in oil prices or a miracle turnaround in the economy. Long-term rates will probably fall to historic norms of 4 percent to 5 percent as Congress and the president respond to public outcry regarding the deficit. While a lot of pork barrels may be overturned, a modest reduction in deficit levels is inevitable. Long-term bonds may not be as attractive as stocks, but they should fare pretty well. Stick with quality, as many lower-grade bonds will face increased risk of default.

The nesting trend will continue. A number of factors will result in the continued cocooning trend. Retirees will be about the only ones living it up—though they may fear venturing out too much and too far. Home electronics, video, music, computers, and any other home-based activity should benefit.

Record growth of overseas economies. Watch China, smaller Asian nations such as Indonesia, Malaysia and Thailand, Latin America and Eastern

Europe. There's nowhere to go but up for many of these countries, as productivity improves. Japan will also see future growth as it switches its export base from the U.S. and Europe to its fast-growing neighbors. Some U.S. companies with a large overseas presence will also benefit. Select emerging markets, such as Latin America, Southeast Asia and Europe, are ripe for higher gains, each for different reasons.

Taxes will go higher. And higher. With the deficit a high priority, and spending cuts coming more slowly, most taxes will rise. Tax-free bonds should shine for the next few years, with high quality crucial to investment success.

More competition among U.S. companies. This competition will encourage profits as layoffs and other cost-cutting measures take effect. Europe won't be far behind.

Emerging technologies will replace many of the growth industries of the last two decades. Just as mainframe computer makers have fallen out of favor during the last three years, PC makers will continue to come under increased competitive pressure, leaving most of the profits in the hands of monopolist supplies such as Intel and Microsoft, or with cutting-edge PC makers who have the cash resources and technological ability to bring out new products that are not easily duplicated.

As the computer business matures, it will be harder for everyone to make the same kind of profits realized in the '80s. Some of the new growth industries that will come of age in the '90s are:

- **Agricultural biotechnology.** A tomato that has a long shelf life is already out. Soon to come, lowfat canola oils, insect-resistant wheat and extra-lean beef.

- **Virtual reality.** Imagine touring a house and seeing the kitchen in 10 different color schemes, all at the push of a button. Put on a helmet and you can "walk" through it, everything in actual scale size and make changes at will. Lower price hardware will make this industry boom.

- **Interactive entertainment.** Do you want to watch a movie? Dial up your local phone or cable company and see anything you want whenever you want. And it's all added to your next bill. No time to go to the bank? Push a button and pay as many bills as you want, right from your TV screen. Or from your laptop computer while you commute to work. It's almost here. Telephone companies and cable operators already have run up in anticipation, perhaps with good reason.

Where to invest in '94

Your best bets for 1994 and beyond might be in some surprising, and not-so-surprising places.

Drug stocks. Some very well-managed companies have had the wind knocked out of them as a result of health care reform. Profits might not be what they used to, but the market is treating the companies as if they'll never see black ink again.

Oversold blue chips. While some are probably destined for the history books, others are restructuring and are likely to weather the economic storm.

Many pay large dividends that can pay better rates than CDs.

Tax-free municipal bonds. Paying historically high yields compared to U.S. governments, these issues will be even more attractive as taxes rise. They've run up a bit in anticipation but could have a lot further to go.

Overseas stocks. Be selective, but many markets are likely to outperform the U.S. because of higher growth rates or current overselling. Europe is an example of the latter; China, Latin America and Southeast Asia the former.

Information technology. Breaking my own rule about popularity, I find there are times when the potential is underestimated by even the bravest bulls. Everything is in place for an information revolution and companies that participate could be well-rewarded, indeed.

There will be investors crushed by the coming changes in the economy. Companies who are unable or unwilling to adapt will fall by the wayside, taking their investors with them. New companies will take their place, benefiting those who invest early. The trick lies in throwing out conventional wisdom. Invest in what you think is an industry or company that will succeed, and don't worry about which way the herd is going.

The 100 Safest Investments for Retirement

What is safe? Safety of principal? Preservation of purchasing power? Shelter from taxes? With everyone from telephone pitchmen to your Uncle Harry dispensing investment advice, it's hard to choose a safe investment. Part of the problem is that everyone has a different opinion. Magazines and newspapers choose "the best" investments every year—but this year's best often seems to be next year's worst. Best does not always seem to mean safest.

The following 100 investments are what I would consider "the best" and the safest investments currently available to an average investor thinking about retirement. Although the selection process was complicated, here's a brief synopsis: The universe of investments was narrowed with the help of a computer. The criteria varied. A weighted value was given to each and investments were scored accordingly. The scoring system considers safety first and performance second when ranking investments. Some of the variables were:

Growth investments. Volatility, liquidity, income and performance.

Equity mutual funds. In addition to the above, asset size, management tenure, management track record, down market performance, expenses and asset turnover were considered.

Fixed income. Quality, price, maturity, tax advantages and volatility.

Fixed-income mutual funds. Asset mix, maturity mix, management tenure, management track record, volatility, asset size, down market performance and turnover.

After the initial selection, the list was narrowed by several subjective factors. Most coincide with an investment theme mentioned in Chapter 9. Those investments mentioned in Turnarounds and Special Situations were added in as a result of their future potential.

No thorough analysis of investments can be based only on the past, since the past often doesn't give an accurate reflection of what's to come. Both the past record and future potential play an important role in selecting an investment.

While no one has a crystal ball, the following 100 investments, in my opinion, offer above-average returns with lower than normal risk levels within their categories.

Chapter 10

Aggressive Growth Investments

Alliance Counterpoint Fund

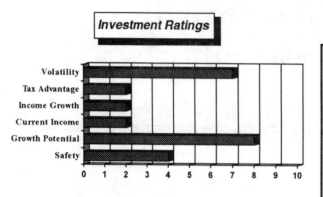

Initial Sales Charge: **5.50%**
B shares available with no initial sales charge

Annual Cost per $1,000: **$26.40**

Annualized Returns

3 Year	*11.14%*
5 Year	*16.45%*
Inception(2/28/85)	*13.51%*

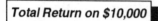

Total Return on $10,000

Income on $10,000 Investment

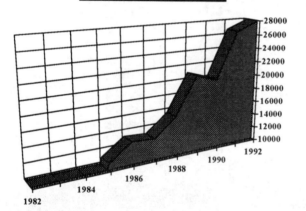

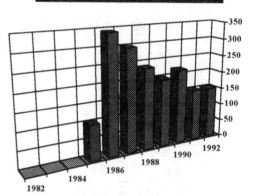

Historic Returns

	1982	1983	1984	1985	1986	1987	1988	1989	1990	1991	1992
Total Return (%)				15.69	20.93	-1.36	19.86	34.20	-4.64	33.47	4.59
S and P 500 (%)	21.47	22.46	6.13	31.64	18.68	5.26	17.50	31.68	-3.20	30.40	7.92
Dividend Yield				1.02	2.94	2.27	1.97	1.45	1.27	1.00	0.81
Income on $10,000 ($)				102	343	298	236	198	219	151	151

Annual Return During Bear Markets

40.00%	
30.00%	
20.00%	
10.00%	
0.00%	
-10.00%	
-20.00%	
-30.00%	
-40.00%	
-50.00%	

1969 1973 1974 1977 1981 1987 1990

■ Alliance Counterpoint ▨ S & P 500

Portfolio Composition

100%
Stocks

As of 6/30/93

Investment Description

Alliance Counterpoint Fund is suffering from an identity crisis. A self-proclaimed contrarian fund, it should be investing in out-of-favor stocks and turnaround situations. While the fund hasn't abandoned its charter, its portfolio looks more like a grab bag than a list of fallen angels. For example, Exxon and Royal Dutch, two undervalued, high-dividend issues, share space with Pepsico, Walt Disney and McDonald's, classic growth stocks. High-tech Intel and Lin Broadcasting are toe-to-

toe with bread-and-butter Kellogg and JM Smucker. Fund manager David Hanke likes a bargain, but he obviously defines a bargain in a variety of ways. A loss of market confidence, an aberration in earnings, or industry fears all could trigger a buy in this fund. This eclectic approach has produced excellent returns without a great deal of risk. While Counterpoint may defy categorization, one label is sure to stay: winner.

Suitability

Age 55 and under	*B+*
Age 55 to 70	*B*
Age 70+	*B-*

Inception: 2/25/85

Manager Tenure: 1985

Telephone: (800) 227-4618

Minimum Initial Investment: $250.00

Direct Deposit: No

Federated Growth

Investment Ratings

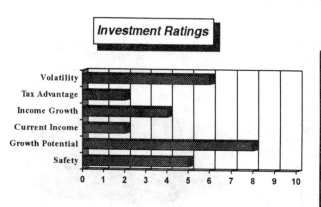

Investment Statistics

Initial Sales Charge: **None**

Annual Cost per $1,000:   **$10.03**

Annualized Returns

3 Year	*9.15%*
5 Year	*12.67%*
Inception(8/23/84)	*16.61%*

Total Return on $10,000

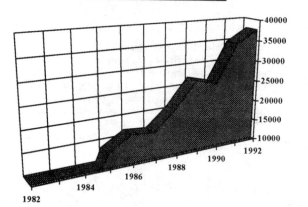

Income on $10,000 Investment

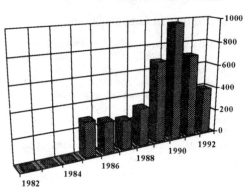

Historic Returns

	1982	1983	1984	1985	1986	1987	1988	1989	1990	1991	1992
Total Return (%)				34.67	24.03	-3.10	28.75	29.24	-4.90	35.11	8.59
S and P 500 (%)	21.47	22.46	6.13	31.64	18.68	5.26	17.50	31.68	-3.20	30.40	7.92
Dividend Yield				2.86	1.96	1.50	2.04	3.50	0.40	3.16	1.35
Income on $10,000 ($)				285	257	239	314	681	976	702	392

Annual Return During Bear Markets

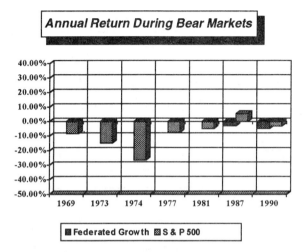

40.00%	
30.00%	
20.00%	
10.00%	
0.00%	
-10.00%	
-20.00%	
-30.00%	
-40.00%	
-50.00%	

1969 1973 1974 1977 1981 1987 1990

■ Federated Growth ▨ S & P 500

Portfolio Composition

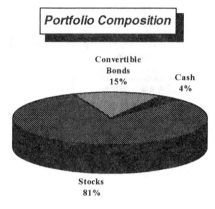

Convertible Bonds 15%

Cash 4%

Stocks 81%

As of 6/30/93

Investment Description

Federated Growth fund defies classification. On one hand, manager Greg Melvin favors classic growth stocks like U.S. Healthcare and Nike. On the other hand, several value-oriented holdings such as Merck and Service Merchandise creep into the portfolio from time to time. Add a sprinkle of small caps and turnaround situations and Federated Growth's strategy emerges. This odd mixture has paid off well for investors. The fund's return since inception runs just a tad over 16%. The only stocks Melvin tends to avoid are slow-growth utilities and some slower-growth blue chips. Growth is definitely the middle name of this fund, but not growth at any price. Most holdings are trading at good valuations and seldom will stocks with outrageously high P/E ratios appear. Cyclicals and financials have boosted performance in the past two quarters, making up for a mediocre 1992. Although the high initial investment ($25,000) might scare off a few smaller investors, for those who have the means, Federated Growth is an excellent choice for a conservative investor.

Suitability

Age 55 and under	*A-*
Age 55 to 70	*A-*
Age 70+	*B-*

Inception Date: 8/23/84

Manager Tenure: 1986

Telephone: (800) 245-5000

Minimum Initial Investment: $25,000.00

Direct Deposit: No

Mutual Benefit Fund

Investment Ratings

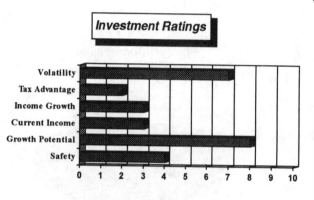

(Volatility, Tax Advantage, Income Growth, Current Income, Growth Potential, Safety — scale 0 to 10)

Investment Statistics

Initial Sales Charge: **4.75%**

Annual Cost per $1,000: **$21.35**

Annualized Returns

3 Year *10.69%*

5 Year *14.53%*

10 Year *13.85%*

Total Return on $10,000

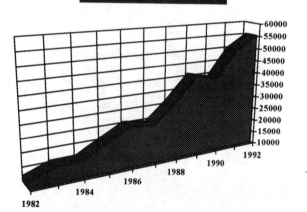

Income on $10,000 Investment

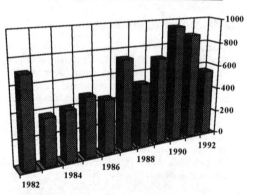

Historic Returns

	1982	1983	1984	1985	1986	1987	1988	1989	1990	1991	1992
Total Return (%)	33.76	26.58	0.31	31.61	22.02	-4.53	29.92	28.23	-5.09	27.69	10.52
S and P 500 (%)	21.47	22.46	6.13	31.64	18.68	5.26	17.50	31.68	-3.20	30.40	7.92
Dividend Yield	7.39	3.19	2.80	3.43	2.48	3.51	2.66	2.87	3.09	3.09	1.58
Income on $10,000 ($)	704	374	402	480	436	734	516	707	955	877	556

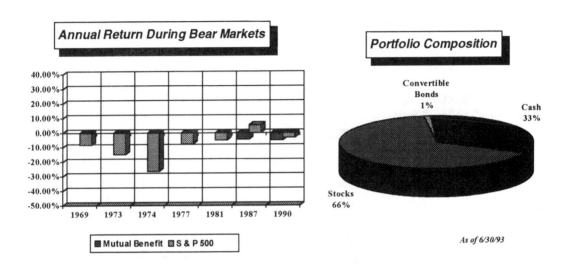

Investment Description

Mutual Benefit's investment strategy defies classification. Side by side with value-oriented blue chips such as Royal Dutch and GTE are small caps like Avnet and Questar. Add a sprinkling of REITs and perennial growth companies such as McDonald's and Coca-Cola, and you have Mutual Benefit's recipe for success. The diversity in strategy comes in part from the funds multi-manager approach. Three managers share a portion of the portfolio, each managing a share independently. John Stone manages 45% with an eye to value and larger cap stocks. Michael Mullarky looks toward small-cap issues for the 45% he manages and Roger Lob, the third manager, focuses on special situations. Each claims to be a value investor but approaches value with an entirely different view. As confusing as it all may sound, shareholders have been rewarded handsomely by this bewildering mixture. Since each strategy tends to go in and out of favor at different times, this approach also tends to limit risk, making this fund not only one of the best performing but also one of the least volatile in the group.

Suitability

Age 55 and under	*A-*
Age 55 to 70	*B*
Age 70+	*B+*

Inception Date: 1/21/71

Manager Tenure: 1981/81/86

Telephone: (800) 323-4726

Minimum Initial Investment: $250.00

Direct Deposit: No

79

Nicholas Fund

Investment Ratings

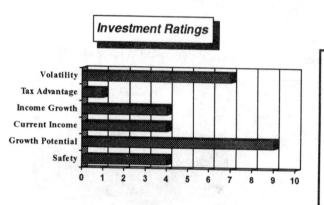

Investment Statistics

Initial Sales Charge:	**None**
Annual Cost per $1,000:	**$9.52**

Annualized Returns

3 Year	*13.50%*
5 Year	*13.92%*
10 Year	*13.12%*

Total Return on $10,000

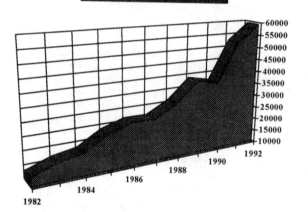

Income on $10,000 Investment

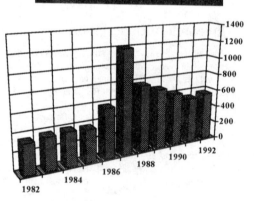

Historic Returns

	1982	1983	1984	1985	1986	1987	1988	1989	1990	1991	1992
Total Return (%)	35.48	23.85	9.89	29.69	11.68	-0.76	18.00	24.53	-4.81	41.98	12.63
S and P 500 (%)	21.47	22.46	6.13	31.64	18.68	5.26	17.50	31.68	-3.20	30.40	7.92
Dividend Yield	3.42	2.87	2.48	2.24	2.73	5.28	3.56	2.82	2.05	1.90	1.44
Income on $10,000 ($)	342	369	384	369	571	1,201	766	694	612	530	562

Annual Return During Bear Markets

40.00%	
30.00%	
20.00%	
10.00%	
0.00%	
-10.00%	
-20.00%	
-30.00%	
-40.00%	
-50.00%	
-60.00%	
	1969 1973 1974 1977 1981 1987 1990

■ Nicholas Fund ▨ S & P 500

Portfolio Composition

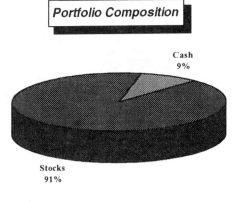

Cash
9%

Stocks
91%

As of 6/30/93

Investment Description

Albert Nicholas is something of an enigma amongst growth fund managers. He doesn't buy the hottest technology or biotech stocks. He always seems to avoid overvalued issues that his fellow managers seem to thrive on. Nicholas buys growth but only at a good price. In short, the Nicholas fund buys growth at a discount, perhaps combining the best traits of growth and value-oriented management styles. It seems to have worked quite well. Nicholas' 13%-plus 3-year, 5-year and 10-year returns are amongst the most consistent of all aggressive growth funds. With only two down-years in the last 12, the Nicholas fund is also one of the safest. Staying with companies whose businesses are easily understood and who dominate their markets, Nicholas' portfolio contains such well-known names as Circuit City, Eli Lilly and Hasbro. A decent dividend makes the Nicholas fund even more attractive to those looking for income in addition to growth. Nicholas' discriminating style has made this fund a winner for over 20 years. Perhaps the best is yet to come.

Suitability

Age 55 and under	*A-*
Age 55 to 70	*B+*
Age 70+	*B-*

Inception Date: 7/14/69

Manager Tenure: 1969

Telephone: (414) 272-6133

Minimum Initial Investment: $500.00

Direct Deposit: No

81

Putnam Voyager Fund

Investment Ratings

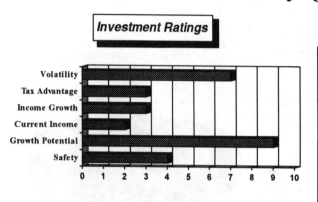

Investment Statistics

Initial Sales Charge: **5.75%**
B shares with no initial sales charge available

Annual Cost per $1,000: **$23.44**

Annualized Returns

3 Year	*14.93%*
5 Year	*16.01%*
10 Year	*13.51%*

Total Return on $10,000

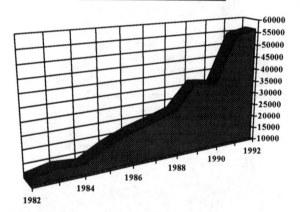

Income on $10,000 Investment

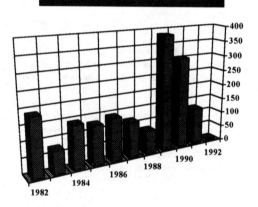

Historic Returns

	1982	1983	1984	1985	1986	1987	1988	1989	1990	1991	1992
Total Return (%)	32.13	14.91	-5.73	37.44	20.06	10.79	11.69	35.11	-2.80	50.31	3.50
S and P 500 (%)	21.47	22.46	6.13	31.64	18.68	5.26	17.50	31.68	-3.20	30.40	7.92
Dividend Yield	1.99	0.59	1.07	1.02	0.79	0.46	0.33	1.66	0.88	0.42	0.50
Income on $10,000 ($)	187	74	141	128	141	117	77	384	303	123	5

Annual Return During Bear Markets

	1969	1973	1974	1977	1981	1987	1990

(chart with y-axis from -50.00% to 40.00% in 10% increments)

■ Putnam Voyager ▨ S & P 500

Portfolio Composition

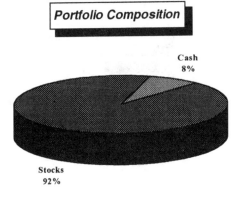

Cash
8%

Stocks
92%

As of 6/30/93

Investment Description

A sheep in wolf's clothing? Putnam Voyager fund is like most aggressive growth funds in name only. Technically classed as a small cap fund, Voyager's mid-cap approach puts it at the top of its class (16%+ 5-year return) without the risk usually associated with aggressive growth funds. Its worst year in the last decade, 1984, was a real bear for most aggressive growth funds but Voyager lost only 5.73%, compared to -11.86% for NASDAQ and -25% or greater for the many small company growth funds.

Mathew Weatherbie, the fund manager since 1983, mixes a core group of small and mid-cap stocks with a sprinkling of larger companies, holding back the fund's returns only slightly in return for greater-than-average stability. By focusing on themes such as high technology and companies providing niche services, Voyager is posed for outstanding future returns without the whipsaw prices most small company fund investors are forced to become accustomed to.

Suitability

Age 55 and under	*A*
Age 55 to 70	*B*
Age 70+	*B-*

Inception Date: 6/1/69

Manager Tenure: 1983

Telephone: (800) 225-1581

Minimum Initial Investment: $500.00

Direct Deposit: Yes

Reich & Tang Equity Fund

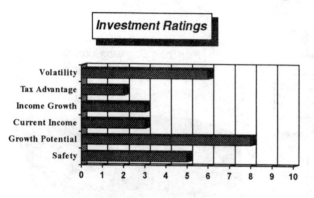

Investment Ratings

Investment Statistics

Initial Sales Charge:	**None**
Annual Cost per $1,000:	**$11.31**

Annualized Returns

3 Year	*13.66%*
5 Year	*12.10%*
Inception(6/1/69)	*15.70%*

Total Return on $10,000

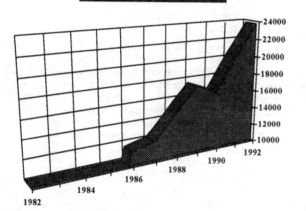

Income on $10,000 Investment

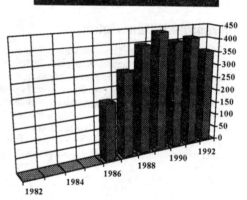

Historic Returns

	1982	1983	1984	1985	1986	1987	1988	1989	1990	1991	1992
Total Return (%)					14.66	5.29	22.86	18.00	-5.83	23.05	17.05
S and P 500 (%)	21.47	22.46	6.13	31.64	18.68	5.26	17.50	31.68	-3.20	30.40	7.92
Dividend Yield					2.08	2.76	3.43	3.19	2.53	2.84	1.98
Income on $10,000 ($)					208	310	396	439	399	410	354

Annual Return During Bear Markets

40.00%	
30.00%	
20.00%	
10.00%	
0.00%	
-10.00%	
-20.00%	
-30.00%	
-40.00%	
-50.00%	

1969 1973 1974 1977 1981 1987 1990

■ Reich & Tang ▨ S & P 500

Portfolio Composition

Cash
10%

Stocks
90%

As of 6/30/93

Investment Description

Reich & Tang is a true "Renaissance" fund. You won't find any of Wall Street's hottest stocks in its portfolio. The fund eschews trendy, high-growth stocks with equally high price earnings ratios. Rather, fund manager Robert Hoerle prefers companies that have recently fallen from grace but still have the potential for earnings recovery. Accordingly, the portfolio is a mish-mash of oil service, publishing, retail and insurance issues, to name a few. Going against the wisdom of the day has its draw-backs, too. During the past few years, Reich & Tang Equity has underperformed other more aggressive counterparts. Still the commitment of management to its idea of value and the recent crash of many glamour stocks should redeem this fund in the years to come. If recent performance is any indication, the fund should continue to produce above-average returns with relatively low risk.

Suitability

Age 55 and under	*B*
Age 55 to 70	*B+*
Age 70+	*B-*

Inception Date: 1/4/85

Manager Tenure: 1985

Telephone: (800) 221-3079

Minimum Initial Investment: $5,000.00

Direct Deposit: No

Sentry Fund

Investment Ratings

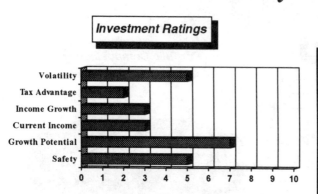

Investment Statistics

Initial Sales Charge:	**None**
Annual Cost per $1,000:	**$7.32**

Annualized Returns

3 Year	*7.40%*
5 Year	*12.60%*
10 Year	*10.40%*

Total Return on $10,000

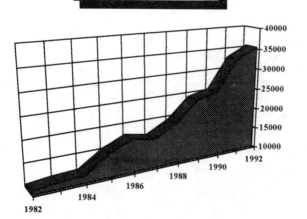

Income on $10,000 Investment

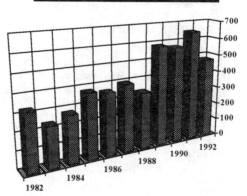

Historic Returns

	1982	1983	1984	1985	1986	1987	1988	1989	1990	1991	1992
Total Return (%)	8.62	5.35	1.84	32.69	14.59	-5.46	16.92	24.04	5.23	28.85	7.46
S and P 500 (%)	21.47	22.46	6.13	31.64	18.68	5.26	17.50	31.68	-3.20	30.40	7.92
Dividend Yield	3.22	2.19	2.51	3.48	2.59	2.36	2.17	3.35	2.17	3.02	1.77
Income on $10,000 ($)	322	230	272	373	357	390	327	581	565	645	472

Annual Return During Bear Markets

40.00%						
30.00%						
20.00%						
10.00%						
0.00%						
-10.00%						
-20.00%						
-30.00%						
-40.00%						
-50.00%	1969	1973	1974	1977	1981	1987	1990

■ Sentry Fund ▨ S & P 500

Portfolio Composition

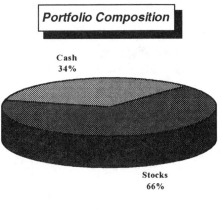

Cash
34%

Stocks
66%

As of 6/30/93

Investment Description

Sentry fund manager Keith Ringberg is looking a tad bearish with over 30% of his fund in cash. The limited number of stocks that meet his low-debt, high-growth criteria has slowed down his acquisition of new stocks. Some signs of speculation, such as the increase in new stock offerings, have also made Ringberg wary of equities. Preferring investments that are easily understood, Sentry avoids high technology industries, which have pushed competing funds to new highs in recent months. Missing the boat in recent months isn't likely to convert Ringberg from his growth at a discount strategy. And why should it? While three year returns have lagged, five-year and ten-year total returns match the best of funds in this category, especially when the level of risk is taken into account. Preferring a buy-and-hold strategy compared to the fast turnover tactics of many others in this group, Sentry fund offers a stable, conservative growth fund for investors looking for above-average returns. It may not have the sizzle of its high-risk counterparts, but Sentry fund has delivered in both good and bad markets.

Suitability

Age 55 and under	*B-*
Age 55 to 70	*B*
Age 70+	*B+*

Inception Date: 5/1/70

Manager Tenure: 1977

Telephone: (800) 533-7827

Minimum Initial Investment: $200.00

Direct Deposit: No

Transamerica Special Emerging Growth

Investment Ratings

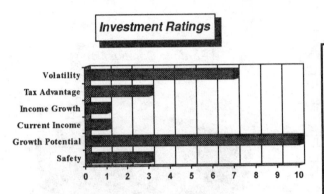

Volatility	
Tax Advantage	
Income Growth	
Current Income	
Growth Potential	
Safety	

Investment Statistics

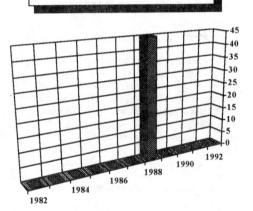

Initial Sales Charge: **None**
5% declining deferred charge

Annual Cost per $1,000:   **$31.22**

Annualized Returns

3 Year	*16.69%*
5 Year	*19.59%*
Inception(10/26/87)	*22.97%*

Total Return on $10,000

Income on $10,000 Investment

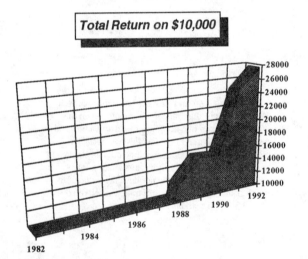

Historic Returns

	1982	1983	1984	1985	1986	1987	1988	1989	1990	1991	1992
Total Return (%)							21.82	28.85	-1.15	58.82	12.13
S and P 500 (%)	21.47	22.46	6.13	31.64	18.68	5.26	17.50	31.68	-3.20	30.40	7.92
Dividend Yield							0.45	0.00	0.00	0.00	0.00
Income on $10,000 ($)							45	0	0	0	0

Annual Return During Bear Markets

	1969	1973	1974	1977	1981	1987	1990

(Chart with y-axis from -50.00% to 40.00% in 10% increments)

■ Transamerica   ▩ S & P 500

Portfolio Composition

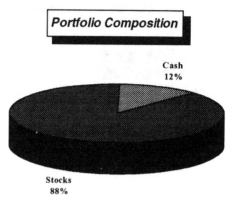

Cash
12%

Stocks
88%

As of 6/30/93

Investment Description

Transamerica Special Emerging Growth fund strives to go where no fund has gone before. Among its holdings are little-known names such as Arkansas Best, Horace Mann Educators and Cordis. Investing in unknown companies has helped propel this fund to astronomical averages, including the highest five-year average of any fund covered in this book, all with surprisingly little risk. The only down year, 1990 (-1.15%), pummeled many better-known competitors with losses of 20% or better. Nevertheless, a short track record and particularily vulnerable sector of the stock market makes Special Emerging Growth suitable only for those willing to ride out the vicissitudes of the over-the-counter marketplace. Manager Ed Larsen balances risk with diversification (the fund has over 400 issues) and indepth research. Since many of the stocks held only have token coverage on Wall Street, Larsen often invests in companies long before earnings and profitability catch the attention of other fund managers and brokerage firms. While the ride might get rocky, aggressive growth funds don't get much better than this.

Suitability

Age 55 and under	*A*
Age 55 to 70	*B-*
Age 70+	*C*

Inception Date: 10/26/87

Manager Tenure: 1987

Telephone: (800) 343-6840

Minimum Initial Investment: $1,000.00

Direct Deposit: No

Wayne Hummer Growth Fund

Investment Ratings

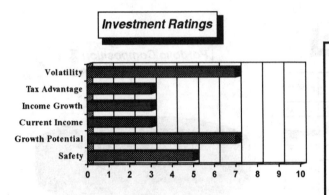

Investment Statistics

| Initial Sales Charge: | **None** |
| Annual Cost per $1,000: | **$14.54** |

Annualized Returns

3 Year	*12.38%*
5 Year	*14.10%*
Inception	*13.70%*

Total Return on $10,000

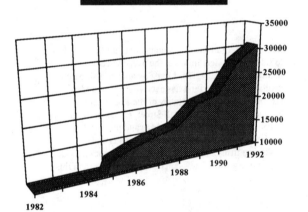

Income on $10,000 Investment

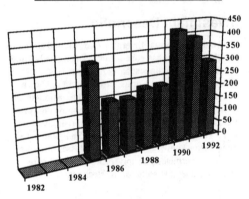

Historic Returns

	1982	1983	1984	1985	1986	1987	1988	1989	1990	1991	1992
Total Return (%)				24 36	13.75	9.27	7.02	24.04	5.01	28.84	10.36
S and P 500 (%)	21.47	22.46	6.13	31.64	18.68	5.26	17.50	31.68	-3.20	30.40	7.92
Dividend Yield				3.34	1.96	1.73	1.82	1.75	2.68	2.44	1.45
Income on $10,000 ($)				335	197	194	221	223	419	389	292

Annual Return During Bear Markets

Year	
40.00%	
30.00%	
20.00%	
10.00%	
0.00%	
-10.00%	
-20.00%	
-30.00%	
-40.00%	
-50.00%	

1969   1973   1974   1977   1981   1987   1990

■ Wayne Hummer   ▨ S & P 500

Portfolio Composition

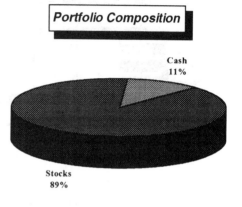

Cash
11%

Stocks
89%

As of 6/30/93

Investment Description

Wayne Hummer Growth's portfolio looks more like Main Street than Wall Street. The asset list reads like the business section of a small-town phone book. In many ways, it is. Focusing on mid-sized, lesser-known companies, managers Alan Bird and Thomas Rowland look for profitable, overlooked businesses far away from the financial mainstream. Many of their holdings are regionally based, dominant in their market and extremely profitable. While not quite big enough to be blue chip, most are larger and have greater financial stability than traditional, small cap stocks. Wayne Hummer's resistance to bear markets seems to have proven their strategy. Boasting above-average returns in both 1987 and 1990 (9.27% and 5.01% respectively), Rowland and Bird guide the fund with an eye toward safety, without sacrificing return in strong markets. With an asset base under $100 million, the fund has the flexibility to invest in smaller companies that other funds lack. An undiscovered value, Wayne Hummer Growth probably won't stay that small for very long.

Suitability

Age 55 and under	*B+*
Age 55 to 70	*B*
Age 70+	*B-*

Inception Date: 12/30/83

Manager Tenure: 1983/1987

Telephone: (800) 621-4477

Minimum Initial Investment: $1,000.00

Direct Deposit: No

91

William Blair Growth Shares

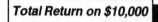

Investment Statistics

Initial Sales Charge:	**None**
Annual Cost per $1,000:	**$8.97**

Annualized Returns

3 Year	*12.60%*
5 Year	*14.60%*
10 Year	*10.30%*

Total Return on $10,000

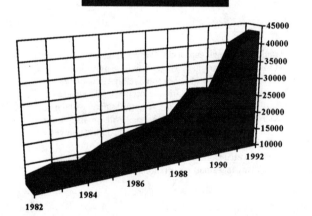

Income on $10,000 Investment

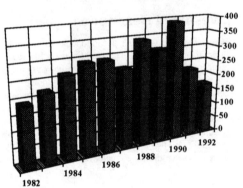

Historic Returns

	1982	1983	1984	1985	1986	1987	1988	1989	1990	1991	1992
Total Return (%)	27.76	13.45	-4.22	23.34	9.79	7.99	7.12	30.45	-2.02	44.37	7.61
S and P 500 (%)	21.47	22.46	6.13	31.64	18.68	5.26	17.50	31.68	-3.20	30.40	7.92
Dividend Yield	1.90	1.76	1.88	2.24	1.86	1.54	1.95	1.66	1.66	1.00	0.53
Income on $10,000 ($)	190	218	260	289	290	256	341	306	389	227	170

Annual Return During Bear Markets

	1969	1973	1974	1977	1981	1987	1990

Y-axis scale: 40.00%, 30.00%, 20.00%, 10.00%, 0.00%, -10.00%, -20.00%, -30.00%, -40.00%, -50.00%

Legend: ▨ William Blair Growth ▨ S & P 500

Portfolio Composition

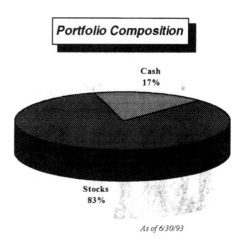

Cash 17%

Stocks 83%

As of 6/30/93

Investment Description

William Blair Growth Shares is singing the blues. Growth stocks that meet manager Neal Seltzer's stringent criteria are becoming harder to come by. Like many other fund managers, Seltzer professes to look for low-debt, high-growth companies at a good price. Earnings must also be predictable. The last criteria eliminates many of the "hot" stocks that have propelled the market in the past few months. Unlike many of his counterparts, Seltzer sticks to his established criteria fairly religiously. A quick review of his holdings reveals very few, if any, stocks outside of his stated parameters. Therein lies

Seltzer's problem. As growth stock multiples have risen, it's become hard to find any good buys meeting his criteria. This devotion to what appears to be a good system for stock picking has left William Blair with ample cash on hand, perhaps to take advantage of future bargains that may come along. Posting excellent returns in both good and bad markets, it's surprising that William Blair Growth Shares has remained relatively unknown. This all-weather growth fund isn't likely to be ignored for long, especially by those with a conservative bent.

Suitability

Age 55 and under	*B+*
Age 55 to 70	*B*
Age 70+	*B*

Inception Date: 3/20/46

Manager Tenure: 1986

Telephone: (800) 742-7272

Minimum Initial Investment: 1000

Direct Deposit: No

93

Chapter 11

Conservative Growth Investments

AARP Growth and Income Fund

Investment Ratings

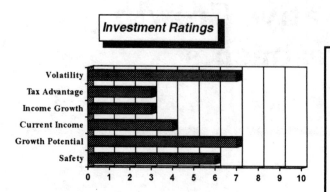

Investment Statistics

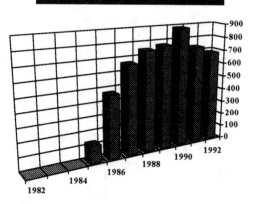

Initial Sales Charge:	**None**
Annual Cost per $1,000:	**$10.90**

Annualized Returns

3 Year	*13.56%*
5 Year	*13.62%*
Inception(11/31/84)	*14.82%*

Total Return on $10,000

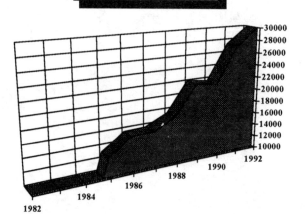

Income on $10,000 Investment

Historic Returns

	1982	1983	1984	1985	1986	1987	1988	1989	1990	1991	1992
Total Return (%)				30.23	19.51	0.87	10.92	26.66	-2.00	26.46	9.22
S and P 500 (%)	21.47	22.46	6.13	31.64	18.68	5.26	17.50	31.68	-3.20	30.40	7.92
Dividend Yield				1.26	3.65	4.46	5.20	5.07	4.81	4.31	3.28
Income on $10,000 ($)				126	469	663	747	769	885	737	682

Annual Return During Bear Markets

	1969	1973	1974	1977	1981	1987	1990

Chart y-axis: 40.00%, 30.00%, 20.00%, 10.00%, 0.00%, -10.00%, -20.00%, -30.00%, -40.00%, -50.00%

■ AARP Growth & Income   ▩ S & P 500

Portfolio Composition

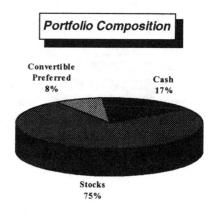

Convertible Preferred 8%

Cash 17%

Stocks 75%

As of 6/30/93

Investment Description

AARP Growth and Income fund takes the income part of its charter rather seriously. Dividend yield is a primary consideration when fund managers choose their invest-ments. Most of the stocks in the portfolio have a higher-than-average yield, allowing the fund to pay out a bit more than the average equity fund. Growth isn't entirely abandoned in the search for more income, however. The fund tries to get the best of both worlds by seeking out high-yielding stocks that also have strong growth prospects. This search takes the fund to unusual places. Almost 15% of assets, for example, are in foreign utilities. These generate decent dividends and more growth potential than their U.S. counterparts because of the undeveloped markets they serve. Turnaround stocks also comprise a healthy piece of the portfolio, meeting the fund's unique requirements for growth and income. An excellent five-year track record and a circumspect approach to stock selection make this fund an excellent choice for investors looking for safety and a little income.

Suitability

Age 55 and under	*A-*
Age 55 to 70	*B*
Age 70+	*B-*

Inception Date: 11/30/84

Manager Tenure: 1986

Telephone: (800) 253-2277

Minimum Initial Investment: $500.00

Direct Deposit: No

American Home Products

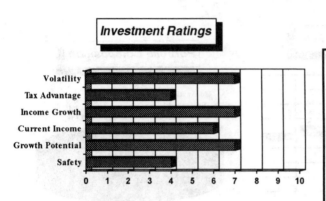

Initial Sales Charge: **NA**
Individual stock, brokerage commissions may apply

Annual Cost per $1,000:   **$0.00**

Annualized Returns

3 Year	*11.78%*
5 Year	*17.41%*
10 Year	*16.37%*

Total Return on $10,000

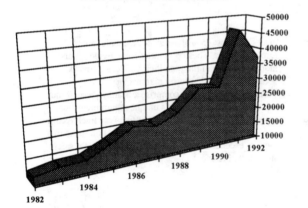

Income on $10,000 Investment

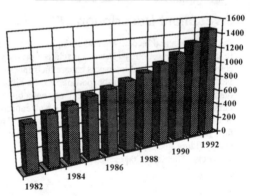

Historic Returns

	1982	1983	1984	1985	1986	1987	1988	1989	1990	1991	1992
Total Return (%)	22.60	10.90	1.76	24.51	22.27	-5.37	14.43	29.13	-2.09	60.81	-20.24
S and P 500 (%)	21.47	22.46	6.13	31.64	18.68	5.26	17.50	31.68	-3.20	30.40	7.92
Dividend Yield	5.92	5.36	5.32	5.74	4.93	4.34	4.95	4.68	4.00	4.52	3.14
Income on $10,000 ($)	591	657	723	794	849	915	986	1,068	1,178	1,304	1,457

40.00%	
30.00%	
20.00%	
10.00%	
0.00%	
-10.00%	
-20.00%	
-30.00%	
-40.00%	
-50.00%	

1969   1973   1974   1977   1981   1987   1990

■ American Home Products ▧ S & P 500

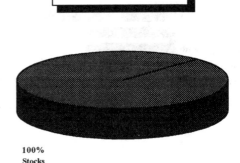

100%
Stocks

As of 6/30/93

Investment Description

While American Home Products might not see the kind of growth experienced during the 1980s (over 500% from 1982 to 1992), Wall Street's RIP for the company, in the words of Mark Twain, "is premature." Prescription drugs like Norplant and Premarin, both in American Home Product's niche of woman's care, should see continued growth during the 1990s. Strength of contraceptive products and over-the-counter brands, such as Advil, Anacin, and Dimetapp should also help push the company's growth, albeit slightly slower due to health care reform. The market has discounted this stock deeply, pushing up the yield and assuming a worst possible scenario. Since American Home Products hasn't experienced the astronomical growth rates of many of its peers over the past few years, it could easily match or even exceed its earnings growth of the past 5 or even 10 years. A healthy dividend makes it easier to be patient while waiting for the market to recognize American Home Product's potential.

Suitability

Age 55 and under	*B+*
Age 55 to 70	*A-*
Age 70+	*B+*

Inception Date:

Manager Tenure:

Telephone: ›

Minimum Initial Investment:

Direct Deposit:

AT&T

Investment Ratings

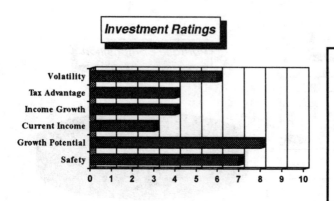

Investment Statistics

Initial Sales Charge: **NA**
Individual stock, brokerage commissions may apply

Annual Cost per $1,000: **$0.00**

Annualized Returns

3 Year	*7.46%*
5 Year	*17.46%*
10 Year	*17.62%*

Total Return on $10,000

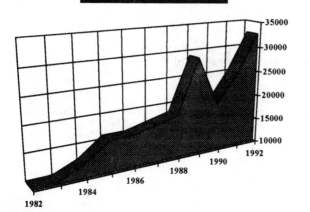

Income on $10,000 Investment

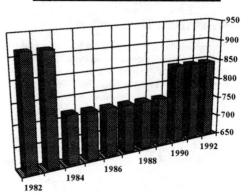

Historic Returns

	1982	1983	1984	1985	1986	1987	1988	1989	1990	1991	1992
Total Return (%)	1.06	3.58	19.31	28.20	0.01	8.00	6.48	58.26	-33.79	29.88	30.35
S and P 500 (%)	21.47	22.46	6.13	31.64	18.68	5.26	17.50	31.68	-3.20	30.40	7.92
Dividend Yield	9.16	9.06	7.34	6.15	4.80	4.80	4.44	4.17	2.90	4.38	3.37
Income on $10,000 ($)	915	915	768	768	768	768	768	768	845	845	845

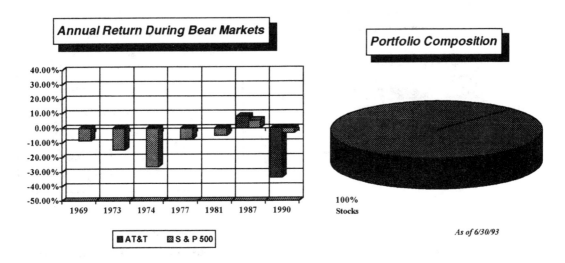

Annual Return During Bear Markets

| | 1969 | 1973 | 1974 | 1977 | 1981 | 1987 | 1990 |

■ AT&T   ▨ S & P 500

Portfolio Composition

100%
Stocks

As of 6/30/93

Investment Description

Ma Bell has a whole new look. Relegated to the shadows of her progeny, the Baby Bells, for years, AT&T finally appears to be "coming into its own." Aggressively pricing long distance rates to compete with competitors who've been nipping at its heals since deregulation, AT&T is beginning to see its market share loss stabilize. And while Baby Bells are crying "foul," AT&T has decided to enter the lucrative cellular market with a vengeance, buying a big stake in mobile phone giant McCaw Cellular. The marketing and technology expertise of AT&T should benefit both companies. By focusing on technology, one of its strengths, the com-

pany hopes to redefine consumer tastes and be at the forefront of a new telecommunications revolution that appears to be looming over the horizon. Interactive video, cable, personal communications and computer technology are all areas in which AT&T has chosen to focus efforts. The recent downfall of IBM has also forced the stock into a bellwether position, which should help support its price as it did for IBM for so many years. All in all, in spite of a smaller dividend than comparable stocks, AT&T promises to be a premier growth and income stock of the 1990s.

Suitability

Age 55 and under	*B+*
Age 55 to 70	*A-*
Age 70+	*B+*

Inception Date:

Manager Tenure:

Telephone:

Minimum Initial Investment:

Direct Deposit:

101

Bristol Myers

Investment Ratings

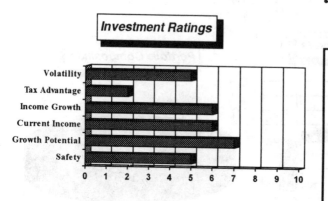

Investment Statistics

Initial Sales Charge:　**NA**
Individual stock, brokerage commissions may apply

Annual Cost per $1,000:　**$0.00**

Annualized Returns

3 Year	*9.96%*
5 Year	*13.95%*
10 Year	*18.58%*

Total Return on $10,000

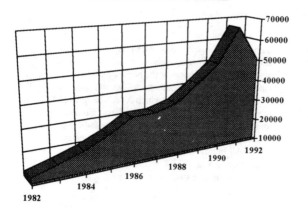

Income on $10,000 Investment

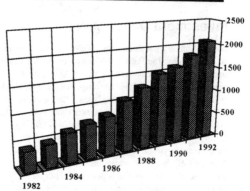

Historic Returns

	1982	1983	1984	1985	1986	1987	1988	1989	1990	1991	1992
Total Return (%)	26.59	25.65	23.97	26.49	24.72	0.76	9.19	23.21	19.64	31.72	-23.51
S and P 500 (%)	21.47	22.46	6.13	31.64	18.68	5.26	17.50	31.68	-3.20	30.40	7.92
Dividend Yield	3.76	3.57	3.79	3.59	3.20	3.39	4.03	4.40	3.79	3.58	3.13
Income on $10,000 ($)	394	451	602	707	798	1,054	1,264	1,505	1,596	1,807	2,078

Annual Return During Bear Markets

40.00%	
30.00%	
20.00%	
10.00%	
0.00%	
-10.00%	
-20.00%	
-30.00%	
-40.00%	
-50.00%	

1969   1973   1974   1977   1981   1987   1990

■ Bristol Myers   ▨ S & P 500

Portfolio Composition

100%
Stocks

As of 6/30/93

Investment Description

When the Clinton administration sneezes at health care costs, the entire drug industry catches a cold. Bristol Myers, trading near a four-year low has been all but written off by Wall Street as a future victim of a health care reform package that has yet to see its final form. Health care regulation will be argued and changed for many years to come, but the stock market has discounted the price of Bristol Myers to reflect the worst possible scenario. Panic often equals opportunity. Yielding over 5% and boasting an 18% per-year dividend growth rate,

Bristol Myers is an excellent addition to a conservative portfolio. While total return might not match the stock's outstanding growth rate during the 1980s, an aging population and ever present need for new drug products should push company earnings higher over the next decade, even if at a slower rate than before. Regardless of the possiblity of future caps on drug prices and other cost controls, it's hard to believe the maker of such household names as Ban, Bufferin, Excederin and Clairol will be unprofitable in future years.

Suitability

Age 55 and under	*B+*
Age 55 to 70	*A*
Age 70+	*B*

Inception Date:

Manager Tenure:

Telephone:

Minimum Initial Investment:

Direct Deposit:

103

Capital Income Builder Fund

Investment Ratings

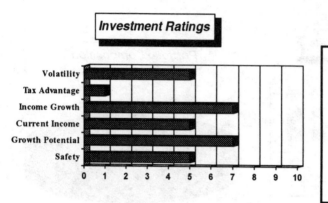

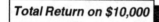

Investment Statistics

Initial Sales Charge:	**5.75%**
Annual Cost per $1,000:	**$21.42**

Annualized Returns

3 Year	*11.99%*
5 Year	*12.20%*
Inception(7/30/87)	*10.89%*

Total Return on $10,000

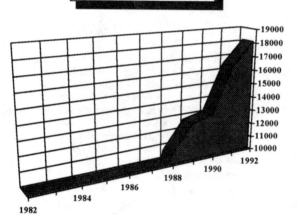

Income on $10,000 Investment

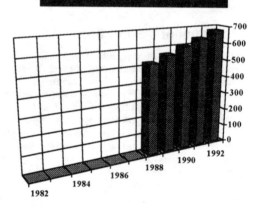

Historic Returns

	1982	1983	1984	1985	1986	1987	1988	1989	1990	1991	1992
Total Return (%)							12.45	19.94	2.89	25.70	10.00
S and P 500 (%)	21.47	22.46	6.13	31.64	18.68	5.26	17.50	31.68	-3.20	30.40	7.92
Dividend Yield							5.54	5.59	5.25	5.65	5.03
Income on $10,000 ($)							521	562	602	637	678

Annual Return During Bear Markets

| | 40.00% |
| 30.00% |
| 20.00% |
| 10.00% |
| 0.00% |
| -10.00% |
| -20.00% |
| -30.00% |
| -40.00% |
| -50.00% |

1969   1973   1974   1977   1981   1987   1990

■ Capital Income Builder ⊠ S & P 500

Portfolio Composition

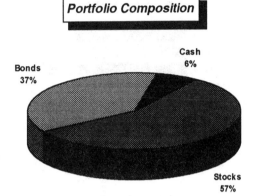

Cash
6%

Bonds
37%

Stocks
57%

As of 6/30/93

Investment Description

Capital Income Builder was created with a very specific purpose in mind: to generate a growing stream of income for investors. Designed as an income-producing fund that consistently increases income, it has certainly accomplished its objective. In the past 5 years, the dividend has been increased every year. Focusing on stocks that produce higher dividends also makes Capital Income Builder a bit of a contrarian play, since most high-yielding stocks also double as out-of-favor issues. Bristol Myers, British Airways and Atlantic Richfield are a few of the less-than-popular stocks included in the portfolio. While equities provide the engine for Capital

Income Builder's income growth, a healthy dose of bonds (37.4%) helps insure that fund holders' current needs are met while they await dividend increases in lower-yielding stocks. Fund managers have shown a predilection for foreign stocks, mostly in the form of ADRs, adding diversification to the fund. Capital Income Builder seems like a fund designed for the retired investor who doesn't want to see his or her income nibbled away at by inflation. A resilience to bear markets only adds to the attraction of this first-class choice for retirement income.

Suitability

Age 55 and under	*B-*
Age 55 to 70	*A*
Age 70+	*A-*

Inception Date: 7/30/87

Manager Tenure: 1987

Telephone: (800) 421-0180

Minimum Initial Investment: $1,000.00

Direct Deposit: No

105

Colonial Utilities Fund

Investment Ratings

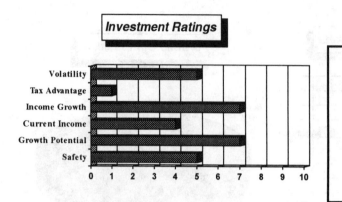

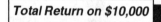

Investment Statistics

Initial Sales Charge: **4.75%**
B shares available with no initial sales charge

Annual Cost per $1,000: **$18.06**

Annualized Returns

3 Year	*16.00%*
5 Year	*13.23%*
10 Year	*11.00%*

Total Return on $10,000

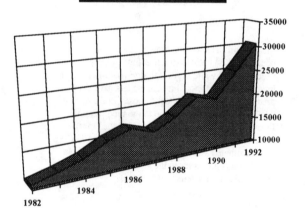

Income on $10,000 Investment

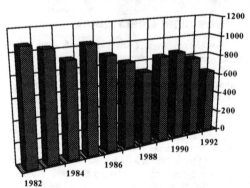

Historic Returns

	1982	1983	1984	1985	1986	1987	1988	1989	1990	1991	1992
Total Return (%)	11.10	11.87	12.52	17.70	9.63	-8.33	13.88	17.73	-5.06	25.91	21.01
S and P 500 (%)	21.47	22.46	6.13	31.64	18.68	5.26	17.50	31.68	-3.20	30.40	7.92
Dividend Yield	11.02	10.22	9.14	10.63	8.90	7.97	8.09	8.99	8.58	9.03	6.22
Income on $10,000 ($)	1,071	1,030	914	1,038	916	828	717	847	869	791	633

Annual Return During Bear Markets

40.00%
30.00%
20.00%
10.00%
0.00%
-10.00%
-20.00%
-30.00%
-40.00%
-50.00%

1969   1973   1974   1977   1981   1987   1990

■ Colonial Utilities   ▨ S & P 500

Portfolio Composition

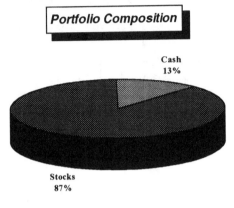

Cash
13%

Stocks
87%

As of 6/30/93

Investment Description

Colonial Utilities is basking in the spotlight of success. Two back-to-back years of extraordinary performance (up 25.91% in 1991 and 21.01% in 1992) have made it the darling of journalists and investors alike. Fund manager John Lennon isn't about to rest on his laurels. He's aggressively buying electric utilities, emphasizing both current yield and dividend growth. The fund makes current yield a priority but also tries to fulfill the shareholders' need for an effective inflation hedge by searching for higher-growth utilities. This balanced approach has served investors well as interest rate declines have made both types of holdings shine. A smaller-than-average telephone and natural gas holding and no foreign utilities makes Colonial Utilities a "bread-and-butter"fund, unlikely to surprise dividend and NAV conscious shareholders. While many utilities funds were off 5% or more during the first quarter of 1993, this fund posted a 6% gain. As fixed income rates fall, it should continue to attract interest as an alternative to bond funds, which offer no dividend growth. A monthly interest check (compared to quaterly on most utility funds) and a more-than-competitive yield make Colonial Utilities one of the best ways to beat the low rate blues.

Suitability

Age 55 and under	*A-*
Age 55 to 70	*A-*
Age 70+	*B+*

Inception Date: 8/3/81

Manager Tenure: 1984

Telephone: (800) 248-2828

Minimum Initial Investment: $1,000.00

Direct Deposit: No

Dreyfus Strategic World Investing Fund

Investment Ratings

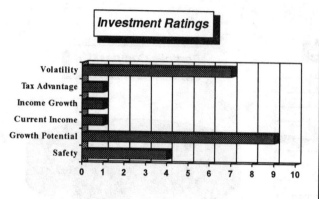

Investment Statistics

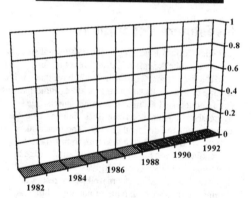

Initial Sales Charge:	**3.00%**
Annual Cost per $1,000:	**$21.82**
Annualized Returns	
3 Year	**5.67%**
5 Year	**9.54%**
Inception(4/10/87)	**14.48%**

Total Return on $10,000

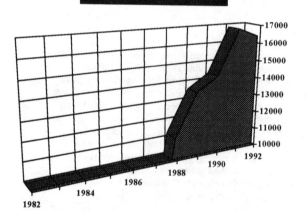

Income on $10,000 Investment

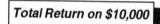

Historic Returns

	1982	1983	1984	1985	1986	1987	1988	1989	1990	1991	1992
Total Return (%)							15.49	21.02	5.79	17.51	-2.73
S and P 500 (%)	21.47	22.46	6.13	31.64	18.68	5.26	17.50	31.68	-3.20	30.40	7.92
Dividend Yield							0.00	0.00	0.00	0.00	0.00
Income on $10,000 ($)							0	0	0	0	0

Annual Return During Bear Markets

	40.00%	30.00%	20.00%	10.00%	0.00%	-10.00%	-20.00%	-30.00%	-40.00%	-50.00%

1969   1973   1974   1977   1981   1987   1990

■ Dreyfus Strategic World   ▩ S & P 500

Portfolio Composition

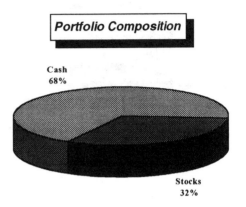

Cash
68%

Stocks
32%

As of 6/30/93

Investment Description

Fund manager Fiona Biggs is looking for a financial Armegeddon. The market crash in Japan, an overvalued U.S. market, sluggish growth worldwide are just the tip of the iceberg, she suggests by her extremely conservative portfolio. While defensive at heart, a least right now, Biggs has proven her worth at making money as well as conserving it. A big bet in Hong Kong when everyone else was diving for cover paid off well for the fund as have selective purchases in gold, oil and European stocks. A large cash position enabled Strategic World Investing to be the only fund to qualify based on the rigorous selection process for this category. While other foreign investments are cited in the Special Situations section of the book, Dreyfus Strategic World Investing's stability and performance allow it to stand out as one of the safest international funds. While returns have been competitive in the past, a large cash position could slow down comparative performance in the future, especially if overseas markets continue to rise. For an average investor looking for a bit of international exposure without the risk usually associated with that type of investment, we whole-heartedly recommend the Dreyfus Strategic World Investing fund.

Suitability

Age 55 and under	A-
Age 55 to 70	B
Age 70+	C

Inception Date: 4/10/87

Manager Tenure: 1988

Telephone: (800) 645-6561

Minimum Initial Investment: $2,500.00

Direct Deposit: No

Eaton Vance Stock Fund

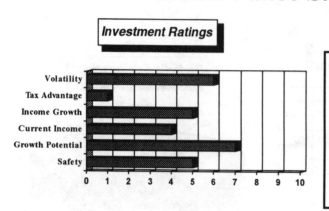

Investment Ratings

Volatility
Tax Advantage
Income Growth
Current Income
Growth Potential
Safety

0 1 2 3 4 5 6 7 8 9 10

Investment Statistics

Initial Sales Charge: **4.75%**

Annual Cost per $1,000: **$17.59**

Annualized Returns

3 Year   *6.10%*

5 Year   *11.70%*

10 Year   *13.00%*

Total Return on $10,000

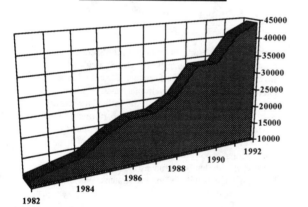

Income on $10,000 Investment

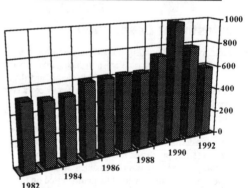

Historic Returns

	1982	1983	1984	1985	1986	1987	1988	1989	1990	1991	1992
Total Return (%)	20.46	14.77	11.35	32.26	15.43	1.99	15.01	28.92	0.59	21.45	6.85
S and P 500 (%)	21.47	22.46	6.13	31.64	18.68	5.26	17.50	31.68	-3.20	30.40	7.92
Dividend Yield	5.54	4.72	4.37	4.86	3.95	3.63	3.68	3.94	4.28	3.52	2.28
Income on $10,000 ($)	527	510	518	604	614	620	618	736	993	784	593

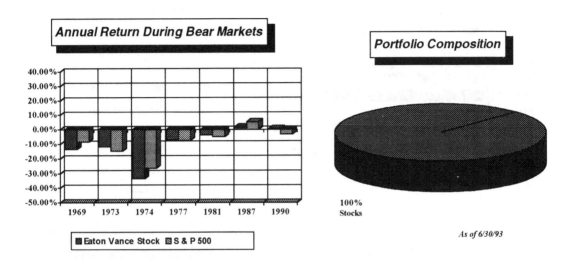

Annual Return During Bear Markets

40.00%
30.00%
20.00%
10.00%
0.00%
-10.00%
-20.00%
-30.00%
-40.00%
-50.00%

1969   1973   1974   1977   1981   1987   1990

■ Eaton Vance Stock ▨ S & P 500

Portfolio Composition

100%
Stocks

As of 6/30/93

Investment Description

Eaton Vance Stock fund seems to have been in the right place at the wrong time during 1992. A large position in drug stocks hurt the fund's performance last year even though drug stocks have begun to rally recently. In spite of the pharmaceutical meltdown, the fund has had a few other winners that help it keep its head above water, including J.C. Penney, Exxon and Walt Disney. Manager Walker Martin has stuck to the bluest of blue chips, allowing the fund to pay a decent dividend while maintaining a cautious posture. The problem is that blue chips have not been the place to be in recent months, causing the fund to lag. Martin's contrarian bent should allow the fund to make up lost ground when the market eventually rotates back to favoring large companies. In the meantime, the fund continues to produce acceptable results and a small but adequete dividend. Investors in Eaton Vance Stock need a good dose of patience but history seems to predict that they will eventually be rewarded. In the meantime, they can sleep well at night knowing that the fund is among the most conservative stock funds around.

Suitability

Age 55 and under	*A-*
Age 55 to 70	*B+*
Age 70+	*B*

Inception Date: 9/23/31

Manager Tenure: 1990

Telephone: (800) 225-6265

Minimum Initial Investment: $1,000.00

Direct Deposit: No

Equifax

Investment Ratings

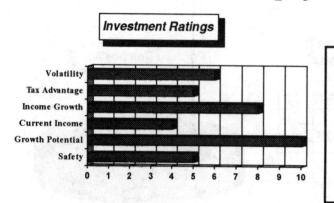

Investment Statistics

Initial Sales Charge: **NA**
Individual stock, brokerage commissions may apply

Annual Cost per $1,000:   **$0.00**

Annualized Returns

3 Year	*12.01%*
5 Year	*11.35%*
10 Year	*20.47%*

Total Return on $10,000

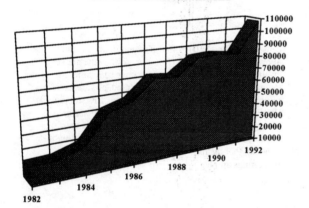

Income on $10,000 Investment

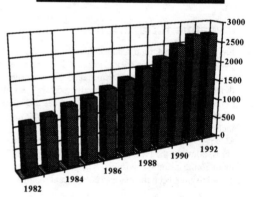

Historic Returns

	1982	1983	1984	1985	1986	1987	1988	1989	1990	1991	1992
Total Return (%)	130.41	3.76	24.11	74.16	10.42	26.85	-2.25	17.97	1.56	-2.31	29.92
S and P 500 (%)	21.47	22.46	6.13	31.64	18.68	5.26	17.50	31.68	-3.20	30.40	7.92
Dividend Yield	11.48	5.43	5.89	5.10	3.23	3.20	2.81	3.17	3.00	3.20	3.28
Income on $10,000 ($)	1,147	1,251	1,408	1,512	1,669	1,825	2,034	2,243	2,503	2,712	2,712

Annual Return During Bear Markets

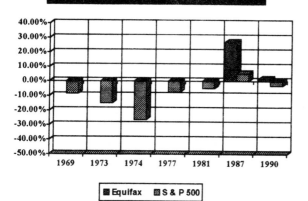

	1969	1973	1974	1977	1981	1987	1990

40.00%
30.00%
20.00%
10.00%
0.00%
-10.00%
-20.00%
-30.00%
-40.00%
-50.00%

■ Equifax ▨ S & P 500

Portfolio Composition

100%
Stocks

As of 6/30/93

Investment Description

Big Brother's watchful eye might be more pervasive than some would like, but Equifax shareholders have been profiting from the boom in personal information services to the tune of over 1,500% in the past decade. Equifax is in the business of supplying infomation: credit, medical, insurance, and checking-account data, which lenders, insurance companies and employers use. Of the Big Three credit suppliers, Equifax is the most diverse and the only one whose prinicipal busines is personal infomation. Riding the credit card and insurance boom of the 1980s, Equifax is poised for future growth as the

company expands to other countries and other businesses, such as personal check guarantees and lottery information. Astute financial management and management's commitment to growth should make this a premier growth stock in the 1990s, albeit an undiscovered one. Financial soundness and a bit of a dividend make this long-term growth holding suitable for investors looking for conservative growth. Strong growth in core businesses and proven management should make Equifax an interesting stock to follow in the years to come.

Suitability

Age 55 and under	A
Age 55 to 70	A-
Age 70+	B+

Inception Date:

Manager Tenure:

Telephone:

Minimum Initial Investment:

Direct Deposit:

113

Franklin Equity Income Fund

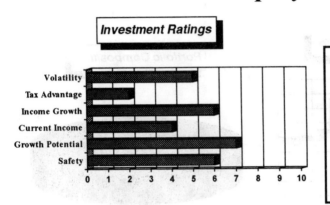

Investment Ratings

Investment Statistics

Initial Sales Charge:	**4.00%**
Annual Cost per $1,000:	**$9.53**

Annualized Returns

3 Year	*12.03%*
5 Year	*12.22%*
Inception(3/15/88)	*12.52%*

Total Return on $10,000

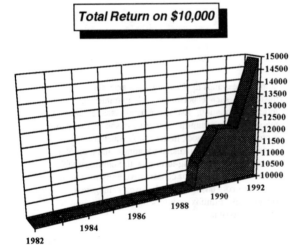

Income on $10,000 Investment

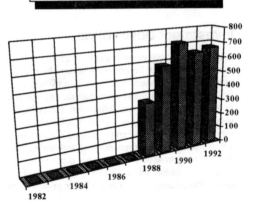

Historic Returns

	1982	1983	1984	1985	1986	1987	1988	1989	1990	1991	1992
Total Return (%)								14.47	11.61	-0.72	22.43
S and P 500 (%)	21.47	22.46	6.13	31.64	18.68	5.26	17.50	31.68	-3.20	30.40	7.92
Dividend Yield								4.47	5.95	6.38	6.20
Income on $10,000 ($)								581	718	647	672

Annual Return During Bear Markets

	1969	1973	1974	1977	1981	1987	1990

40.00%
30.00%
20.00%
10.00%
0.00%
-10.00%
-20.00%
-30.00%
-40.00%
-50.00%

■ Franklin Equity Income   ▨ S & P 500

Portfolio Composition

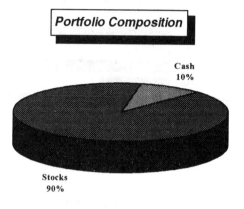

Cash
10%

Stocks
90%

As of 6/30/93

Investment Description

Virtually unknown, this little fund packs a wallop in both performance and dividend yield. One of the few non-utility funds paying over 4%, Franklin Equity Income focuses on high-yielding, conservative but out-of-favor stocks. The high-yielding nature of these investments provides a stable income (paid monthly) while the out-of-favor holdings tend to outperform the stock market. This fund has posted a 12% average return during its relatively short life. With holdings such as Great Western Financial, Eastman Kodak and Mobil, the fund errs to safety when seeking its above-average yield. A small percentage of utilities (11%) and preferred stocks (23%) round out a very balanced, basically nonbond income portfolio. Given the performance and conservative makeup of Franklin Equity Income, the only surprise a shareholder may have is that more investors haven't recognized its value. Its assets hover just below $30 million and hardly anyone has recognized its value, yet. Given the economic outlook for the next decade and current interest rate levels, Franklin Equity Income won't remain anonymous for long.

Suitability

Age 55 and under	*A-*
Age 55 to 70	*A*
Age 70+	*A-*

Inception Date: 3/15/88

Manager Tenure: 1988

Telephone: (800) 342-5236

Minimum Initial Investment: $100.00

Direct Deposit: Yes

115

Franklin Rising Dividends Fund

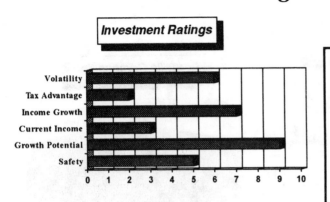

Investment Ratings

Volatility
Tax Advantage
Income Growth
Current Income
Growth Potential
Safety

0 1 2 3 4 5 6 7 8 9 10

Investment Statistics

Initial Sales Charge:	**4.00%**
Annual Cost per $1,000:	**$22.07**

Annualized Returns

3 Year	*10.68%*
5 Year	*10.63%*
Inception(1/14/87)	*8.83%*

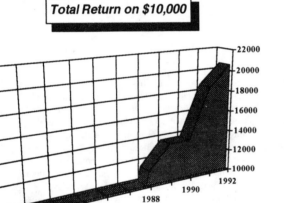

Total Return on $10,000

22000
20000
18000
16000
14000
12000
10000

1982 1984 1986 1988 1990 1992

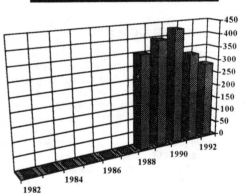

Income on $10,000 Investment

450
400
350
300
250
200
150
100
50
0

1982 1984 1986 1988 1990 1992

Historic Returns

	1982	1983	1984	1985	1986	1987	1988	1989	1990	1991	1992
Total Return (%)							18.80	19.60	0.26	35.96	10.38
S and P 500 (%)	21.47	22.46	6.13	31.64	18.68	5.26	17.50	31.68	-3.20	30.40	7.92
Dividend Yield							3.67	3.60	3.37	2.68	1.74
Income on $10,000 ($)							352	396	429	330	286

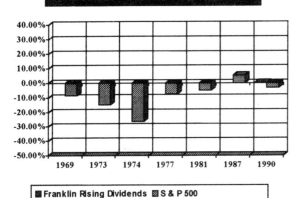

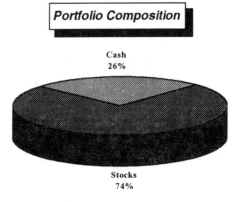

Cash
26%

Stocks
74%

As of 6/30/93

■ Franklin Rising Dividends ▨ S & P 500

Investment Description

Franklin Rising Dividend fund managers are willing to search just about anywhere to find stocks that meet their stringent criteria. The resulting hodge-podge of blue chips, out-of-favor and virtually unknown companies has become a trademark of the fund's portfolio. Side by side with blue chips, such as Philip Morris, are beaten-down drug stocks like Bristol Myers and Merck, and little-known Rite Aid and Dirrell Brothers. The fund 's strict rising dividend criteria is the only common factor amongst all its holdings. Managers Bruce Baughman and Bill Lippman look only for stocks that have consistantly raised their dividend, are profitable and

have a low-debt ratio. In addition, below-market price/earnings ratios are considered essential. Unfortunately, the popularity of rising dividend funds in the past few years, coupled with a market rise, makes it increasingly difficult to find stocks that meet this management team's criteria. Most of what they've bought recently is either undiscovered or lacking investors' favor. In any case, Franklin Rising Dividend's track record speaks for itself. All this in a market that isn't favoring earnings growth. Perhaps the encore will be better than its past decade star performance.

Suitability

Age 55 and under	*A-*
Age 55 to 70	*A-*
Age 70+	*B+*

Inception Date: 1/14/87

Manager Tenure: 1987

Telephone: (800) 342-5236

Minimum Initial Investment: $100.00

Direct Deposit: Yes

117

Franklin Utilities Fund

Investment Ratings

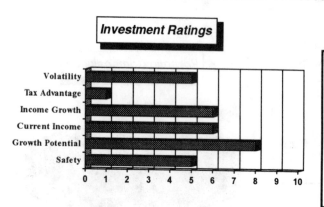

Investment Statistics

Initial Sales Charge: **4.00%**

Annual Cost per $1,000: **$14.37**

Annualized Returns

3 Year	*15.84%*
5 Year	*13.87%*
10 Year	*14.46%*

Total Return on $10,000

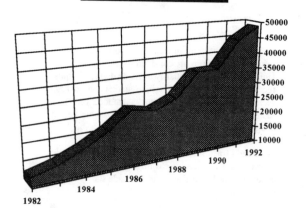

Income on $10,000 Investment

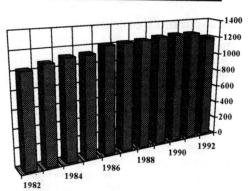

Historic Returns

	1982	1983	1984	1985	1986	1987	1988	1989	1990	1991	1992
Total Return (%)	31.34	15.75	21.43	22.85	23.77	-5.49	11.64	25.83	0.38	24.18	9.08
S and P 500 (%)	21.47	22.46	6.13	31.64	18.68	5.26	17.50	31.68	-3.20	30.40	7.92
Dividend Yield	10.76	9.40	9.22	8.49	7.90	6.97	7.93	7.80	6.79	7.27	5.85
Income on $10,000 ($)	1,022	1,075	1,118	1,129	1,205	1,217	1,228	1,249	1,262	1,262	1,191

Annual Return During Bear Markets

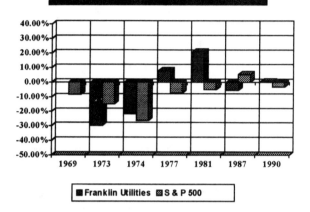

Legend: ■ Franklin Utilities ▨ S & P 500

Portfolio Composition

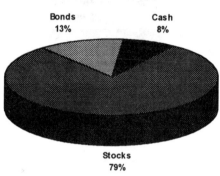

Bonds 13% Cash 8% Stocks 79%

As of 6/30/93

Investment Description

Remember the story of the tortoise and the hare? Franklin Utilities Fund plods along, year after year, leaving many more aggressive funds behind in a cloud of dust. A 15.84% three-year average return belies the fund's humble objective of buying conservative, income-paying utility stocks. Unlike many other utility funds, Franklin resisted diversifying from its bread-and-butter electric utilities stocks. While others have loaded their portofolios with telephone stocks, bonds, and more speculative electric companies, co-managers Greg Johnson and C. Johnson focus on high-yielding stocks with solid prospects for dividend growth. Only recently have they added bonds to the seldom-traded portfolio, and only in an effort to combat falling yields in some stocks. The fund's low expense ratio helps keep dividends high while a low turnover rate (1% in 1992) keeps capital gains distributions low. For the conservative investor looking for a little income, few investments look better.

Suitability

Age 55 and under	B
Age 55 to 70	A
Age 70+	B

Inception Date: 9/30/48

Manager Tenure: 1957/1987

Telephone: (800) 342-5236

Minimum Initial Investment: $100.00

Direct Deposit: Yes

Heinz (H.J.)

Investment Ratings

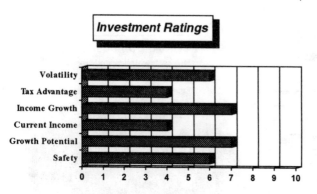

Investment Statistics

Initial Sales Charge: **NA**
Individual stock, brokerage commissions may apply

Annual Cost per $1,000: **$0.00**

Annualized Returns

3 Year	*10.92%*
5 Year	*20.04%*
10 Year	*24.16%*

Total Return on $10,000

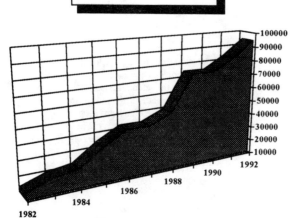

Income on $10,000 Investment

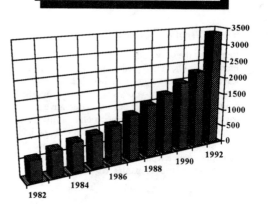

Historic Returns

	1982	1983	1984	1985	1986	1987	1988	1989	1990	1991	1992
Total Return (%)	44.18	41.18	13.16	50.59	25.09	-0.31	15.79	49.73	-0.36	11.47	13.50
S and P 500 (%)	21.47	22.46	6.13	31.64	18.68	5.26	17.50	31.68	-3.20	30.40	7.92
Dividend Yield	5.79	5.05	4.11	4.09	3.15	3.01	3.47	3.47	2.66	3.01	3.01
Income on $10,000 ($)	578	728	835	942	1,092	1,307	1,499	1,735	1,992	2,249	3,373

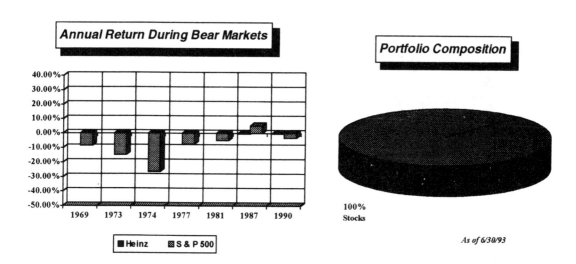

Annual Return During Bear Markets

40.00%
30.00%
20.00%
10.00%
0.00%
-10.00%
-20.00%
-30.00%
-40.00%
-50.00%

1969   1973   1974   1977   1981   1987   1990

■ Heinz   ▨ S & P 500

Portfolio Composition

100%
Stocks

As of 6/30/93

Investment Description

"Heinz 57" might very well describe this changing company. While its fortunes don't rise and fall with the price of ketchup anymore, Heinz faces daunting challenges during the next few years after a decade of meteoric growth. The rise of private-label brands has limited the company's ability to raise prices, and a strong dollar has hurt foreign earnings. Cost reductions have helped partially offset these earnings obstacles, but you can't help question the company's long-term prospects, given changing consumer attitudes toward brand names and the flatness in general of food companies' earnings in the past couple of years. Heinz's strength lies not in the industry it happens to be a part of, but in its exposure to growing overseas markets, where brand-name recognition is still important, and its competitiveness in markets where it doesn't yet dominate, such as baby foods, diet foods and diet centers. Capitalizing on name recognition and marketing savvy should help Heinz gain market share in both areas. Close attention to costs should also help the company maintain its competitive edge. While Heinz might not provoke the excitement of the latest biotechnology or computer offering, its reputation as an excellent growth holding should be retained well into the 1990s.

Suitability

Age 55 and under	*B+*
Age 55 to 70	*A-*
Age 70+	*B-*

Inception Date:

Manager Tenure:

Telephone:

Minimum Initial Investment:

Direct Deposit:

Ingersoll Rand

Investment Ratings

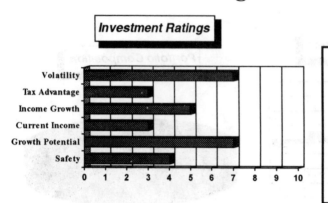

Investment Statistics

Initial Sales Charge: **NA**
Individual stock, brokerage commissions may apply

Annual Cost per $1,000: **$0.00**

Annualized Returns

3 Year	*7.91%*
5 Year	*13.40%*
10 Year	*18.11%*

Total Return on $10,000

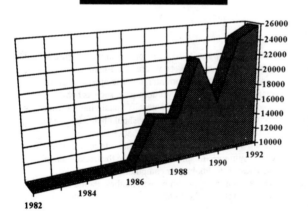

Income on $10,000 Investment

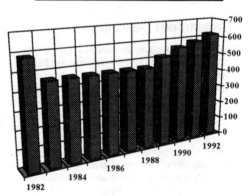

Historic Returns

	1982	1983	1984	1985	1986	1987	1988	1989	1990	1991	1992
Total Return (%)	-30.09	32.59	-13.13	17.58	4.21	59.19	-3.52	46.72	-25.87	47.65	5.91
S and P 500 (%)	21.47	22.46	6.13	31.64	18.68	5.26	17.50	31.68	-3.20	30.40	7.92
Dividend Yield	5.84	6.58	4.96	5.71	4.86	4.66	2.93	3.39	2.51	3.54	2.55
Income on $10,000 ($)	584	460	460	460	460	460	460	513	557	584	619

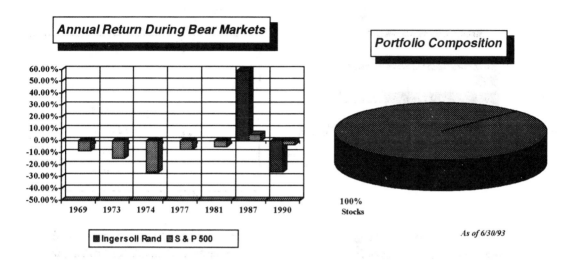

Annual Return During Bear Markets

| | 1969 | 1973 | 1974 | 1977 | 1981 | 1987 | 1990 |

■ Ingersoll Rand ▨ S & P 500

Portfolio Composition

100%
Stocks

As of 6/30/93

Investment Description

Ingersoll Rand is poised to ride the wave of infrastructure rebuilding that will eventually sweep the world. For years, analysts have talked about the decline in roads, bridges, streets and other essential parts of publically funded services worldwide. During that time, budget deficits and other fiscal constraints have left the problem intact and most analysts moved on to some other "hot" theme. The problem hasn't gone away and will have to be corrected at some point. Ingersoll Rand is positioned both domestically and internationally to benefit from this recurring problem, and its solution. The company makes construction equipment and air compressors, along with several other industrially oriented products. A large percentage of its sales (over 40%) and profit come from overseas. As economies recover worldwide, this company should benefit disproportionately because of its leverage and large investment in plant and other capital improvements. As businesses and municipalities come out of their economic bomb shelters, and a recovery seems more obvious, Ingersoll Rand should see drastic improvements in sales and profits. This cyclical holding could be one of the great growth opportunities of the decade.

Suitability

Age 55 and under	*B*+
Age 55 to 70	*B*+
Age 70+	*B*+

Inception Date:

Manager Tenure:

Telephone:

Minimum Initial Investment:

Direct Deposit:

123

John Hancock Sovereign Investors

Investment Ratings

Investment Statistics

Initial Sales Charge:	**5.00%**
Annual Cost per $1,000:	**$19.54**

Annualized Returns

3 Year	*12.64%*
5 Year	*13.00%*
10 Year	*14.51%*

Total Return on $10,000

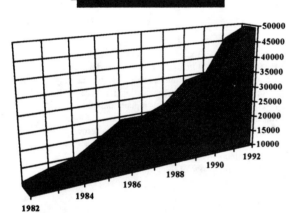

Income on $10,000 Investment

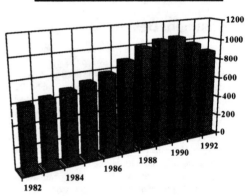

Historic Returns

	1982	1983	1984	1985	1986	1987	1988	1989	1990	1991	1992
Total Return (%)	21.81	19.61	11.18	30.54	21.80	0.20	11.23	23.76	4.38	30.49	7.23
S and P 500 (%)	21.47	22.46	6.13	31.64	18.68	5.26	17.50	31.68	-3.20	30.40	7.92
Dividend Yield	6.41	5.88	5.53	5.61	4.86	4.69	5.47	5.45	4.68	4.36	3.14
Income on $10,000 ($)	609	638	682	727	784	885	991	1,042	1,054	975	884

Annual Return During Bear Markets

40.00%						
30.00%						
20.00%						
10.00%						
0.00%						
-10.00%						
-20.00%						
-30.00%						
-40.00%						
-50.00%	1969	1973 1974	1977	1981	1987	1990

■ John Hancock Sovereign Investors ▨ S & P 500

Portfolio Composition

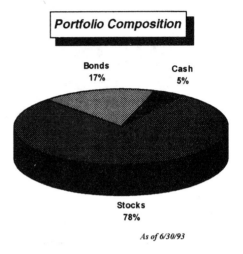

Bonds 17%

Cash 5%

Stocks 78%

As of 6/30/93

Investment Description

John Hancock Sovereign Investors takes the rising dividends part of its charter very seriously. A member of a small cadre of mutual funds focusing on growth of dividends, Sovereign Investors only purchases stocks in companies that have raised their dividends every year in the last 10. As a result, the portfolio looks like a who's who of growth stocks. McDonald's, Pepsico, Procter & Gamble and VF Corp. are but a few of the more famous growth offerings with a sprinkling of lesser-known companies like Alltell and Corestates added for good measure. The results have been predictable. The fortunes of the fund have followed the fortunes of growth stocks, rising sharply during most of the decade (up 14.51% annually for 10 years) and suffering a setback the past few months as growth stocks have fallen out of favor. Nevertheless, the fund manages to keep risk low by sticking with larger growth issues and, although it hasn't really participated in the the OTC rally as some of its peers have, the conservative nature of its holding should comfort investors concerned about inevitable down markets. A low-risk approach to growth investing and a consistent performance record should make John Hancock Sovereign Investors attractive for growth-oriented investors who want to avoid the roller-coaster ride of a more aggressive fund.

Suitability

Age 55 and under	*A-*
Age 55 to 70	*B+*
Age 70+	*B-*

Inception Date: 5/1/36

Manager Tenure: NA

Telephone: (800) 225-5291

Minimum Initial Investment: $1,000.00

Direct Deposit: No

125

Johnson & Johnson

Investment Ratings

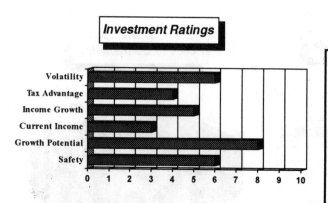

Investment Statistics

Initial Sales Charge: **NA**
Individual stock, brokerage commissions may apply

Annual Cost per $1,000:   **$0.00**

Annualized Returns

3 Year	*21.34%*
5 Year	*24.17%*
10 Year	*17.57%*

Total Return on $10,000

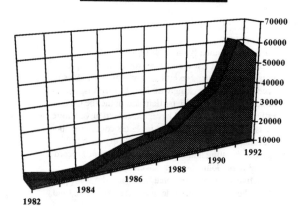

Income on $10,000 Investment

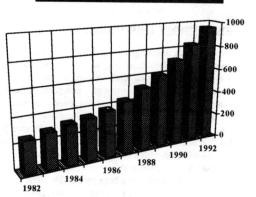

Historic Returns

	1982	1983	1984	1985	1986	1987	1988	1989	1990	1991	1992
Total Return (%)	33.67	-17.63	-11.63	45.68	24.70	14.10	13.69	39.50	20.84	59.58	-11.79
S and P 500 (%)	21.47	22.46	6.13	31.64	18.68	5.26	17.50	31.68	-3.20	30.40	7.92
Dividend Yield	2.59	2.18	2.94	3.54	2.66	2.44	2.56	2.63	2.22	2.15	1.55
Income on $10,000 ($)	258	290	323	344	377	430	517	603	711	829	958

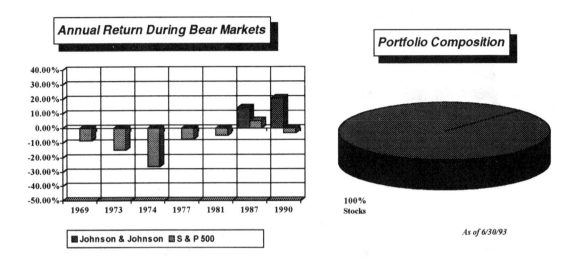

Annual Return During Bear Markets

■ Johnson & Johnson ▨ S & P 500

Portfolio Composition

100%
Stocks

As of 6/30/93

Investment Description

Johnson & Johnson might be most familiar as a maker of baby products or Band-Aid's, but investors are discovering that it's so much more. Most of the company's earnings come from pharmaceuticals, which recently have fallen out of favor with Wall Street as health care reform begins to take shape. While the price of the stock has fallen along with other drug companies, Johnson and Johnson's breadth of diversification should shelter it from the worst-case scenario, which industry bears have already discounted into its price. For investors feeling a bit queasy about the drug industry, this stock allows you to test the water before jumping in to the drug industry as a whole. The company's huge research and development budget has allowed it to fill a pipeline full of new drugs but the strength of its non-pharmaceutical consumer businesses means it doesn't have to depend on drug profits entirely. Its strong finances and decent dividend also make the stock suitable for most types of investors. This lower-risk, blue chip should continue to please shareholders in spite of whatever the future might have in store.

Suitability

Age 55 and under	*A-*
Age 55 to 70	*B+*
Age 70+	*B+*

Inception Date:

Manager Tenure:

Telephone:

Minimum Initial Investment:

Direct Deposit:

127

MFS Total Return

Investment Ratings

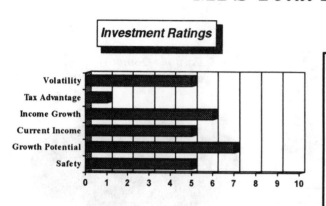

Investment Statistics

Initial Sales Charge:	**4.75%**
Annual Cost per $1,000:	**$16.61**

Annualized Returns

3 Year	*10.70%*
5 Year	*12.09%*
10 year	*10.51%*

Total Return on $10,000

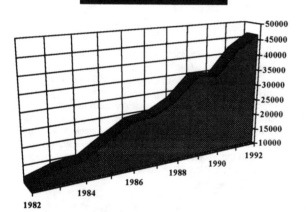

Income on $10,000 Investment

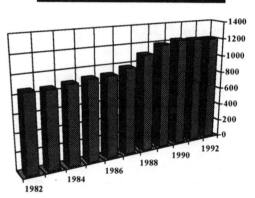

Historic Returns

	1982	1983	1984	1985	1986	1987	1988	1989	1990	1991	1992
Total Return (%)	28.58	19.09	6.96	30.21	19.39	3.43	14.91	23.06	-2.32	21.62	10.07
S and P 500 (%)	21.47	22.46	6.13	31.64	18.68	5.26	17.50	31.68	-3.20	30.40	7.92
Dividend Yield	8.98	7.51	7.03	7.27	5.93	5.60	6.44	6.45	5.79	6.21	5.39
Income on $10,000 ($)	857	853	880	906	916	971	1,097	1,186	1,220	1,212	1,202

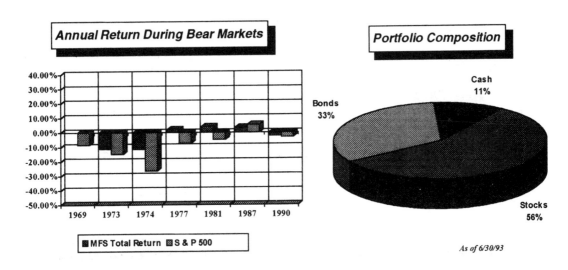

Annual Return During Bear Markets

■ MFS Total Return ▨ S & P 500

Portfolio Composition

Cash 11%
Bonds 33%
Stocks 56%

As of 6/30/93

Investment Description

MFS Total Return hopes to ride the crest of the economic recovery. Cyclical stocks dominate the fund's portfolio, not only for macro-economic reasons but also because most high-yielding stocks currently are cyclical. Since income is a primary goal of the fund, a large percentage of assets are deployed in stocks such as Eastman Kodak, Texaco and Ford Motor. A remaining one-third sits in longer-term bonds and the rest is divided between convertible bonds and cash. Manager Dick Dahlberg has moved the fund away from traditional growth issues such as Coca-Cola and Philip Morris as price earnings ratios soared in the group and relative dividend-yields fell.

In hindsight, it seems like a prescient move. While taking a more conservative tack with the equity portion of the portfolio, Dahlberg has been aggressive with bonds. With a fairly long duration, MFS Total Return is cashing in on declining long-term rates, adding to the fund's impressive total returns for the past two years. A seemingly typical balanced fund, MFS Total Return fund has rewarded shareholders with atypically good total returns for over a decade and remains a strong offering for those looking for a balanced approach to investing.

Suitability

Age 55 and under	*A-*
Age 55 to 70	*A*
Age 70+	*B+*

Inception Date: 10/6/70

Manager Tenure: 1985

Telephone: (800) 225-2606

Minimum Initial Investment: $1,000.00

Direct Deposit: Yes

Oppenheimer Equity Income

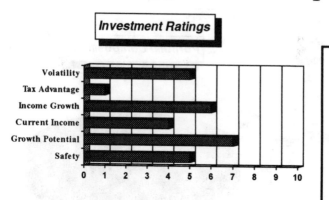

Investment Ratings

Volatility
Tax Advantage
Income Growth
Current Income
Growth Potential
Safety

0 1 2 3 4 5 6 7 8 9 10

Investment Statistics

Initial Sales Charge: **5.75%**
B shares available with no initial

Annual Cost per $1,000: **$18.70**

Annualized Returns

3 Year *7.95%*
5 Year *9.23%*
10 Year *11.25%*

Total Return on $10,000

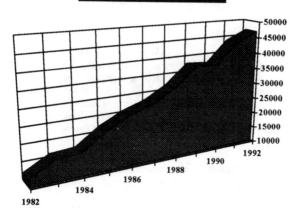

50000
45000
40000
35000
30000
25000
20000
15000
10000

1982 1984 1986 1988 1990 1992

Income on $10,000 Investment

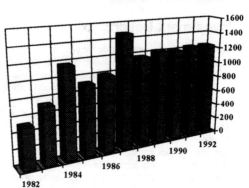

1600
1400
1200
1000
800
600
400
200
0

1982 1984 1986 1988 1990 1992

Historic Returns

	1982	1983	1984	1985	1986	1987	1988	1989	1990	1991	1992
Total Return (%)	30.49	33.33	3.25	30.98	15.56	9.30	14.02	18.56	-1.37	17.27	7.06
S and P 500 (%)	21.47	22.46	6.13	31.64	18.68	5.26	17.50	31.68	-3.20	30.40	7.92
Dividend Yield	6.43	5.48	5.89	5.83	6.55	5.66	0.71	6.11	5.92	5.20	5.77
Income on $10,000 ($)	512	726	1,168	914	989	1,475	1,165	1,215	1,197	1,230	1,236

Annual Return During Bear Markets

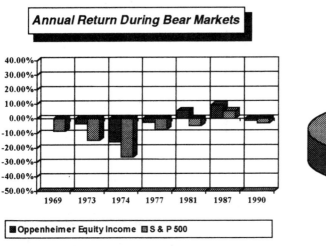

■ Oppenheimer Equity Income ⊠ S & P 500

Portfolio Composition

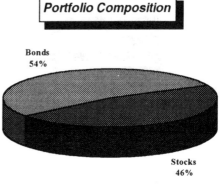

Bonds
54%

Stocks
46%

As of 6/30/93

Investment Description

"Value" should be added to the name of Oppenheimer's flagship conservative equity fund. While many funds preach the merits of value investing, few fund managers truly practice it. You won't find any gold or biotech stocks in this portfolio, at least not anymore. John Doney, formerly of National's Total Return fund, has a reputation as a diehard value investor. Seldom buying companies not paying dividends, Doney's predilection for high yields is a big plus for income-oriented investors. High-yielding stocks such as Texaco, Sears and

Tenneco litter the portfolio, allowing the fund to pay an abnormally high yield. The search for high yields often leads Doney to battered stocks and industries often ripe for turnaround, adding a nice capital gains bonus to the rich dividend. It's worked rather nicely so far. Since Doney's arrival, Equity Income is once again producing above-average returns after a brief hiatus from the list of top performers. If his track record at National Total Return is any indication of Doney's ability, we'll be hearing a lot more about this fund in the future.

Suitability

Age 55 and under	B
Age 55 to 70	B+
Age 70+	B-

Inception Date: 12/1/70

Manager Tenure: 06/92

Telephone: (800) 525-7048

Minimum Initial Investment: $1,000.00

Direct Deposit: No

131

PAX World

Investment Ratings

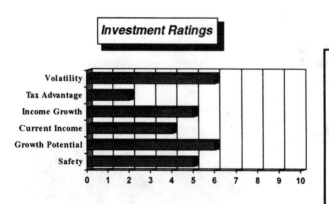

Investment Statistics

Initial Sales Charge:	**None**
Annual Cost per $1,000:	**$10.81**

Annualized Returns

3 Year	*8.10%*
5 Year	*11.36%*
10 Year	*11.22%*

Total Return on $10,000

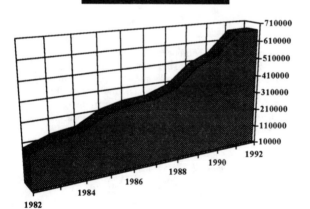

Income on $10,000 Investment

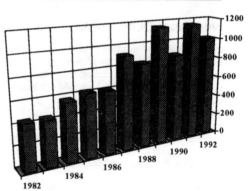

Historic Returns

	1982	1983	1984	1985	1986	1987	1988	1989	1990	1991	1992
Total Return (%)	826.00	24.17	7.39	25.79	8.45	2.49	11.70	24.81	10.53	20.71	0.63
S and P 500 (%)	21.47	22.46	6.13	31.64	18.68	5.26	17.50	31.68	-3.20	30.40	7.92
Dividend Yield	4.36	3.86	4.61	4.53	3.75	5.69	5.27	6.96	4.36	5.51	4.47
Income on $10,000 ($)	435	433	565	615	608	912	821	1,152	862	1,154	1,004

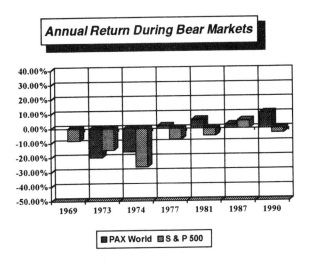

Annual Return During Bear Markets

40.00%	
30.00%	
20.00%	
10.00%	
0.00%	
-10.00%	
-20.00%	
-30.00%	
-40.00%	
-50.00%	

1969 1973 1974 1977 1981 1987 1990

■ PAX World ▨ S & P 500

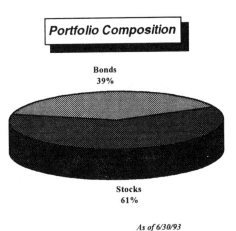

Portfolio Composition

Bonds
39%

Stocks
61%

As of 6/30/93

Investment Description

PAX World fund has been the victim of a series of mis-steps in the past two years that every fund is likely to be subject to at least once in its lifetime. Fund manager Anthony Brown acted on his belief that interest rates had bottomed out, and shifted funds to growth stocks, which he felt would benefit. The resulting one-two punch of further declines in interest rates and earnings disappointments in many well-known growth stocks sent the fund reeling. Slow to recover, the fund has staggered since but it's begining to find its stride again. Perennial growth holdings such as Merck and Heinz are starting to recover. The fund has once again boosted its holding in bonds and other interest sensitive stocks and the total return for 1993 should be decent. PAX World's resilence should help it bounce back to the 11% to 12% returns investors are accustomed to. The fund's past track record and its socially conscious charter will always make it attractive for high-minded investors, even though returns will usually be slightly lower than similar, less altruistic offerings.

Suitability

Age 55 and under	*A*
Age 55 to 70	*A*
Age 70+	*A*

Inception Date: 9/30/71

Manager Tenure: 1971

Telephone: (800) 767-1729

Minimum Initial Investment: $250.00

Direct Deposit: No

133

The George Putnam Fund

Investment Ratings

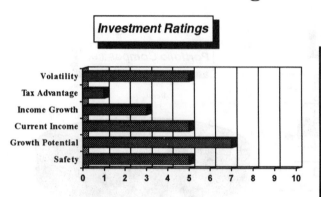

Investment Statistics

Initial Sales Charge: **5.75%**
B shares with no initial sales charge available

Annual Cost per $1,000: **$17.18**

Annualized Returns

3 Year *9.28%*

5 Year *10.76%*

10 Year *11.10%*

Total Return on $10,000

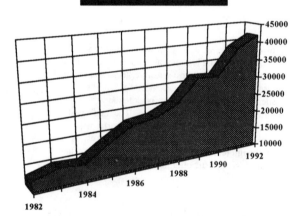

Income on $10,000 Investment

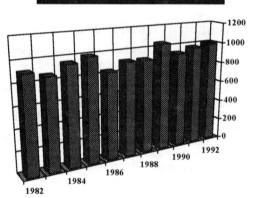

Historic Returns

	1982	1983	1984	1985	1986	1987	1988	1989	1990	1991	1992
Total Return (%)	35.48	14.96	-2.22	29.84	18.84	3.70	12.10	23.60	-0.92	22.80	7.96
S and P 500 (%)	21.47	22.46	6.13	31.64	18.68	5.26	17.50	31.68	-3.20	30.40	7.92
Dividend Yield	9.26	7.34	6.56	8.77	6.09	5.46	6.05	6.57	5.05	5.62	4.95
Income on $10,000 ($)	904	859	948	990	830	908	904	1,040	931	973	999

Annual Return During Bear Markets

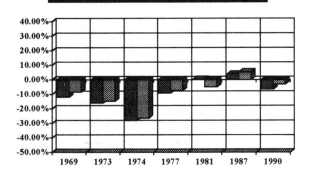

■ The George Putnam Fund ▨ S & P 500

Portfolio Composition

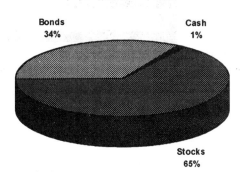

Bonds
34%

Cash
1%

Stocks
65%

As of 6/30/93

Investment Description

The George Putnam Fund of Boston has been accused of being a model of mediocrity. The conservative blue chips that comprise the stock portion of the portfolio have never had the blazing returns of some more aggressive funds. Bonds chosen by co-manager John Geissinger, similarly, have never had the highest yield or the strongest ratings. Yet the fund delivers better than decent performance without the accompanying levels of risk usually found in more aggressive peers. Recently, as the market has rediscovered value-oriented blue chips, George Putnam's performance has picked up considerably. Holdings in turnaround situations like Sears and Eastman Kodak have boosted year-to-date

returns, after a couple years of blue-chip doldrums. The bond portion of the fund continues to find value in BB or BBB bonds, especially in those likely to have ratings changes in the next few months. With better yields than higher-grade bonds, without the risk often accompanying lower-grade junk, the fund's bond holdings pass on a decent yield to shareholders with reasonable risk levels. Overall, the George Putnam Fund should be attractive for investors looking for a moderate income and participation in the market without the risk often found in more aggressive mutual funds.

Suitability

Age 55 and under	*B+*
Age 55 to 70	*A-*
Age 70+	*A-*

Inception Date: 11/5/37

Manager Tenure: 1984/1986

Telephone: (800) 225-1581

Minimum Initial Investment: $500.00

Direct Deposit: Yes

135

Putnam Fund for Growth and Income

Investment Ratings

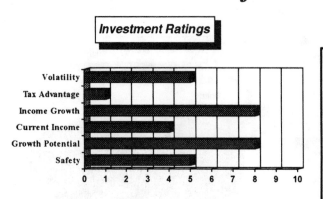

Investment Statistics

Initial Sales Charge: **5.75%**
B shares with no initial sales charge available

Annual Cost per $1,000: **$21.30**

Annualized Returns

3 Year	*10.28%*
5 Year	*12.09%*
10 Year	*13.34%*

Total Return on $10,000

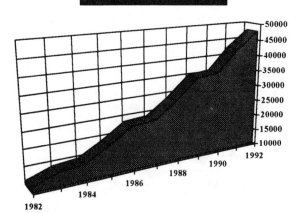

Income on $10,000 Investment

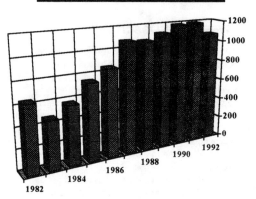

Historic Returns

	1982	1983	1984	1985	1986	1987	1988	1989	1990	1991	1992
Total Return (%)	22.44	21.91	5.39	28.47	22.85	2.43	20.72	20.70	2.39	19.18	11.78
S and P 500 (%)	21.47	22.46	6.13	31.64	18.68	5.26	17.50	31.68	-3.20	30.40	7.92
Dividend Yield	6.13	4.10	3.89	5.68	5.07	5.33	6.01	5.53	5.12	5.29	4.20
Income on $10,000 ($)	634	459	566	738	845	1,073	1,058	1,114	1,183	1,189	1,073

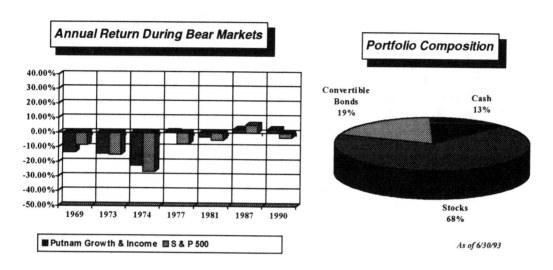

Annual Return During Bear Markets

40.00%	
30.00%	
20.00%	
10.00%	
0.00%	
-10.00%	
-20.00%	
-30.00%	
-40.00%	
-50.00%	

1969 1973 1974 1977 1981 1987 1990

■ Putnam Growth & Income ▨ S & P 500

Portfolio Composition

Convertible Bonds 19%

Cash 13%

Stocks 68%

As of 6/30/93

Investment Description

Putnam Growth and Income is part of a dying breed; a value-oriented fund that hasn't lost money in any calender year since 1981 (a 2.85% loss). Former fund manager John Maurice, who managed the fund since 1968, recently retired but not without leaving the fund in capable hands. Gerald Zukowski continues to manage a portion of the portfolio, along with former Putnam Convertible fund managers Tony Kreisel and Dave King, who manage the remainder. Accordingly, the fund's convertible holdings have increased substantially, but otherwise Maurice's strategy remains intact. The contin-uous search for undervalued stocks should serve investors well in the future as in the past. A higher-than-average dividend payout and excellent dividend growth history is a big plus for retired investors. Although this fund underperformed growth funds during the past decades, its strength lies in its resilience to downturns. An emphasis on strong balance sheets and out-of-favor stocks should continue to propel Putnam Growth & Income with above-average returns in the years to come.

Suitability

Age 55 and under	*B+*
Age 55 to 70	*A*
Age 70+	*B+*

Inception Date: 11/6/57

Manager Tenure: 1991/1993

Telephone: (800) 225-1581

Minimum Initial Investment: $500.00

Direct Deposit: Yes

Rubbermaid

Investment Ratings

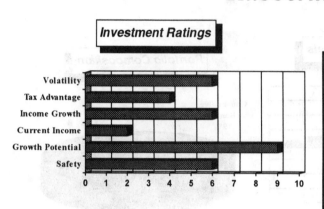

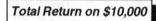

Investment Statistics

Initial Sales Charge: **NA**
Individual stock, brokerage commissions may apply

Annual Cost per $1,000: **$0.00**

Annualized Returns

3 Year	*21.28%*
5 Year	*22.05%*
10 Year	*25.45%*

Total Return on $10,000

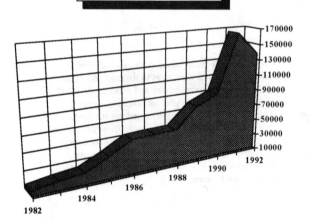

Income on $10,000 Investment

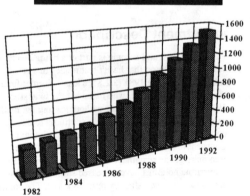

Historic Returns

	1982	1983	1984	1985	1986	1987	1988	1989	1990	1991	1992
Total Return (%)	62.69	30.43	13.74	55.04	40.58	2.58	1.00	46.26	14.29	82.14	-16.99
S and P 500 (%)	21.47	22.46	6.13	31.64	18.68	5.26	17.50	31.68	-3.20	30.40	7.92
Dividend Yield	3.47	2.40	2.04	1.98	1.51	1.32	1.53	1.83	1.47	1.48	0.92
Income on $10,000 ($)	347	390	433	477	563	694	824	997	1,171	1,344	1,518

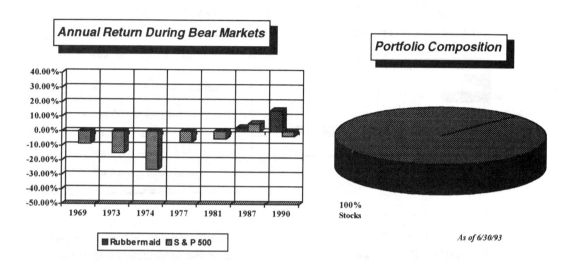

Annual Return During Bear Markets

40.00%
30.00%
20.00%
10.00%
0.00%
-10.00%
-20.00%
-30.00%
-40.00%
-50.00%

1969   1973   1974   1977   1981   1987   1990

■ Rubbermaid ▨ S & P 500

Portfolio Composition

100%
Stocks

As of 6/30/93

Investment Description

Rubbermaid's business might seem mundane at first glance, but a closer look at this company's financial history reveals a growth record nothing short of astonishing. One of the fastest-growing companies of the past decade, Rubbermaid continues to flourish with an eye set on the future and new markets. The company's 1984 acquisition of Little Tykes toys makes it the third largest preschool toymaker in the country. The 1991 purchase of Eldon industries put Rubbermaid in the tool business. Traditional products such as plastic storage containers and other plastic housewares continue to sell well. The company recently began branching out into the ready-to-assemble furniture business, making products designed to appeal to children. Rubbermaid has always limited its expansion and acquisitions to lines that complement its primary business, plastic accessories. The company has yet to make a marketing misstep and for that reason should continue to grow at an above-average rate along with its product lines.

Suitability

Age 55 and under	*A*
Age 55 to 70	*A-*
Age 70+	*B+*

Inception Date:

Manager Tenure:

Telephone:

Minimum Initial Investment:

Direct Deposit:

SteinRoe Prime Equities

Investment Ratings

Investment Statistics

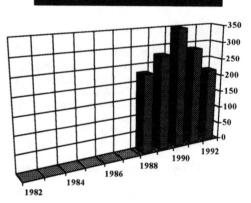

Initial Sales Charge:	**None**
Annual Cost per $1,000:	**$12.78**

Annualized Returns

3 Year	*9.86%*
5 Year	*15.89%*
Inception(3/23/87)	*10.07%*

Total Return on $10,000

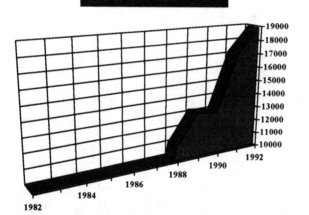

Income on $10,000 Investment

Historic Returns

	1982	1983	1984	1985	1986	1987	1988	1989	1990	1991	1992
Total Return (%)							9.02	21.00	-1.72	32.42	10.01
S and P 500 (%)	21.47	22.46	6.13	31.64	18.68	5.26	17.50	31.68	-3.20	30.40	7.92
Dividend Yield							2.28	2.59	2.55	2.18	1.28
Income on $10,000 ($)							228	276	348	285	216

Annual Return During Bear Markets

40.00%	
30.00%	
20.00%	
10.00%	
0.00%	
-10.00%	
-20.00%	
-30.00%	
-40.00%	
-50.00%	

1969 1973 1974 1977 1981 1987 1990

■ SteinRoe Prime Equities ▧ S & P 500

Portfolio Composition

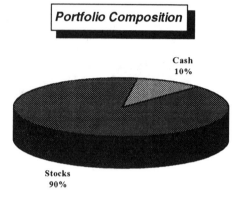

Cash
10%

Stocks
90%

As of 6/30/93

Investment Description

Steinroe Prime Equities doesn't have much in common with other growth & income funds. It doesn't have much of a yield, hold any bonds, or invest heavily in blue chips. The title "growth and opportunity" would probably more aptly describe this offering. Manager Ralph Segall's portfolio looks more like a smorgasbord than it does a structured portfolio relying on a particular theme. Among classic growth stocks such as Home Depot, Abbott Labs and Sun Microsystems are value offering such as Dun & Bradstreet and El Paso Natural Gas. Throw in a pinch of foreign holdings like Banco LatinoAmer de Export and Telefonos de Mexico and

SteinRoe Prime Equities' unique recipe for success emerges. Its 15.89% five-year return bears witness to its success. The mid-cap orientation of the fund also protects it from the ups and downs that so often accompany more aggressive, small-company funds, without giving up too much return. Segall's willingness to look for value just about anywhere should make this an interesting fund to follow as value becomes harder to find in traditional places. No one may understand Steinroe Prime Equities's secret of success but as the old adage goes, if it ain't broke....

Suitability

Age 55 and under	*B+*
Age 55 to 70	*B*
Age 70+	*B-*

Inception Date: 3/23/87

Manager Tenure: 1987

Telephone: (800) 338-2550

Minimum Initial Investment: $1,000.00

Direct Deposit: No

141

Vanguard Quantitative

Investment Ratings

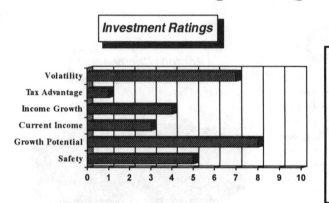

Investment Statistics

Initial Sales Charge:	**None**
Annual Cost per $1,000:	**$5.25**

Annualized Returns

	3 Year	*12.67%*
	5 Year	*14.71%*
Inception(12/10/86)		*13.43%*

Total Return on $10,000

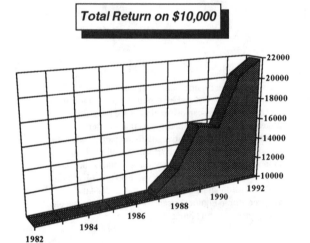

Income on $10,000 Investment

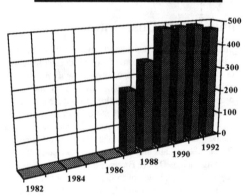

Historic Returns

	1982	1983	1984	1985	1986	1987	1988	1989	1990	1991	1992
Total Return (%)						4.04	16.80	32.00	-2.44	30.29	7.01
S and P 500 (%)	21.47	22.46	6.13	31.64	18.68	5.26	17.50	31.68	-3.20	30.40	7.92
Dividend Yield						2.58	3.57	4.24	3.32	3.54	2.70
Income on $10,000 ($)						257	363	488	488	489	470

Annual Return During Bear Markets

40.00%
30.00%
20.00%
10.00%
0.00%
-10.00%
-20.00%
-30.00%
-40.00%
-50.00%

1969   1973   1974   1977   1981   1987   1990

■ Vanguard Quantitative ▨ S & P 500

Portfolio Composition

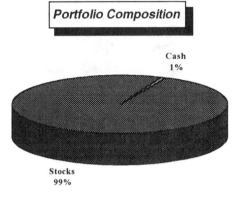

Cash
1%

Stocks
99%

As of 6/30/93

Investment Description

Vanguard Quantitative fund looks a bit like an index fund on steroids. Fund manager John Nagoriak and his co-manager, a computer, try to mimic the S&P 500 index with a few important differences, overweighting favorable stocks and underweighting unfavorable stocks should allow the fund to outperform a standard index fund. Stocks are chosen by a proprietary computer program that takes earnings, price momentum and dividends, among other factors, into account. So far, the strategy has worked magnificently. By outperforming a standard index fund by a small margin, Vanguard Quantitative has also outperfomed over 90% of all fund managers. Naturally Vanguard's abnormally low expense structure helps returns greatly, but Nagorniak and his computer add value to an otherwise boring investment strategy. The last six years' performance, however, may be a hard act to follow. Since the broad market has risen so sharply in the past decade, it's been pretty easy for index funds to beat money managers. In the next few years, however, a good stock picker might become a more valuable commodity. Time will test Vanguard Quantitative's philosophy, but so far, Nagorniak's batting a thousand. He can afford to have his average lowered a little.

Suitability

Age 55 and under	*A*
Age 55 to 70	*A-*
Age 70+	*B*

Inception Date: 12/10/86

Manager Tenure: 1986

Telephone: (800) 662-7447

Minimum Initial Investment: $3,000.00

Direct Deposit: No

Washington Mutual Investors

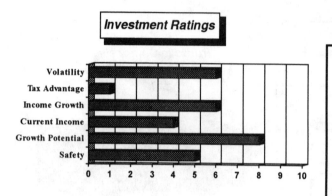

Investment Ratings

Volatility
Tax Advantage
Income Growth
Current Income
Growth Potential
Safety

0 1 2 3 4 5 6 7 8 9 10

Investment Statistics

Initial Sales Charge:	**5.75%**
Annual Cost per $1,000:	**$16.98**

Annualized Returns

3 Year	*9.15%*
5 Year	*12.04%*
10 Year	*14.13%*

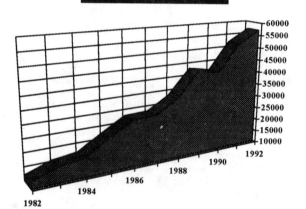

Total Return on $10,000

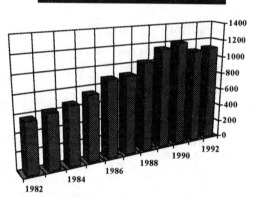

Income on $10,000 Investment

Historic Returns

	1982	1983	1984	1985	1986	1987	1988	1989	1990	1991	1992
Total Return (%)	34.68	26.18	8.28	32.12	22.50	1.42	17.66	28.99	-3.82	25.53	9.44
S and P 500 (%)	21.47	22.46	6.13	31.64	18.68	5.26	17.50	31.68	-3.20	30.40	7.92
Dividend Yield	6.04	5.22	4.68	5.11	4.62	4.23	3.86	4.91	4.16	4.11	3.52
Income on $10,000 ($)	569	618	663	742	881	898	1,019	1,150	1,203	1,091	1,112

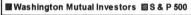

Annual Return During Bear Markets

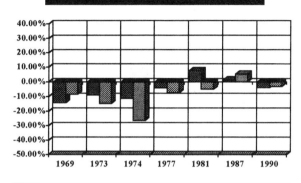

40.00%
30.00%
20.00%
10.00%
0.00%
-10.00%
-20.00%
-30.00%
-40.00%
-50.00%

1969   1973   1974   1977   1981   1987   1990

■ Washington Mutual Investors ▨ S & P 500

Portfolio Composition

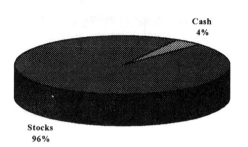

Cash
4%

Stocks
96%

As of 6/30/93

Investment Description

Washington Mutual Investors isn't in the business of timing the market. By prospectus, the fund must have at least 95% of all funds invested in stocks. It's further restricted by the types of equities it can invest in. Companies must have a consistent history of paying dividends, be listed on a stock exchange, and have a certain capitalization. Only a small percentage of all stocks make the cuts from which fund managers cull the best for their portfolio. While it might seem like the portfolio needs little attention, management does add a great deal of value to the fund. Having earned an annual spot in most top-performer lists, Washington Mutual

Investors should not be confused with an index fund. Overweighting out-of-favor stocks such as Mobil, Texaco and several financial stocks, Capital Research, which manages the fund, has produced above-average returns with the fund's customary low risk. While not producing the sizzling hot returns of other more aggressive funds, the performance during bear markets has been admirable. Investors looking for reliability without sacrificing returns should continue to flock to Washington Mutual Investors fund as a safe haven in an increasingly treacherous marketplace.

Suitability

Age 55 and under	*A*
Age 55 to 70	*A-*
Age 70+	*B+*

Inception Date: 7/31/52

Manager Tenure: NA

Telephone: (800) 421-0180

Minimum Initial Investment: $250.00

Direct Deposit: No

Wellesley Income

Investment Ratings

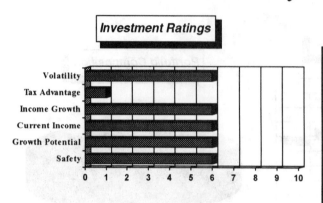

Investment Statistics

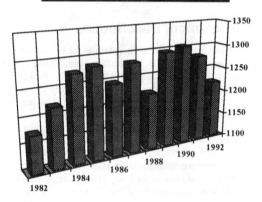

Initial Sales Charge: **None**

Annual Cost per $1,000:   **$5.24**

Annualized Returns

3 Year	*14.46%*
5 Year	*13.70%*
10 Year	*14.12%*

Total Return on $10,000

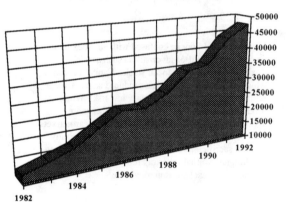

Income on $10,000 Investment

Historic Returns

	1982	1983	1984	1985	1986	1987	1988	1989	1990	1991	1992
Total Return (%)	23.30	18.60	16.64	27.41	18.34	-1.92	13.61	20.93	3.76	21.57	8.67
S and P 500 (%)	21.47	22.46	6.13	31.64	18.68	5.26	17.50	31.68	-3.20	30.40	7.92
Dividend Yield	11.73	11.08	10.82	10.39	8.69	6.40	8.44	8.58	7.73	7.93	6.70
Income on $10,000 ($)	1,173	1,219	1,275	1,284	1,246	1,282	1,216	1,296	1,304	1,280	1,220

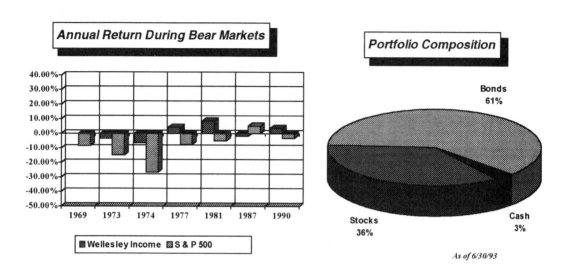

Investment Description

Balanced investing doesn't get much better than this. The Wellesley fund seems to be a jack of all trades. Using a one-third stock, two-third bond portfolio, Wellesley has consistently been a top performer year after year. While Vanguard's low expense ratios help raise the fund's relative performance, credit should also be given to equity manager Jack Ryan and bond manager Earl McEvoy's skills. The fund has always lived up to the "income" part of its name by investing in conservative (usually A-rated or better) bonds, but the real zip in its total return comes from the slightly contrarian way it views the market. While utilities continue to be the stock of choice with many stock-based income funds, equity manager Ryan has been abandoning this traditional total-return investment in favor of better-valued drug stocks and convertible bonds. Oil stocks and retailers round out the stock part of the portfolio. Somewhat less interest-rate sensitive, the fund is seeking to insure future growth as utilities become less attractive. Wellesley's income and total return are second to none, and the low expenses appeal to the miser in all of us. Even though assets have tripled in the last three years, Wellesley Income fund should continue to shine in the years to come.

Suitability

Age 55 and under	*B*+
Age 55 to 70	*A*
Age 70+	*A-*

Inception Date: 7/1/70

Manager Tenure: 1982/1986

Telephone: (800) 662-7447

Minimum Initial Investment: $3,000.00

Direct Deposit: No

147

Chapter 12

Income Investments

Benham GNMA Income

Investment Ratings

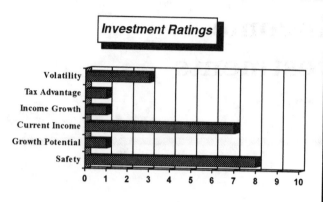

Investment Statistics

| Initial Sales Charge: | **None** |
| Annual Cost per $1,000: | **$6.57** |

Annualized Returns

3 Year	*11.52%*
5 Year	*10.85%*
Inception(9/23/85)	*10.30%*

Total Return on $10,000

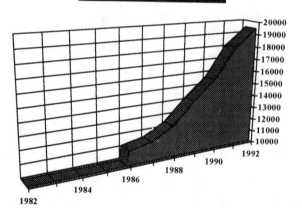

Income on $10,000 Investment

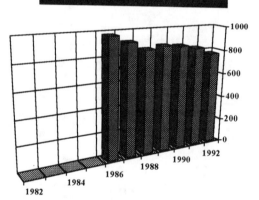

Historic Returns

	1982	1983	1984	1985	1986	1987	1988	1989	1990	1991	1992
Total Return (%)					11.37	3.59	8.29	13.90	10.14	15.57	7.54
Lehman Index (%)	31.30	8.00	15.00	21.30	15.60	2.30	7.60	14.20	8.30	16.10	7.60
Dividend Yield					9.77	9.10	9.00	9.90	8.83	8.47	7.40
Income on $10,000 ($)					976	918	851	870	860	831	773

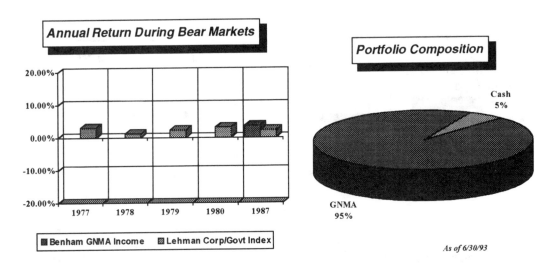

Annual Return During Bear Markets

	1977	1978	1979	1980	1987

■ Benham GNMA Income   ▨ Lehman Corp/Govt Index

Portfolio Composition

Cash
5%

GNMA
95%

As of 6/30/93

Investment Description

Benham GNMA Income fund is staying with what's tried and true. While other U.S. government funds look toward reverse floaters, Collateralized Mortgage Obligations, and other derivative securities, this fund has decided to concentrate on the plain, old regular GNMA securities. Fund manager Randy Merk chooses to look for value right in the backyard rather than in arcane new bond types. By focusing on the underlying mortgages in a GNMA pool, Merk seeks mortgages that will tend to postpone paying off. Since the market usually discounts premium mortgages by an average payoff time, which adjusts as interest rates change, finding a mortgage bond that prepays more slowly than average can be like finding a pot of gold. An in-depth look at origination date, type of loan and the region from which it comes, and comparing it to past experience, Benham GNMA hopes to find high-yielding bonds that will continue to pay high rates for some time to come. While this approach isn't particularly original, in the case of Benham, it does seem to work exceptionally well. The yield, while helped by a low expense structure, has been consistently high. For the risk-adverse investor seeking better-than-average returns, Benham GNMA Income delivers.

Suitability

Age 55 and under	*B-*
Age 55 to 70	*A-*
Age 70+	*A*

Inception Date: 9/23/85

Manager Tenure: 1987/1992

Telephone: (800) 472-3389

Minimum Initial Investment: $1,000.00

Direct Deposit: No

Bond Fund of America

Investment Ratings

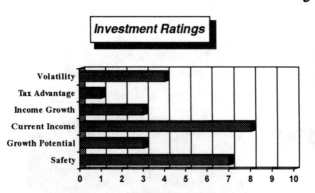

	Initial Sales Charge:	**4.75%**

Annual Cost per $1,000:   **$14.80**

Annualized Returns

3 Year	*9.30%*
5 Year	*10.53%*
10 Year	*11.62%*

Total Return on $10,000

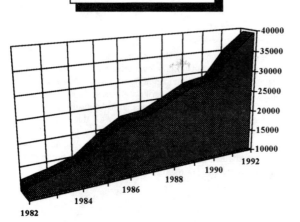

Income on $10,000 Investment

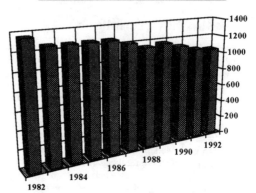

Historic Returns

	1982	1983	1984	1985	1986	1987	1988	1989	1990	1991	1992
Total Return (%)	33.01	9.41	11.84	26.63	15.16	2.70	10.70	10.13	3.27	21.04	11.34
Lehman Index (%)	31.30	8.00	15.00	21.30	15.60	2.30	7.60	14.20	8.30	16.10	7.60
Dividend Yield	14.25	11.36	11.60	11.68	10.28	9.43	9.67	9.82	9.37	9.52	8.47
Income on $10,000 ($)	1,356	1,260	1,260	1,260	1,260	1,206	1,143	1,170	1,116	1,062	1,044

Annual Return During Bear Markets

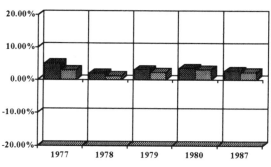

| | 1977 | 1978 | 1979 | 1980 | 1987 |

▨ Bond Fund of America   ▨ Lehman Corp/Govt Index

Portfolio Composition

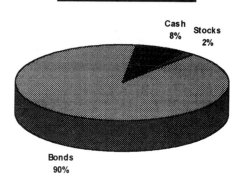

Cash 8% Stocks 2%

Bonds 90%

As of 6/30/93

Investment Description

Somtimes bigger is better, as the Bond Fund of America has been out to prove for the past decade. No one manager is responsible for this goliath's extraordinary performance. In fact, some would say that the lack of one central manager is its secret to success. Since different managers tend to have a variety of opinions, bulls are often balanced by bears, creating a sort of hedging effect that has served the fund well.

With an astonishing $4 billion in assets, this largest of large corporate funds continues to defy critics who say it shouldn't perform any better than the market averages. The broad portfolio includes such diverse holdings as U.S. Treasuries and lower than investment-grade bonds. While Bond Fund of America's strength lies in its diversity, fund managers certainly aren't afraid to take a plunge. Look at the effects of big bets in low-grade bonds and financial services issues, both of which have helped push the fund's returns 4.92% and 3.77% above-market averages in 1991 and 1992 respectively. Investors may not see that kind of bull market performance over the next few years, but can expect above-market performance from this large but potent mutual fund offering.

Suitability

Age 55 and under	*B*
Age 55 to 70	*B+*
Age 70+	*B+*

Inception Date: 5/28/74

Manager Tenure: NA

Telephone: (800) 421-0180

Minimum Initial Investment: $1,000.00

Direct Deposit: No

Circle Income Shares

Investment Ratings

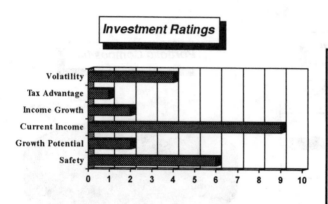

Investment Statistics

Initial Sales Charge:	**None**
Closed end fund	
Annual Cost per $1,000:	**$10.12**

Annualized Returns

3 Year	*10.66%*
5 Year	*7.01%*
10 Year	*8.75%*

Total Return on $10,000

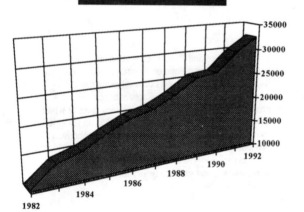

Income on $10,000 Investment

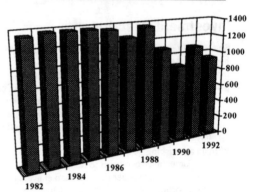

Historic Returns

	1982	1983	1984	1985	1986	1987	1988	1989	1990	1991	1992
Total Return (%)	2.89	35.94	9.64	15.80	10.92	5.22	10.40	11.85	1.92	14.51	8.81
Lehman Index (%)	31.30	8.00	15.00	21.30	15.60	2.30	7.60	14.20	8.30	16.10	7.60
Dividend Yield	13.60	11.58	11.17	11.77	11.15	10.33	11.76	9.62	7.57	9.96	8.23
Income on $10,000 ($)	1,346	1,374	1,374	1,374	1,355	1,260	1,365	1,097	878	1,088	935

Annual Return During Bear Markets

	1977	1978	1979	1980	1987

(Y-axis: 20.00%, 10.00%, 0.00%, -10.00%, -20.00%)

■ Circle Income Shares   ▨ Lehman Corp/Govt Index

Portfolio Composition

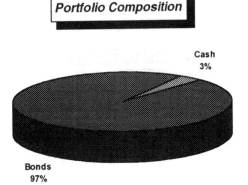

Cash 3%

Bonds 97%

As of 6/30/93

Investment Description

Circle Income Shares takes its "barbell" strategy seriously. Familiar to many government funds, a barbell strategy usually involves buying both short-term and long-term bonds to lower volatility while increasing return. Circle Income Shares puts a unique spin on the strategy. Almost a third of its assets are invested in government bonds while the remaining two-thirds goes into medium-grade bonds, the bulk in BBB-rated issues. A stable net asset value with an above-average yield has been the result for the past decade. While Circle Income Shares might not deliver the kind of total return some of

its more aggressive rivals promise, risk level falls dramatically compared to them, while the yield is considerably higher than most 100% U.S. government alternatives. The only problem lately has been bond calls and mortgage bond prepayments, which have forced income down during the past few years. Nevertheless, the fund still yields around 7% and the discount to net asset value makes it a true bargain when compared to other alternatives. For an income-oriented investor looking for higher yields without higher risk, Circle Income Shares fits the bill.

Suitability

Age 55 and under	*A*
Age 55 to 70	*A-*
Age 70+	*B+*

Inception Date: 7/31/73

Manager Tenure: 1990

Telephone: (317) 321-8180

Minimum Initial Investment: NA

Direct Deposit: NA

155

Convertible Bonds

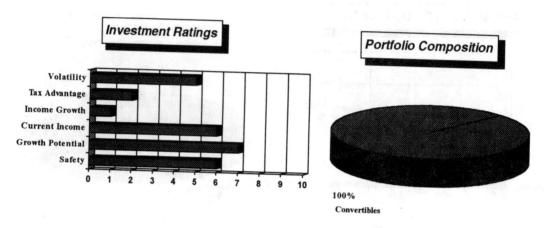

Investment Ratings

- Volatility
- Tax Advantage
- Income Growth
- Current Income
- Growth Potential
- Safety

0 1 2 3 4 5 6 7 8 9 10

Portfolio Composition

100%
Convertibles

As of 6/30/93

Investment Description

Growth without risk? Convertible bonds have long been favored by conservative investors who desire the growth of a stock with the safety and income of a bond. Convertible bonds are classified as debt and resemble bonds in their priority of stocks in the event of liquidation, interest payments and guarantee of principal by the company upon maturity. Unlike regular bonds, convertibles can be exchanged for stock in the company at a given price, usually higher than the current market price. Investors enjoy the security of being bondholders without giving up potential appreciation in the price of

the stock, the best of both worlds. Convertible bonds fell out of Wall Street's favor right after the market crash of 1987 but have recently begun a comeback. While the investment sounds ideal, the problem is finding bonds that are convertible. As the junk bond market heats up, most lower-rated companies that have traditionally issued this type of debt haven't needed any help in selling their low-grade bonds recently. Still, good buys can be found in companies like Pennzoil, OfficeDepot and U.S. West to name a few.

Suitability

Age 55 and under	B
Age 55 to 70	A-
Age 70+	B+

Inception Date:

Manager Tenure:

Telephone:

Minimum Initial Investment:

Direct Deposit: No

Convertible Preferred Stock

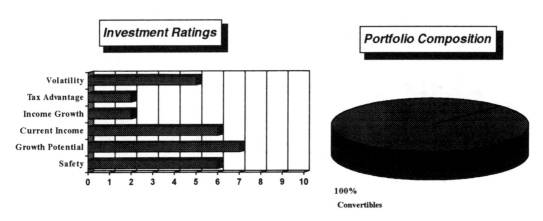

Investment Ratings

- Volatility
- Tax Advantage
- Income Growth
- Current Income
- Growth Potential
- Safety

0 1 2 3 4 5 6 7 8 9 10

Portfolio Composition

100%
Convertibles

As of 6/30/93

Investment Description

Convertible preferred stock isn't a very exciting investment. Preferred prices seldom move as much as common stock or trade more than a 10,000 shares a day. Traditionally a corporate investment, preferred stock has been virtually ignored by most investors for years, until now. What changed? Interest rates. While a 7% or 8% yield seemed unexciting when CDs were paying 8%, a 6 or 7% yield looks pretty good now that rates are hovering around 3%. While convertible preferred stocks don't enjoy the preferential treatment of bonds, they are slightly more secure than common stock. The conversion feature allows investors to enjoy a better yield than common stockholders, while being able to participate in the common stock's appreciation. Income-oriented investors can expect yields as high as 8% in relatively conservative issues. Several companies recommended issue convertible preferred stock including K-Mart and Great Western. For the investor who wants it all (income and growth), this is about as close as you can get.

Suitability

Age 55 and under	*B+*
Age 55 to 70	*A-*
Age 70+	*B*

Inception Date:

Manager Tenure:

Telephone:

Minimum Initial Investment:

Direct Deposit: No

Dreyfus Short-Intermediate Govt

Investment Ratings

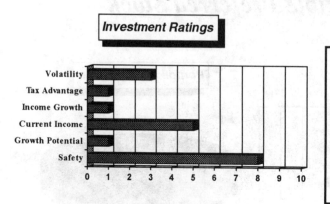

Investment Statistics

Initial Sales Charge: **None**

Annual Cost per $1,000:   **$4.20**

Annualized Returns
3 Year	*10.65%*
5 Year	*9.81%*
Inception(4/6/87)	*8.74%*

Total Return on $10,000

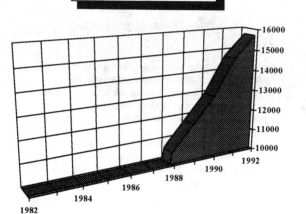

Income on $10,000 Investment

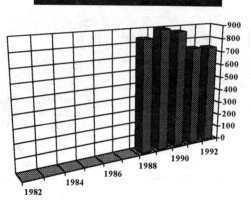

Historic Returns

	1982	1983	1984	1985	1986	1987	1988	1989	1990	1991	1992
Total Return (%)							5.64	11.29	10.04	13.50	7.03
Lehman Index (%)	31.30	8.00	15.00	21.30	15.60	2.30	7.60	14.20	8.30	16.10	7.60
Dividend Yield							8.36	9.24	8.84	7.45	7.01
Income on $10,000 ($)							836	897	871	739	734

Annual Return During Bear Markets

	1977	1978	1979	1980	1987

20.00%
10.00%
0.00%
-10.00%
-20.00%

■ Dreyfus Short-Intermediate ■ Lehman Corp/Govt Index Gov't

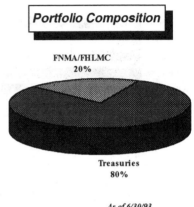

Portfolio Composition

FNMA/FHLMC
20%

Treasuries
80%

As of 6/30/93

Investment Description

Dreyfus Short-Intermediate Government fund is chomping at the bit. The fund's prospectus allows only bonds with maturities of 3 1/2 years or less, so fund manager Barbara Kenworthy has been venturing into more aggressive bonds. Zero coupon bonds and deep-discount issues have provided a vehicle by which the fund can participate in the recent bull market in bonds. As a result, capital gains have pushed this fund's total return very near many of its longer-term competitors, especially since the slide in short-term rates has been more severe than in long-term rates. A large holding of Treasuries as compared to mortgage bonds has strength-ened this intermediate fund's performance since prepayments, which plague other government funds, have had a negligable effect here. The fund's low expense ratio adds to its competitiveness, boosting its return considerably over many rivals. While Kenworthy might be at a loss to produce an encore of the past 4 years, especially if short-term rates are near a bottom, the stability of this fund's price and the relative yield compared to longer, riskier alternatives make Dreyfus Short-Intermediate Government attractive to anyone looking for a better yield without the risk associated with longer-term bonds.

Suitability

Age 55 and under	*A-*
Age 55 to 70	*A-*
Age 70+	*B+*

Inception Date: 4/6/87

Manager Tenure: 1987

Telephone: (800) 645-6561

Minimum Initial Investment: $2,500

Direct Deposit: No

159

Ellsworth Convertible Growth & Income

Investment Ratings

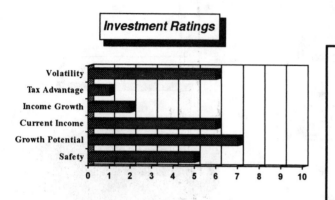

Total Return on $10,000

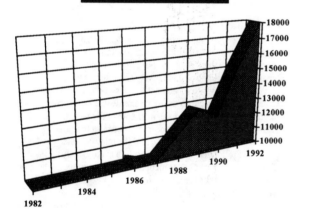

Income on $10,000 Investment

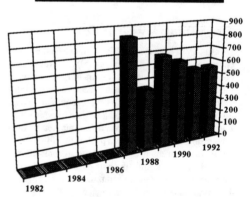

Historic Returns

	1982	1983	1984	1985	1986	1987	1988	1989	1990	1991	1992
Total Return (%)					3.49	-4.43	15.02	12.50	-4.20	24.86	17.35
Lehman Index (%)	31.30	8.00	15.00	21.30	15.60	2.30	7.60	14.20	8.30	16.10	7.60
Dividend Yield						8.42	5.48	7.78	7.09	7.12	6.12
Income on $10,000 ($)						833	448	677	625	552	552

Annual Return During Bear Markets

20.00%				
10.00%				
0.00%				
-10.00%				
-20.00%	1977	1978	1979	1980	1987

■ Elsworth Convertible   ⊠ Lehman Corp/Govt Index

Portfolio Composition

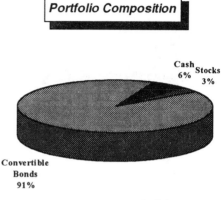

Cash 6%   Stocks 3%

Convertible Bonds 91%

As of 6/30/93

Investment Description

In spite of falling interest rates, Ellsworth Convertible Growth and Income fund has managed to maintain an above-average yield and an even better total return during the past two years. Investing only in convertible bonds, fund managers Ron and Tom Dinsmore focus on issues that not only pay a decent yield but also have attractive underlying stocks. As interest rates have fallen, the Dinsmores' average maturity has lengthened, to prop up sagging yields, but their basic strategy remains intact. Holdings such as Freeport McMoran, Cigna, and Pennzoil illustrate the fund's predisposition to conservative,value-oriented issues. As a result, the risk

level is well below most competitors, even though performance hasn't suffered; the fund's 13.21% three return looks more like a growth fund than a bond fund. Convertible bonds have been overlooked by investors ever since the 1987 crash tarnished their image. The Ellsworth Convertible Growth and Income fund is a particularly good way to buy into this rapidly recovering market, since it trades at a hefty discount to its net asset value. The 8%-plus discount allows investors to buy $1 worth of assets for only $.92. Who said there aren't any bargains left in the market?

Suitability

Age 55 and under	*A-*
Age 55 to 70	*A*
Age 70+	*B*

Inception Date: 6/30/86

Manager Tenure: 1986

Telephone: (212) 269-9236

Minimum Initial Investment: NA

Direct Deposit: No

161

Federated GNMA

Investment Ratings

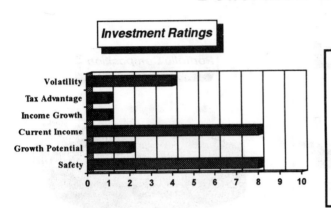

Investment Statistics

Initial Sales Charge:	**None**
Annual Cost per $1,000:	**$4.98**

Annualized Returns

3 Year	*10.90%*
5 Year	*11.13%*
10 Year	*11.83%*

Total Return on $10,000

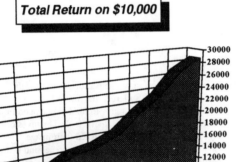

Income on $10,000 Investment

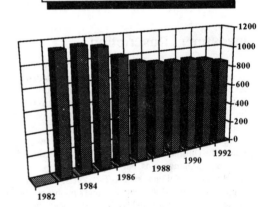

Historic Returns

	1982	1983	1984	1985	1986	1987	1988	1989	1990	1991	1992
Total Return (%)		7.50	14.88	19.52	10.93	3.50	8.22	15.06	10.38	15.33	6.52
Lehman Index (%)	31.30	8.00	15.00	21.30	15.60	2.30	7.60	14.20	8.30	16.10	7.60
Dividend Yield		11.31	12.01	11.54	9.83	9.10	9.39	9.43	8.98	8.73	7.91
Income on $10,000 ($)		1,131	1,149	1,122	1,021	951	923	914	914	896	859

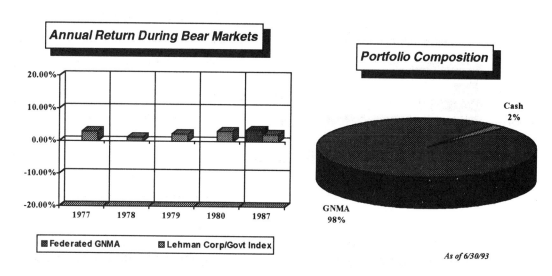

Annual Return During Bear Markets

| | 1977 | 1978 | 1979 | 1980 | 1987 |

☒ Federated GNMA   ☒ Lehman Corp/Govt Index

Portfolio Composition

Cash
2%

GNMA
98%

As of 6/30/93

Investment Description

Federated GNMA fund is shopping for bonds, carefully. Reasoning that prepayments are likely to continue, manager Gary Madich intends to focus on current and high coupon bonds. Most have either already been through a wave of refinancing and contain loans more likely to remain intact, or are made up of lower rate mortgages. Looking at individual mortgage pools and choosing bonds in areas where prepayments are slow, such as the economically depressed Northeast, should help Federated GNMA raise its yield. While neither of the strategies are particularily original, the fund should

continue to post above-average returns by sticking to a basic strategy that's worked well in the past. While many funds are reaching for higher yields in exotic bonds such as inverse floaters and unusual Collateralized Mortgage Obligations, Federated Income maintains a "vanilla" strategy and competes by keeping management and operation expenses to a minimum, passing on the saving to investors. While the high initial investment may keep smaller investors away, for those willing to ante up, this fund should pay off rather well.

Suitability

Age 55 and under	*B-*
Age 55 to 70	*A-*
Age 70+	*A*

Inception Date: 3/23/82

Manager Tenure: 1987

Telephone: (800) 245-5000

Minimum Initial Investment: $25,000.00

Direct Deposit: No

Federated Income Trust

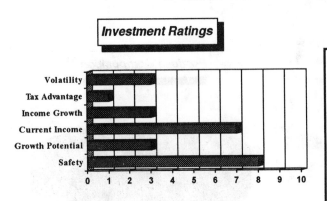

Initial Sales Charge:	**None**
Annual Cost per $1,000:	**$5.00**

Annualized Returns

3 Year	*10.07%*
5 Year	*9.80%*
10 year	*10.47%*

Total Return on $10,000

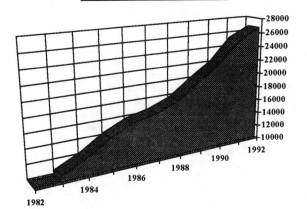

Income on $10,000 Investment

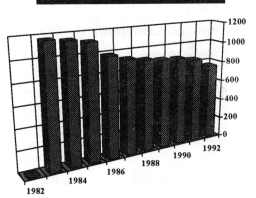

Historic Returns

	1982	1983	1984	1985	1986	1987	1988	1989	1990	1991	1992
Total Return (%)		7.93	14.44	17.15	9.60	4.63	7.62	12.47	10.42	13.90	5.67
Lehman Index (%)	31.30	8.00	15.00	21.30	15.60	2.30	7.60	14.20	8.30	16.10	7.60
Dividend Yield		11.67	12.00	11.56	9.66	9.22	9.39	9.38	9.05	8.68	7.47
Income on $10,000 ($)		1,167	1,148	1,120	980	930	902	883	874	845	761

Annual Return During Bear Markets

	1977	1978	1979	1980	1987

(Y-axis: 20.00%, 10.00%, 0.00%, -10.00%, -20.00%)

■ Federated Income   ▨ Lehman Corp/Govt Index

Portfolio Composition

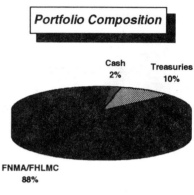

Cash 2%   Treasuries 10%

FNMA/FHLMC 88%

As of 6/30/93

Investment Description

Federated seems to be working very hard to keep this gem a secret. It's never advertised, you'll never see it on anyone's recommended list and the fund doesn't even have a color sales brochure. Part of the reason for this lack of publicity comes from the institutional nature of the fund. Until recently, the fund sold shares only to large investors, such as banks and pension funds. While some discount brokerage firms now offer the Federated Income Trust to the general public, the large-ish

$25,000 minimum might turn some investors off. Paying 7.5% currently and boasting a very stable net asset value, this fund also keeps an extremely short average maturity, approximately 4.9 years currently. Managers Kathy Foody-Malus and Gary Madich find higher returns with shorter maturities in stable PAC CMOs. In spite of the hefty minimum purchase, conservative investors worried about rising rates will find an excellent package in the Federated Income Trust.

Suitability

Age 55 and under	*C*
Age 55 to 70	*B*+
Age 70+	*A*

Inception Date: 3/30/82

Manager Tenure: 1986/1990

Telephone: (800) 245-5000

Minimum Initial Investment: $25,000

Direct Deposit: No

165

FNMA/FHLMC CMO - Broken PAC

Investment Ratings

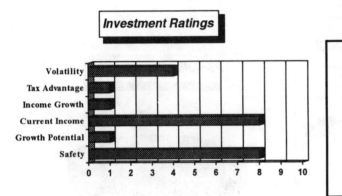

Investment Statistics

Initial Sales Charge: **Varies**
Markups between 1/2% and 3% typical

Annual Cost per $1,000: **$0.00**

Annualized Returns

3 Year *11.08%*

5 Year *11.44%*

10 Year *12.50%*

Total Return on $10,000

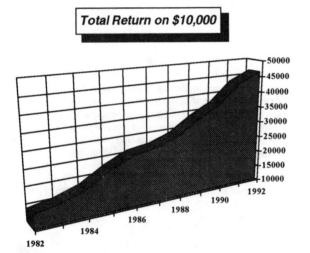

Income on $10,000 Investment

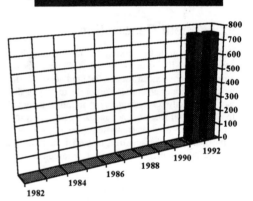

Historic Returns

	1982	1983	1984	1985	1986	1987	1988	1989	1990	1991	1992
Total Return (%)	43.00	10.10	15.80	25.20	13.40	4.30	8.70	15.40	10.70	15.70	7.00
Lehman Index (%)	31.30	8.00	15.00	21.30	15.60	2.30	7.60	14.20	8.30	16.10	7.60
Dividend Yield	14.00	12.10	13.40	11 60	8.70	9.40	9.90	9.50	9.60	8.90	8.00
Income on $10,000 ($)										750	750

Annual Return During Bear Markets

	1977	1978	1979	1980	1987

20.00%
10.00%
0.00%
-10.00%
-20.00%

■ FNMA/FHLMC   ▨ Lehman Corp/Govt Index

Portfolio Composition

100%
FNMA/FHMLC

As of 6/30/93

Investment Description

As interest rate fell precipitously the past two years, many longer-term Collateralized Mortgage Obligations paid off early or had their average life reduced drastically. While some investors received money back from more speculative support bonds, some higher-quality PACs were left intact, even though their prepayment rates had fallen out of the band that the issuers had guaranteed the bond's maturity at. Generally negative public sentiment has left many of these "broken" PACs in limbo, as individual investors are frightened off because of previous experience with more volatile CMOs,

and institutions are hesitant to carry a bond that has fallen outside of its band. The result is a buying opportunity for relative short term bonds (3-8 years) that have limited risk. The bond's maturity, at most, would extend to the original bond's maturity, should interest rates rise dramatically, while prepayment risk has stabilized recently along with interest rates. An above-average yield, principal guarantee at maturity and the AAA-safety of a U.S. government agency all make Broken PAC Collateralized Mortgage Obligations attractive for income-oriented investors.

Suitability

Age 55 and under	*B*
Age 55 to 70	*A-*
Age 70+	*A*

Inception Date:

Manager Tenure:

Telephone:

Minimum Initial Investment:

Direct Deposit:

FNMA/FHLMC CMO - PAC

Investment Ratings

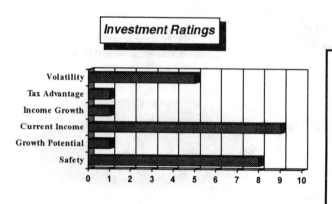

Investment Statistics

Initial Sales Charge: **Varies**
Markups between 1/2% and 3% typical

Annual Cost per $1,000: **$0.00**

Annualized Returns

3 Year	*11.08%*
5 Year	*11.44%*
10 Year	*12.50%*

Total Return on $10,000

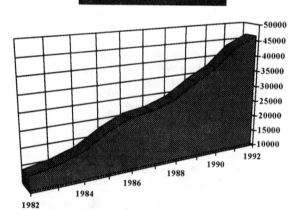

Income on $10,000 Investment

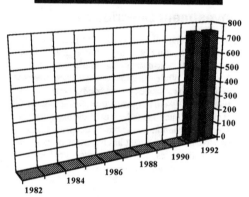

Historic Returns

	1982	1983	1984	1985	1986	1987	1988	1989	1990	1991	1992
Total Return (%)	43.00	10.10	15.80	25.20	13.40	4.30	8.70	15.40	10.70	15.70	7.00
Lehman Index (%)	31.30	8.00	15.00	21.30	15.60	2.30	7.60	14.20	8.30	16.10	7.60
Dividend Yield	14.00	12.10	13.40	11.60	8.70	9.40	9.90	9.50	9.60	8.90	8.00
Income on $10,000 ($)										750	750

Annual Return During Bear Markets

	1977	1978	1979	1980	1987

Y-axis: 20.00%, 10.00%, 0.00%, -10.00%, -20.00%

■ FNMA/FHLMC   ▨ Lehman Corp/Govt Index

Portfolio Composition

100%
FNMA/FHMLC

As of 6/30/93

Investment Description

Collateralized Mortgage Obligations have really gotten a bad rap in the past two years, often unjustly. Many brokerage firms were reprimanded by the SEC for advertising CMOs without revealing prepayment risk. Many brokerage clients purchased bonds with an 8-year or longer average life, which they equated to maturity. When interest fell dramatically, and bonds paid off early, many investors shunned CMOs, blaming the investment for the unexpected payoff. While many brokerage firms recommend what are called support bonds, because of higher yields, other more conservative Collateralized Mortgage Obligations can be found. PAC bonds are one such alternative. Much more stable than support bonds, PACs offer investors a fixed maturity with a higher yield than Treasury obligations. Most investors are attracted to these bonds because of monthly payments and a fixed-interest check, which, unlike mutual funds, doesn't flucuate with interest rates.

Suitability

Age 55 and under	*B*
Age 55 to 70	*A-*
Age 70+	*A-*

Inception Date:

Manager Tenure:

Telephone:

Minimum Initial Investment:

Direct Deposit:

169

FPA New Income

Investment Ratings

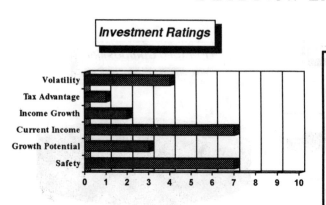

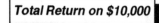

Investment Statistics

Initial Sales Charge:	**4.50%**
Annual Cost per $1,000:	**$20.66**

Annualized Returns

3 Year	*8.02%*
5 Year	*10.66%*
10 Year	*11.67%*

Total Return on $10,000

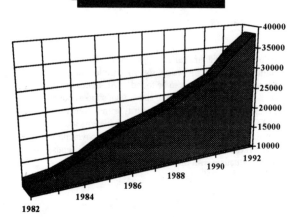

Income on $10,000 Investment

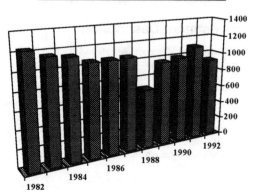

Historic Returns

	1982	1983	1984	1985	1986	1987	1988	1989	1990	1991	1992
Total Return (%)	27.85	6.17	16.43	21.31	11.11	7.87	8.55	12.23	8.38	18.80	11.12
Lehman Index (%)	31.30	8.00	15.00	21.30	15.60	2.30	7.60	14.20	8.30	16.10	7.60
Dividend Yield	12.89	10.74	11.03	9.88	8.96	8.84	5.76	7.91	7.86	8.74	6.72
Income on $10,000 ($)	1,231	1,156	1,130	1,055	1,055	1,058	680	959	989	1,098	920

Annual Return During Bear Markets

■ FPA New Income   ▤ Lehman Corp/Govt Index

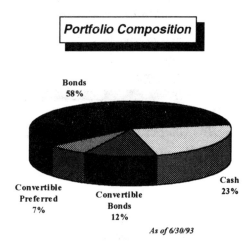

Portfolio Composition

Bonds
58%

Convertible
Preferred
7%

Convertible
Bonds
12%

Cash
23%

As of 6/30/93

Investment Description

FPA New Income fund has never been afraid to blaze its own trail. As fixed-income mutual funds become increasingly difficult to differentiate, FPA stands out for its unabashed bearishness. Manager Bob Rodriguez simply doesn't find the bond market attractive at the current low yields and, as a result, cash has risen to close to 23%. Other than venturing into some more obscure issues, such as high-coupon GNMA-backed mobile home bonds and some foreign government securities, Rodriguez would rather wait for higher yields than risk

being run over by a bond market selloff. While his caution might be overstated, Rodriguez's conservative bent should attract cautious investors looking for above-average returns without the exposure to interest risk that accompanies so many fixed-income funds. While the performance may lag some of its more aggressive competitors in the next few months, FPA New Income's bearish stance could well be vindicated during the next year. If not, a decent yield and a stable NAV should assuage most investors.

Suitability

Age 55 and under	*B*
Age 55 to 70	*B+*
Age 70+	*A-*

Inception Date: 4/1/69

Manager Tenure: 1984

Telephone: (800) 982-4372

Minimum Initial Investment: $1,500.00

Direct Deposit: No

Franklin U.S. Govt Securities

Investment Ratings

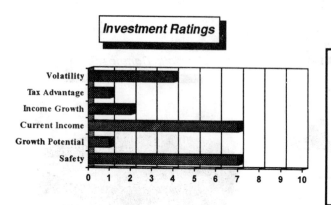

Investment Statistics

Initial Sales Charge:	**4.00%**
Annual Cost per $1,000:	**$11.55**

Annualized Returns

3 Year	*9.21%*
5 Year	*9.03%*
10 Year	*9.94%*

Total Return on $10,000

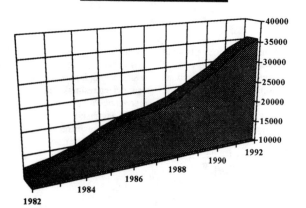

Income on $10,000 Investment

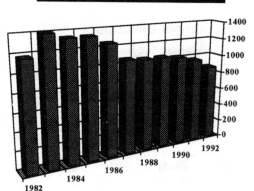

Historic Returns

	1982	1983	1984	1985	1986	1987	1988	1989	1990	1991	1992
Total Return (%)	32.23	9.14	12.88	19.97	10.74	4.32	7.45	13.11	10.78	13.71	7.40
Lehman Index (%)	31.30	8.00	15.00	21.30	15.60	2.30	7.60	14.20	8.30	16.10	7.60
Dividend Yield	12.20	12.60	12.55	12.68	11.17	9.57	9.99	10.26	9.76	9.30	8.00
Income on $10,000 ($)	1,171	1,397	1,337	1,337	1,248	1,054	1,036	1,036	1,015	965	863

Annual Return During Bear Markets

20.00%	
10.00%	
0.00%	
-10.00%	
-20.00%	
	1977 1978 1979 1980 1987

■ Franklin U.S. Gov't   ▣ Lehman Corp/Govt Index

Portfolio Composition

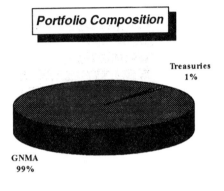

Treasuries
1%

GNMA
99%

As of 6/30/93

Investment Description

Critics of Franklin U.S. Government Securities fund abound. It's too big, they say, to take advantage of special niches, such as multi-family housing bonds and other special-interest bonds. A fund with over $14 billion would simply overwhelm the market. The same is true of special opportunities in Collateralized Mortgage Obligation or inverse floaters. Rather than hinder performance, Franklin U.S. Government's absence from these "niches" has helped it avoid the volatility other government funds have had over the years. Using a straightforward portfolio, the fund takes advantage of lower expense ratios to compete in a marketplace where other funds are taking more risks to keep their sinking yields afloat. Fund manager Jack Lemein simply buys current coupon GNMAs and holds them. While individual pool selection does play a role in buying bonds, the fund size precludes it from doing a lot of in-depth research. Investors may not always agree with this simple strategy but at least they can understand it. For that, Franklin should be praised and its U.S. Government Securities fund deserves the attention of anyone looking for a plain-old government fund.

Suitability

Age 55 and under	*B*
Age 55 to 70	*A-*
Age 70+	*B+*

Inception Date: 4/3/82

Manager Tenure: 1984

Telephone: (800) 342-5236

Minimum Initial Investment: $100.00

Direct Deposit: Yes

Great Western Financial

Investment Ratings

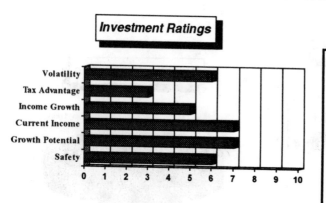

Investment Statistics

Initial Sales Charge: **NA**
Individual stock, brokerage commissions may apply

Annual Cost per $1,000: **$0.00**

Annualized Returns

3 Year	*5.60%*
5 Year	*8.20%*
10 Year	*9.16%*

Total Return on $10,000

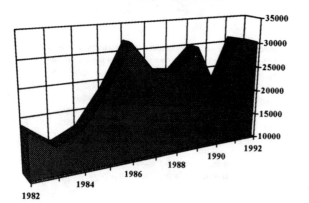

Income on $10,000 Investment

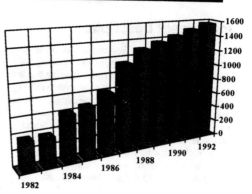

Historic Returns

	1982	1983	1984	1985	1986	1987	1988	1989	1990	1991	1992
Total Return (%)	88.79	-19.63	15.34	36.45	34.30	-18.01	-1.64	16.67	-30.00	46.94	-2.78
S and P 500 (%)	21.47	22.46	6.13	31.64	18.68	5.26	17.50	31.68	-3.20	30.40	7.92
Dividend Yield	3.62	1.92	3.98	3.74	3.32	3.55	4.92	5.27	4.74	7.10	5.06
Income on $10,000 ($)	362	362	603	655	793	1,137	1,293	1,362	1,431	1,500	1,568

Annual Return During Bear Markets

40.00%							
30.00%							
20.00%							
10.00%							
0.00%							
-10.00%							
-20.00%							
-30.00%							
-40.00%							
-50.00%	1969	1973	1974	1977	1981	1987	1990

■ Great Western ▨ S & P 500

Portfolio Composition

100%
Stocks

As of 6/30/93

Investment Description

California thrifts aren't finding their way to many stock analysts' recommended lists, and with good reason. California is in the midst of a deep recession while other areas of the country seem to be emerging from tough economic times. Real estate prices have fallen for the first time in recent memory in the Golden State, and most big thrifts' experiments with commercial real estate have ended abruptly just as commercial values only recently ended a free fall. Still, Great Western represents an often-overlooked gem in the rubble of what used to be a thriving California thrift industry. Its focus on single family residential lending, especially variable-rate loans

should help boost its loan quality over time. With its commercial real estate debacle almost behind it, and deposit rates at 30-year lows, Great Western is poised to deliver excellent earnings when the California real estate market begins to turn around. Add in a cost-cutting program that was recently announced, and a large mutual fund company delivering additional fee income, and there's a compelling argument for making a long-term investment in the company. A healthy dividend should make the most impatient investor better able to wait out a turnaround in this stock.

Suitability

Age 55 and under	*B*
Age 55 to 70	*A-*
Age 70+	*A-*

Inception Date:

Manager Tenure:

Telephone:

Minimum Initial Investment:

Direct Deposit:

175

K-Mart

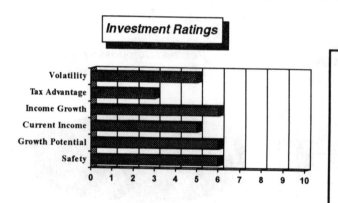

Initial Sales Charge: **NA**
Individual stock, brokerage commissions may apply

Annual Cost per $1,000:   **$0.00**

Annualized Returns

3 Year	*16.90%*
5 Year	*15.34%*
10 Year	*17.33%*

Total Return on $10,000

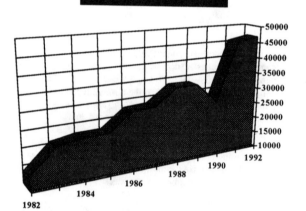

Income on $10,000 Investment

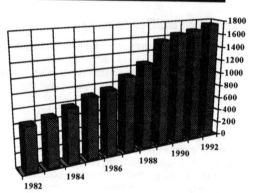

Historic Returns

	1982	1983	1984	1985	1986	1987	1988	1989	1990	1991	1992
Total Return (%)	39.68	51.14	6.02	0.36	24.02	1.71	18.07	-0.36	-18.93	68.28	2.62
S and P 500 (%)	21.47	22.46	6.13	31.64	18.68	5.26	17.50	31.68	-3.20	30.40	7.92
Dividend Yield	6.29	4.91	3.70	4.00	4.24	3.97	4.44	4.67	4.91	6.20	3.85
Income on $10,000 ($)	628	685	780	895	952	1,104	1,257	1,561	1,638	1,676	1,752

Annual Return During Bear Markets

40.00%						
30.00%						
20.00%						
10.00%						
0.00%						
-10.00%						
-20.00%						
-30.00%						
-40.00%						
-50.00%						

1969   1973   1974   1977   1981   1987   1990

■ K-Mart   ▨ S & P 500

Portfolio Composition

100%
Stocks

As of 6/30/93

Investment Description

K-mart has been rebuilding itself from top to bottom during the past few years. Gone are the blue-light specials, polyester ties and messy, understocked shelves. Even the ice-cream bar and snack counter has all but vanished. Enter a whole new store, with wide isles, expanded merchandise and even a pizza restaurent operated by an outside company. But will it be too little, too late? Market leader Wal-Mart is expanding quickly, as is third-place Target, although both have been stumbling somewhat lately in earnings growth. Chairman Joseph Antonini isn't taking any chances. In addition to an aggressive revitaliization effort in existing stores, the company is experimenting with super stores, which combine general merchandise and groceries. K-mart's expansion efforts also take it into other areas of the retail market. PACE Warehouses, OfficeMax, Sports Authority and Waldenbooks are all owned by the company. Some sales and earnings disappointments might come during the next few quarters but the results of store modernization and expansion will make its way to the bottom line within the next few years. While investors wait, an above-average dividend more than makes up for any lost income from other investment alternatives.

Suitability

Age 55 and under	*A-*
Age 55 to 70	*A*
Age 70+	*A-*

Inception Date:

Manager Tenure:

Telephone:

Minimum Initial Investment:

Direct Deposit:

177

Kemper U.S. Govt

Investment Ratings

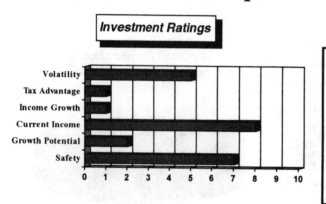

Investment Statistics

Initial Sales Charge: **4.50%**

Annual Cost per $1,000: **$12.38**

Annualized Returns

3 Year	*9.57%*
5 Year	*9.20%*
10 year	*10.76%*

Total Return on $10,000

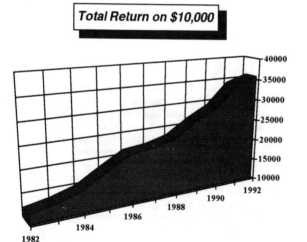

Income on $10,000 Investment

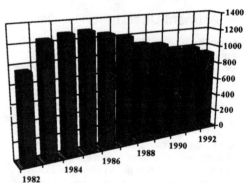

Historic Returns

	1982	1983	1984	1985	1986	1987	1988	1989	1990	1991	1992
Total Return (%)	28.53	8.91	12.25	22.32	16.24	2.68	6.35	14.00	9.68	17.25	4.61
Lehman Index (%)	31.30	8.00	15.00	21.30	15.60	2.30	7.60	14.20	8.30	16.10	7.60
Dividend Yield	13.20	11.34	12.15	12.37	10.98	10.20	10.07	10.25	9.28	9.31	7.98
Income on $10,000 ($)	948	1,239	1,284	1,296	1,248	1,206	1,104	1,080	1,008	1,003	923

Annual Return During Bear Markets

| | 1977 | 1978 | 1979 | 1980 | 1987 |

(chart y-axis: 20.00%, 10.00%, 0.00%, -10.00%, -20.00%)

■ Kemper U.S. Gov't   ▨ Lehman Corp/Govt Index

Portfolio Composition

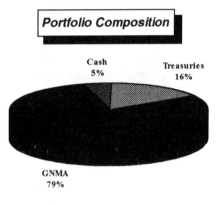

Cash 5%

Treasuries 16%

GNMA 79%

As of 6/30/93

Investment Description

Kemper U.S. Government is well on the road to recovery from a disastrous year in 1992. Using a strategy of rapid swapping between mortgage bonds and Treasuries, and supplementing this trading with forward contracts, the fund performed quite well until 1992, on a total return basis. One can only surmise that 1992's poor showing helped placed the fund on a more conservative path recently. A more traditional portfolio of GNMAs, Treasuries and other straight mortgage bonds has already strengthened performance considerably through the first six months of 1993. The more aggressive trading strate-gies now confined to a mere 10% of the total fund assets, Kemper U.S. Government should return to a more stable footing, without sacrificing the high returns its shareholders have become accustomed to. Fund management's commitment to a shorter duration should also protect investors from interest-rate spikes like the one that sent it reeling in 1992. The shorter maturities and more conservative portfolio will no doubt return Kemper U.S. Government to the winner's circle, where investors are accustomed to seeing it.

Suitability

Age 55 and under	*B+*
Age 55 to 70	*B+*
Age 70+	*B*

Inception Date: 6/24/77

Manager Tenure: 1981/1991

Telephone: (800) 621-1048

Minimum Initial Investment: $1,000.00

Direct Deposit: No

179

Low Investment Grade Bonds

Investment Ratings

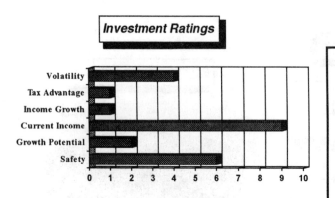

Investment Statistics

Initial Sales Charge: **NA**
Markup or brokerage commission varies

Annual Cost per $1,000: **$0.00**

Annualized Returns

3 Year	*9.71%*
5 Year	*10.03%*
10 Year	*11.15%*

Total Return on $10,000

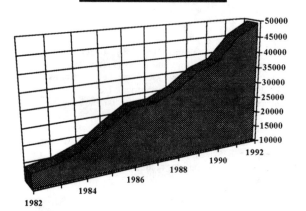

Income on $10,000 Investment

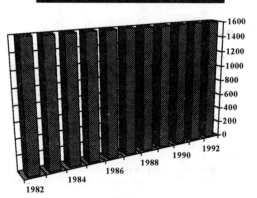

Historic Returns

	1982	1983	1984	1985	1986	1987	1988	1989	1990	1991	1992
Total Return (%)	44.50	8.30	17.70	28.00	18.70	1.50	10.50	15.30	6.40	18.50	8.00
Lehman Index (%)	31.30	8.00	15.00	21.30	15.60	2.30	7.60	14.20	8.30	16.10	7.60
Dividend Yield	16.10	13.60	14.20	12.70	10.40	10.60	10.80	10.20	10.40	9.80	9.00
Income on $10,000 ($)	1,600	1,600	1,600	1,600	1,600	1,600	1,600	1,600	1,600	1,600	1,600

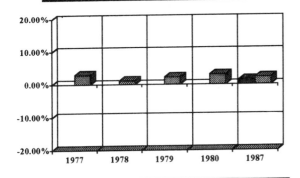

Annual Return During Bear Markets

■ Low Investment Grade Bonds ⊠ Lehman Corp/Govt Index

Portfolio Composition

100%
Bonds

As of 6/30/93

Investment Description

It's no coincidence that many of the mutual funds listed in this book buy lower-grade bonds. Not bottom-of-the-barrel "junk bonds," which often teeter on default and rise and fall with the companies' fortunes, but lower-grade debt issued by large companies who simply don't rate in comparison with larger, better capitalized companies. Some are the product of an early age of leveraged buyouts and takeovers. Most are simply companies that lack the resources to rate A or better. A sampling from a list in the bonds section of a newspaper includes names like Turner Broadcasting (CNN, WTBS cable), Chrysler

and Westinghouse, all with yields from 8 to 10%. Selectivity is the key to success in this marketplace. Steady earnings and good future prospects are more desireable for a conservative investor than recently so-called "fallen angels." A company in rapid decline can often continue to decline while a lower-grade bond that's settled in at a lower rating has greater potential to rebuild and catch the market's attention once again. Caution is essential in this market, as is good information. A little research and a lot of patience goes a long way in this under-recognized market.

Suitability

Age 55 and under	*A-*
Age 55 to 70	*B+*
Age 70+	*B-*

Inception Date:

Manager Tenure: NA

Telephone:

Minimum Initial Investment: $1,000.00

Direct Deposit:

181

Lutheran Brotherhood Income

Investment Ratings

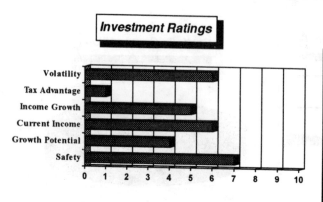

Investment Statistics

Initial Sales Charge: **5.00%**

Annual Cost per $1,000: **$17.74**

Annualized Returns

3 Year

5 Year *9.90%*

10 Year *10.29%*

Total Return on $10,000

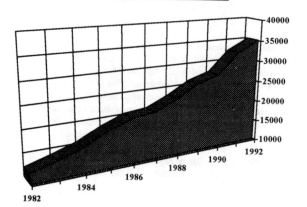

Income on $10,000 Investment

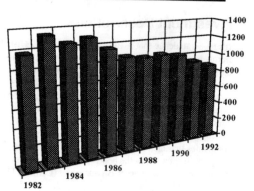

Historic Returns

	1982	1983	1984	1985	1986	1987	1988	1989	1990	1991	1992
Total Return (%)	30.40	12.76	13.29	17.23	10.26	2.73	10.89	12.44	5.68	17.24	8.01
Lehman Index (%)	31.30	8.00	15.00	21.30	15.60	2.30	7.60	14.20	8.30	16.10	7.60
Dividend Yield	12.40	12.21	11.38	11.64	10.01	9.14	9.55	9.59	9.13	8.64	7.49
Income on $10,000 ($)	1,177	1,346	1,255	1,294	1,164	1,061	1,035	1,048	1,022	931	867

Annual Return During Bear Markets

	20.00%					
10.00%						
0.00%						
-10.00%						
-20.00%	1977	1978	1979	1980	1987	

■ Lutheran Brotherhood Income ▨ Lehman Corp/Govt Index

Portfolio Composition

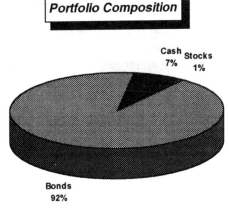

Cash 7% Stocks 1%

Bonds 92%

As of 6/30/93

Investment Description

Lutheran Brotherhood Income fund is a model of moderation. With a large U.S government position and almost no corporates without an investment-grade rating, its financial temperance has given the fund a level of safety many others in this category can only envy. Fund manager Charles Heeren's view of future interest-rate trends has resulted in further retrenching during the past few months, with the average bond maturity shortening and average bond quality rising from its already lofty position. While Heeren isn't afraid of risk, as he demonstrated in 1992 and early 1993 by making a big bet on corporate bonds, his disdain for volatility has generally kept the fund on a more moderate course. A smattering of mortgage-backed securities and high-yielding Canadian government bonds round out the portfolio, adding a slight boost to the portfolio yield. While its plain vanilla approach to investing might be something less than inspiring, Lutheran Brotherhood Income fund's consistently stable NAV and above-average return should be attractive to the circumspect investor.

Suitability

Age 55 and under	*B-*
Age 55 to 70	*B+*
Age 70+	*A-*

Inception Date: 6/1/72

Manager Tenure: 1986

Telephone: 8(00-) 328-4552

Minimum Initial Investment: $500.00

Direct Deposit: No

MFS Worldwide Govt

Investment Ratings

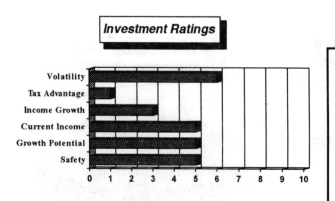

Investment Statistics

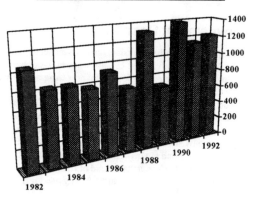

Initial Sales Charge: **4.75%**

Annual Cost per $1,000: **$22.35**

Annualized Returns
3 Year   *12.10%*
5 Year   *11.10%*
10 Year   *13.70%*

Total Return on $10,000

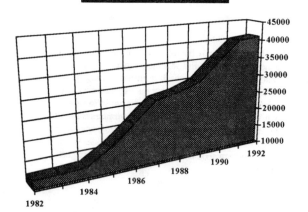

Income on $10,000 Investment

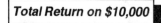

Historic Returns

	1982	1983	1984	1985	1986	1987	1988	1989	1990	1991	1992
Total Return (%)	29.46	1.55	2.34	29.79	30.17	24.42	4.38	7.37	17.90	13.42	1.35
Lehman Index (%)	31.30	8.00	15.00	21.30	15.60	2.30	7.60	14.20	8.30	16.10	7.60
Dividend Yield	11.06	7.47	7.95	7.91	7.76	4.97	7.59	4.23	8.30	6.25	6.18
Income on $10,000 ($)	1,053	831	831	778	926	725	1,316	687	1,390	1,147	1,215

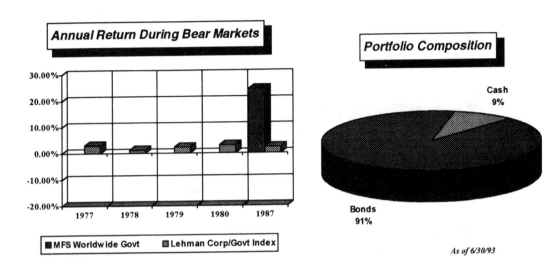

Annual Return During Bear Markets

	30.00%	20.00%	10.00%	0.00%	-10.00%	-20.00%

1977 1978 1979 1980 1987

■ MFS Worldwide Govt ▨ Lehman Corp/Govt Index

Portfolio Composition

Cash
9%

Bonds
91%

As of 6/30/93

Investment Description

MFS Worldwide Government Fund is a survivor. After being pummeled by the currency crisis of 1992, the fund is sticking to its guns and expecting to ride a wave of interest rate cuts just beginning to sweep Europe. Manager Leslie Nanberg has learned from the past and now employs currency hedges to help prevent a repeat of last year's roller-coaster ride. Even if the U.S. dollar should rise as a result of European rates, the fund should reap the benefits of a bond rally in Europe. Countries such as France and Denmark remain favorites and accordingly garner the largest positions in the fund, with Sweden and the UK not far behind. While Worldwide Government sports a relatively short duration (5.2 years), Nanberg has longer maturities in countries such as France and Denmark, while bonds from weaker economies such as Italy and Spain have very short maturities. This barbell strategy, commonly used in U.S. government funds, should allow the fund to participate in a strong European bond market. As U.S. investors hungrily eye higher yields overseas, MFS Worldwide Government offers a package of stability and performance not surpassed by any other overseas bond fund.

Suitability

Age 55 and under	*B+*
Age 55 to 70	*B-*
Age 70+	*C*

Inception Date: 2/25/81

Manager Tenure: 1984

Telephone: (800) 225-2606

Minimum Initial Investment: $1,000.00

Direct Deposit: Yes

Nicholas Income

Investment Ratings

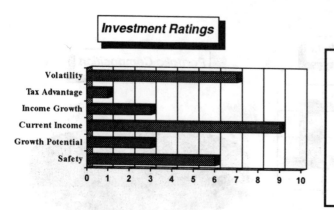

Investment Statistics

Initial Sales Charge: **None**

Annual Cost per $1,000: **$8.68**

Annualized Returns

3 Year	*12.27%*
5 Year	*9.29%*
10 Year	*10.50%*

Total Return on $10,000

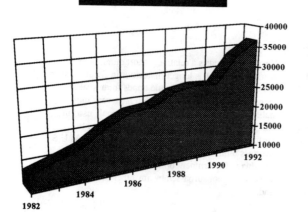

Income on $10,000 Investment

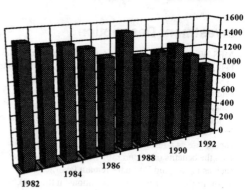

Historic Returns

	1982	1983	1984	1985	1986	1987	1988	1989	1990	1991	1992
Total Return (%)	35.14	12.33	12.70	21.29	11.43	2.53	11.55	3.04	-1.03	23.05	10.33
Lehman Index (%)	31.30	8.00	15.00	21.30	15.60	2.30	7.60	14.20	8.30	16.10	7.60
Dividend Yield	12.65	11.96	11.99	11.51	9.60	11.72	10.16	10.33	11.63	11.63	8.98
Income on $10,000 ($)	1,464	1,401	1,401	1,337	1,209	1,496	1,178	1,210	1,273	1,114	955

Annual Return During Bear Markets

40.00%	
30.00%	
20.00%	
10.00%	
0.00%	
-10.00%	
-20.00%	
-30.00%	
-40.00%	
-50.00%	

1969   1973   1974   1977   1981   1987   1990

■ Nicholas Income   ▨ S & P 500

Portfolio Composition

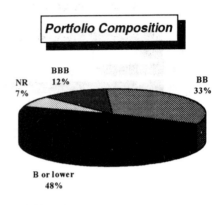

NR
7%

BBB
12%

BB
33%

B or lower
48%

As of 6/30/93

Investment Description

The Nicholas Income fund will probably never be accused of following the crowd. As junk bond funds have jumped into more speculative issues to maintain high payouts, and the whole market for lower-grade bonds has exploded this past year, Albert Nicholas has stayed with what's tried and true. Buying lower-grade bonds might be the central theme of Nicholas' strategy, but calling this fund a junk bond fund simply doesn't do it justice. There aren't any PIK's (payment in kind), deferred interest bonds, or the lowest-rated bonds. Rather, only established companies in solid industries which happen to have below investment-grade ratings. Household

names such as Playtex, Revlon and Unisys provide the bulk of the holdings with a token amount in investment-grade bonds and stocks. Interest rates on bonds from this overlooked niche, while not offering the double-digit returns of more speculative junk issues, produce yields far above comparable government and blue-chip corporate debt. An improving economy should add some capital appreciation to returns as many lower-grade bonds see their ratings upgraded as their financial conditions improve. Shell-shocked fixed-income investors couldn't ask for more.

Suitability

Age 55 and under	*B*
Age 55 to 70	*A-*
Age 70+	*B*

Inception Date: 5/1/30

Manager Tenure: 1977

Telephone: (414) 272-6133

Minimum Initial Investment: $500.00

Direct Deposit: No

187

Oppenheimer High Yield

Investment Ratings

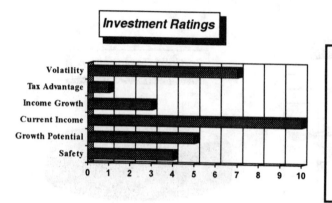

Investment Statistics

Initial Sales Charge: **4.75%**
B shares available with no initial charge

Annual Cost per $1,000: **$16.87**

Annualized Returns

3 Year *13.85%*

5 Year *10.15%*

10 Year *10.08%*

Total Return on $10,000

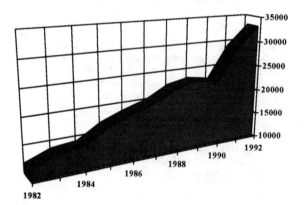

Income on $10,000 Investment

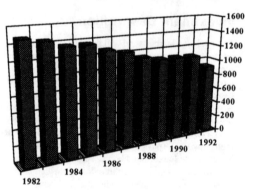

Historic Returns

	1982	1983	1984	1985	1986	1987	1988	1989	1990	1991	1992
Total Return (%)	28.62	14.66	3.54	18.84	9.76	7.20	11.94	3.89	-3.21	28.60	13.85
Lehman Index (%)	31.30	8.00	15.00	21.30	15.60	2.30	7.60	14.20	8.30	16.10	7.60
Dividend Yield	15.50	13.63	12.88	14.28	12.90	12.91	12.68	12.34	13.47	16.02	12.23
Income on $10,000 ($)	1,477	1,436	1,359	1,359	1,269	1,223	1,133	1,087	1,087	1,079	918

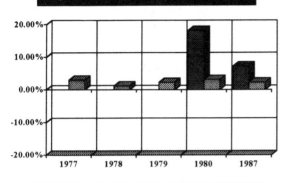

Annual Return During Bear Markets

20.00%
10.00%
0.00%
-10.00%
-20.00%

1977   1978   1979   1980   1987

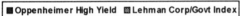

■ Oppenheimer High Yield   ▧ Lehman Corp/Govt Index

Portfolio Composition

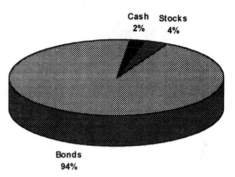

Cash 2%   Stocks 4%

Bonds 94%

As of 6/30/93

Investment Description

The Oppenheimer High Yield fund is anything but a "junk" bond fund. While most of its competitors dredge the depths of the corporate bond universe, this fund seeks a more conservative approach. Bond quality remains firmly in the BB to B range, mostly with interest-paying bonds in solid industries. Loathing bottom-of-the-barrel corporate junk such as PIKs and zero coupons, fund manager Ralph Stellmacher searches for "fallen angels," which have the potential for turnaround given enough time. Held back by a conservative philosophy, this fund will rarely be found in the top 10 performing list of junk funds during a good market. But when the lower-grade bond prices turn south, Oppenheimer High Yield really shines. In 1990, for example, when the bottom fell out of the market, the fund turned in a scant 3.21% loss compared to 20% to 50% losses many other fund passed on to shareholders. Stellmacher's current bond mix includes such household names as Gillette, Unisys and Borg Warner. For investors tempted by high-yielding corporate bonds, there couldn't be a more obvious choice.

Suitability

Age 55 and under	*B+*
Age 55 to 70	*C*
Age 70+	*C-*

Inception Date: 7/28/78

Manager Tenure: 1988

Telephone: (800) 525-7048

Minimum Initial Investment: $1,000.00

Direct Deposit: Yes

189

Putnam Global Govt Income

Investment Ratings

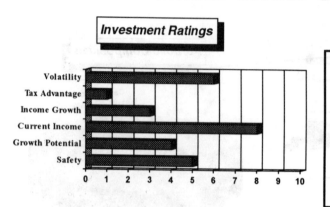
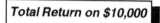

Investment Statistics

Initial Sales Charge: **4.75%**
B shares with no initial sales charge available

Annual Cost per $1,000: **$23.56**

Annualized Returns

3 Year	*10.24%*
5 Year	*10.36%*
Inception(6/1/87)	*12.45%*

Total Return on $10,000

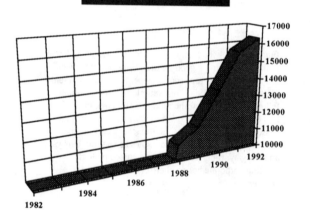

Income on $10,000 Investment

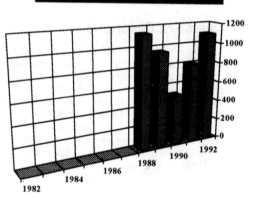

Historic Returns

	1982	1983	1984	1985	1986	1987	1988	1989	1990	1991	1992
Total Return (%)							14.89	7.65	16.33	15.15	4.41
Lehman Index (%)	31.30	8.00	15.00	21.30	15.60	2.30	7.60	14.20	8.30	16.10	7.60
Dividend Yield							11.96	9.82	8.55	8.00	10.26
Income on $10,000 ($)							1,139	956	502	806	1,099

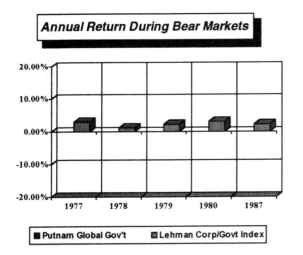

Annual Return During Bear Markets

1977	1978	1979	1980	1987

■ Putnam Global Gov't ▨ Lehman Corp/Govt Index

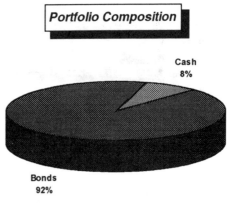

Portfolio Composition

Cash
8%

Bonds
92%

As of 6/30/93

Investment Description

Putnam Global Government Income shareholders probably feel like they've been on a roller coaster the past few months. When the bottom fell out of the European currency market last year, free-for-all trading in European bonds sent this fund's price gyrating for several months. Compared to other global bond funds, this fund's NAV remained intact, thanks to managers Lawrence Daly and Dave Jallit's skill. After the dust had cleared, the fund began a steady climb, which is continuing through this year. Both managers seem convinced that European rates will drop, and have positioned themselves appro-

priately. France, Denmark and Spain are top holdings, all chosen for their yields and the effect falling European interest should have on their respective bonds. Fairly well-hedged going into 1992's crisis, Global Government Income has scaled back its hedging strategy to take full advantage of falling rates overseas. Not afraid to be selectively aggressive is what's made this fund the top performer in this category. Investors looking for diversification,higher yields and safety in a global bond fund should look no further than Putnam Global Government Income.

Suitability

Age 55 and under	*B+*
Age 55 to 70	*B*
Age 70+	*B-*

Inception Date: 6/1/87

Manager Tenure: 1989/1992

Telephone: (800) 225-1581

Minimum Initial Investment: $500.00

Direct Deposit: Yes

Scudder Income

Investment Ratings

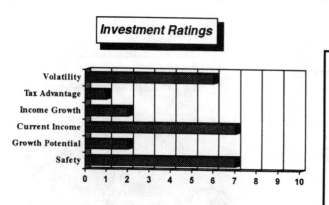

Investment Statistics

Initial Sales Charge:	**None**
Annual Cost per $1,000:	**$9.48**

Annualized Returns

3 Year	*12.68%*
5 Year	*11.48%*
10 Year	*11.32%*

Total Return on $10,000

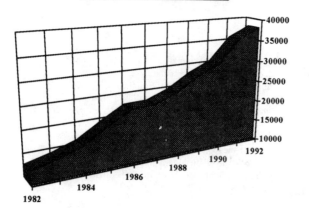

Income on $10,000 Investment

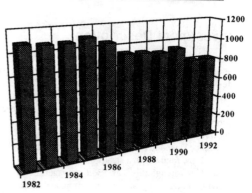

Historic Returns

	1982	1983	1984	1985	1986	1987	1988	1989	1990	1991	1992
Total Return (%)	30.37	10.88	12.27	21.80	14.75	0.67	8.99	12.75	8.32	17.32	6.74
Lehman Index (%)	31.30	8.00	15.00	21.30	15.60	2.30	7.60	14.20	8.30	16.10	7.60
Dividend Yield	12.56	10.71	10.74	11.03	9.52	8.13	8.11	8.54	8.46	7.33	6.69
Income on $10,000 ($)	1,088	1,071	1,071	1,105	1,045	934	925	908	934	805	803

Annual Return During Bear Markets

20.00%					
10.00%					
0.00%					
-10.00%					
-20.00%	1977	1978	1979	1980	1987

■ Low Investment Grade Bonds ▨ Lehman Corp/Govt Index

Portfolio Composition

100%
Bonds

As of 6/30/93

Investment Description

Scudder Income fund doesn't have a short-term prospective. The fund is a raging bull when it comes to bonds and the portfolio is structured accordingly. While the fund's charter states that the average maturity of the portfolio will be 8 years or more, manager Bill Hutchinson takes that directive a step further by concentrating in discount bonds and callable issues, which perform better when interest rates decline. His strategy paid off handsomely in the last half of 1992 and the beginning of 1993, as long-term interest rates declined. The fund's emphasis on total returns has given it an enviable track record, up 10.29% annually for the past 10 years. In spite of a seemingly aggressive stance,

the fund takes a lot less risk than you'd think. A majority of bonds fall into the solid AAA or AA categories, with the remainder BBB or better. Once again, the charter mandates the majority of the bonds held must be rated A or better, and no non-investments grade holdings are allowed. Recently, the proscription from holding junk bonds has hurt total return compared to rival funds but over the long haul, this defensive structure should serve shareholders well. Investors wanting to profit from a falling bond market as well as collect more than a little interest should consider the Scudder Income fund very seriously.

Suitability

Age 55 and under	*B*
Age 55 to 70	*A-*
Age 70+	*B+*

Inception Date: 5/10/28

Manager Tenure: 1986/1990

Telephone: (800) 225-2470

Minimum Initial Investment: $1,000.00

Direct Deposit: No

193

State Street Research Govt Income

Investment Ratings

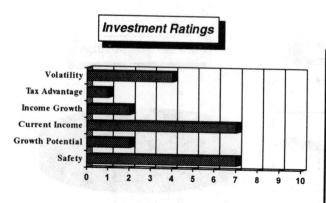

Investment Statistics

Initial Sales Charge:	**None**
Annual Cost per $1,000:	**$10.43**

Annualized Returns

3 Year	*12.09%*
5 Year	*10.57%*
Inception(3/23/87)	*9.13%*

Total Return on $10,000

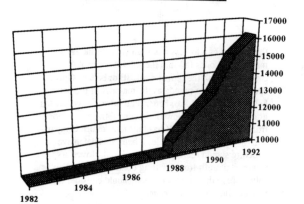

Income on $10,000 Investment

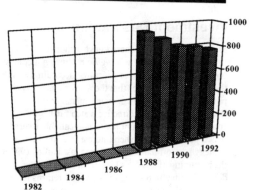

Historic Returns

	1982	1983	1984	1985	1986	1987	1988	1989	1990	1991	1992
Total Return (%)							6.56	12.54	8.93	16.08	6.75
Lehman Index (%)	31.30	8.00	15.00	21.30	15.60	2.30	7.60	14.20	8.30	16.10	7.60
Dividend Yield							9.51	9.20	8.25	8.08	7.21
Income on $10,000 ($)							951	891	822	805	771

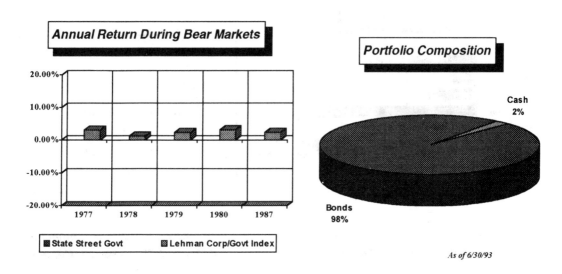

Annual Return During Bear Markets

20.00%	
10.00%	
0.00%	
-10.00%	
-20.00%	

1977   1978   1979   1980   1987

■ State Street Govt   ▨ Lehman Corp/Govt Index

Portfolio Composition

Cash 2%

Bonds 98%

As of 6/30/93

Investment Description

Just like the Phoenix of ancient legend, State Street Research Government Income fund has risen from the ashes of investor scorn to take a place among top-performing government funds. Originally sold through brokerage firms as Met Life/State Street U.S. Government fund, brokers offered this fund to the public right before the bond debacle of 1987. Fund assets have been declining ever since as burned investors sought higher yields elsewhere. As they say, things change. Manager John Kallis' large position in zero coupon

bonds helped turn around performance in 1991 and the fund's been on a winning streak ever since. While Kallis isn't afraid to take a large position, such as the zero coupons in 1991, State Street Research U.S. Government basically follows a cautious path. While other government funds might bounce back and forth between top-performing and bottom-performing lists, State Street U.S. Government is happy to occupy the middle, providing an above-average return with a minimal amount of risk.

Suitability

Age 55 and under	*B-*
Age 55 to 70	*B+*
Age 70+	*A-*

Inception Date: 3/23/87

Manager Tenure: 1987

Telephone: (800) 882-0052

Minimum Initial Investment: $10,000.00

Direct Deposit: No

195

Vanguard Fixed-Income GNMA

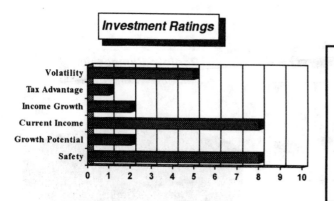

Investment Ratings

- Volatility
- Tax Advantage
- Income Growth
- Current Income
- Growth Potential
- Safety

0 1 2 3 4 5 6 7 8 9 10

Investment Statistics

Initial Sales Charge:	**None**
Annual Cost per $1,000:	**$3.97**

Annualized Returns

3 Year	*11.59%*
5 Year	*11.05%*
10 Year	*11.46%*

Total Return on $10,000

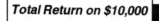

Income on $10,000 Investment

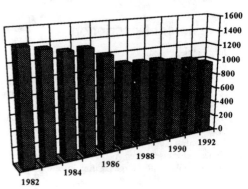

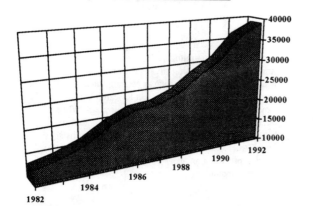

Historic Returns

	1982	1983	1984	1985	1986	1987	1988	1989	1990	1991	1992
Total Return (%)	31.56	9.65	14.03	20.68	11.69	2.15	8.81	14.77	10.32	16.77	6.85
Lehman Index (%)	31.30	8.00	15.00	21.30	15.60	2.30	7.60	14.20	8.30	16.10	7.60
Dividend Yield	14.08	11.82	11.71	11.70	9.96	8.86	9.41	9.49	8.76	8.58	7.51
Income on $10,000 ($)	1,407	1,358	1,309	1,321	1,211	1,089	1,077	1,077	1,040	1,028	966

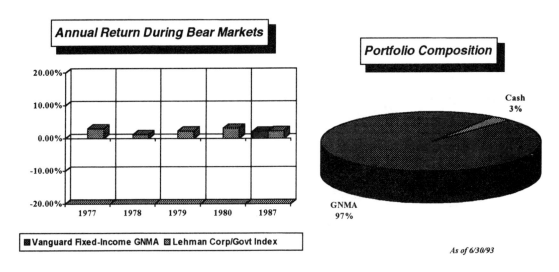

Annual Return During Bear Markets

■ Vanguard Fixed-Income GNMA ☒ Lehman Corp/Govt Index

Portfolio Composition

Cash
3%

GNMA
97%

As of 6/30/93

Investment Description

Vanguard Fixed-Income GNMA fund disproves the old adage that you get what you pay for. Boasting the lowest expense ratio of any GNMA fund covered, by no coincidence, this fund also has one of the highest payouts. Manager Paul Sullivan invests almost solely in GNMAs, holding few, if any, Treasuries or other government securities. While this simplifies the fund structure and limits its risk, it can lag behind other government funds in good bond markets. Even so,

competing solely on the basis of yield, Vanguard Fixed-Income fund has attracted its share of followers. Fund assets have swelled from $298 million in 1985 to over $7.5 billion. New money flows into current coupon bonds, only slightly diluting existing shareholders. While the fund takes very little risk and is seldom traded, it consistently appears in the top 25% of all government funds and pays a more-than-competitive yield. What more could you ask for?

Suitability

Age 55 and under	*B*
Age 55 to 70	*A*
Age 70+	*A-*

Inception Date: 6/27/80

Manager Tenure: 1980

Telephone: (800) 662-7447

Minimum Initial Investment: $3,000.00

Direct Deposit: No

Chapter 13

Tax Advantaged Investments

Alliance Muni Income Fund

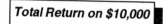

Investment Ratings

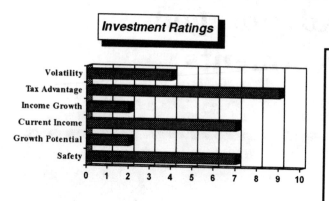

Volatility	
Tax Advantage	
Income Growth	
Current Income	
Growth Potential	
Safety	

0 1 2 3 4 5 6 7 8 9 10

Investment Statistics

Initial Sales Charge: **4.50%**
B shares available with no initial sales charge

Annual Cost per $1,000: **$13.07**

Annualized Returns

3 Year	*9.89%*
5 Year	*9.94%*
Inception(12/29/86)	*8.76%*

Total Return on $10,000

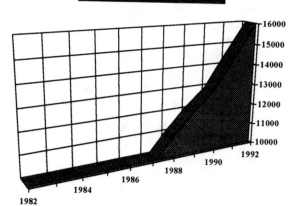

Income on $10,000 Investment

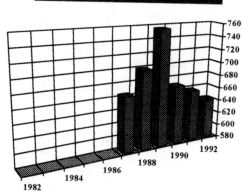

Historic Returns

	1982	1983	1984	1985	1986	1987	1988	1989	1990	1991	1992
Total Return (%)						1.29	12.80	10.10	7.39	11.84	10.43
Lehman Index (%)	31.30	8.00	15.00	21.30	15.60	2.30	7.60	14.20	8.30	16.10	7.60
Dividend Yield						7.40	7.78	7.44	6.97	6.86	6.36
Income on $10,000 ($)						664	699	756	669	658	640

Annual Return During Bear Markets

20.00%				
10.00%				
0.00%				
-10.00%				
-20.00%	1977	1978	1979	1980	1987

■ Alliance Muni Income   ▨ Lehman Corp/Govt Index

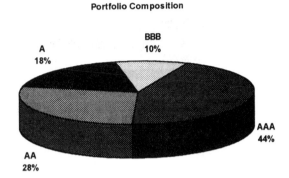

Portfolio Composition

A 18%
BBB 10%
AAA 44%
AA 28%

As of 6/30/93

Investment Description

You won't find many bears at Alliance Muncipal Income fund. Manager Susan Peabody, who also manages Alliance's California fund, doesn't see any dark clouds on the horizon for tax-free bonds. She's posi-tioned the fund accordingly. A contrarian by nature, Peabody believes that future increases in tax rates should help support tax-free bond prices, even though conventional wisdom has many muni bond watchers worried about interest rates. While Peabody doesn't see spectacular capital gains in store in the next few years, she believes that interest payments from tax-free bonds will provide superior returns compared to other fixed- income investments,

especially to those in ever-increasing tax brackets. While Peabody's contrianism extends to individual issues (Denver airport, California, and Massachusetts), her against-the- grain philosophy has its limits. For example, she avoids COPs (certificates of participation) and health care issues because of uncertainty of revenues that support the interest payments. The fund also eschews more speculative derivative bonds, such as inverse floaters and the like. This balanced and well-thought-out approach to tax-free investing makes the Alliance Municipal Income Fund one of the best all-round buys in this category.

Suitability

Age 55 and under	*B+*
Age 55 to 70	*B+*
Age 70+	*B+*

Inception Date: 12/29/86

Manager Tenure: 1986

Telephone: (800) 227-4618

Minimum Initial Investment: $250.00

Direct Deposit: No

Calvert T/F Reserves Limited-Term

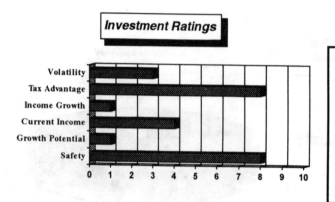

Investment Ratings

- Volatility
- Tax Advantage
- Income Growth
- Current Income
- Growth Potential
- Safety

0 1 2 3 4 5 6 7 8 9 10

Investment Statistics

Initial Sales Charge:	**2.00%**
Annual Cost per $1,000:	**$10.92**

Annualized Returns

3 Year	*4.78%*
5 Year	*5.49%*
10 Year	*6.17%*

Total Return on $10,000

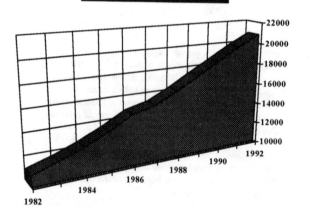

Income on $10,000 Investment

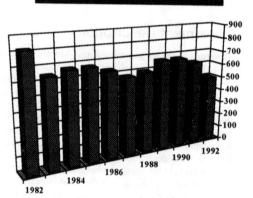

Historic Returns

	1982	1983	1984	1985	1986	1987	1988	1989	1990	1991	1992
Total Return (%)	12.45	6.35	7.36	8.33	8.53	3.47	6.80	7.12	6.50	6.46	5.08
Lehman Index (%)	31.30	8.00	15.00	21.30	15.60	2.30	7.60	14.20	8.30	16.10	7.60
Dividend Yield	8.31	6.30	6.61	6.58	6.11	5.44	5.74	6.35	6.31	5.94	4.70
Income on $10,000 ($)	815	640	670	670	632	574	594	664	664	624	495

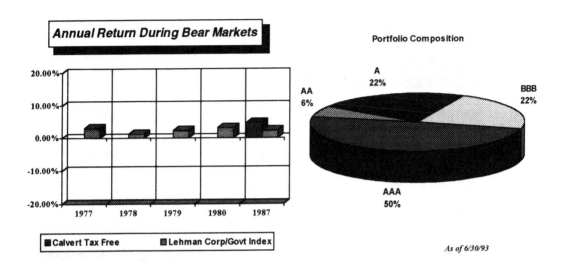

Annual Return During Bear Markets

Portfolio Composition

■ Calvert Tax Free   ▨ Lehman Corp/Govt Index

As of 6/30/93

Investment Description

A tax-free money market its not, but Calvert Tax-Free Reserves Limited-Term comes about as close as it can without giving up a juicy 1% to 2% yield advantage. Keeping the average maturity under 1 year, this fund is one step beyond a money market fund (it yields just under 4% compared to 2% on many money markets) without being a full-blown medium-term tax-free mutual fund (4.5% yields with a more potential fluctuation in principal). While the yields might not be eye-popping, the stability of NAV is impressive enough to satisfy any skeptic. A high-quality portfolio (mostly A and above) adds to the low-risk image that the fund seeks to project. A hefty portion of the portfolio is kept in cash substitutes, such as floating rate securities and short-term paper, to insure liquidity in the event of massive withdrawals. Calvert's unique niche fund may not be all things to all people. Investors looking for a better-than-average tax-exempt return and a safe haven in what can be a tumultuous market shouldn't look any further than Calvert Tax Free Reserves Limited-Term.

Suitability

Age 55 and under	*B+*
Age 55 to 70	*A-*
Age 70+	*A-*

Inception Date: 3/4/81

Manager Tenure: 1981/1983

Telephone: (800) 368-2748

Minimum Initial Investment: $2,000

Direct Deposit: No

203

Colonial California Tax Exempt

Investment Ratings

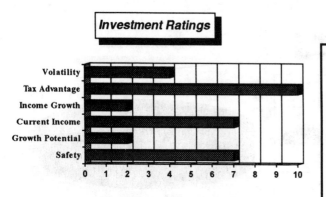

Investment Statistics

Initial Sales Charge: **4.75%**
B shares available with no initial sales charge

Annual Cost per $1,000: **$13.80**

Annualized Returns

3 Year	*7.81%*
5 Year	*8.05%*
Inception(6/16/86)	*7.17%*

Total Return on $10,000

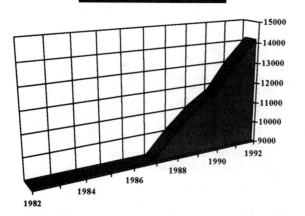

Income on $10,000 Investment

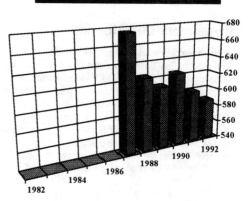

Historic Returns

	1982	1983	1984	1985	1986	1987	1988	1989	1990	1991	1992
Total Return (%)						-4.34	11.98	9.13	5.99	11.21	7.81
S and P 500 (%)	21.47	22.46	6.13	31.64	18.68	5.26	17.50	31.68	-3.20	30.40	7.92
Dividend Yield						7.10	7.40	6.96	6.97	6.77	6.37
Income on $10,000 ($)						676	625	612	625	600	587

Annual Return During Bear Markets

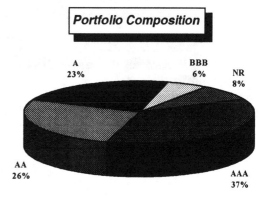

Chart legend: ■ Colonial Cal. Tax Free ▨ Lehman Corp/Govt Index

Y-axis values: 20.00%, 10.00%, 0.00%, -10.00%, -20.00%
X-axis: 1977, 1978, 1979, 1980, 1987

Portfolio Composition

A 23%
BBB 6%
NR 8%
AA 26%
AAA 37%

As of 6/30/93

Investment Description

Quality is the watch word at Colonial California Tax Exempt fund. While still convinced that California tax-free bonds offer the best returns to Californians in high tax brackets, manager Bill Loring shuns most lower-quality issues in an effort to weather the state's economic storm. Since yields vary little from high-to low-quality bonds, the fund has given up very little income in return for one of the strongest bond portfolios in its class. Managed to maximize tax-free income and minimize taxable capital gains, Colonial California Tax Exempt fund favors premium and current coupon bonds. The absence of zero coupon and discount issues should enable the fund to better weather an adverse market in the event of a rise in interest rates. Emphasizing education and hospital bonds, Loring hopes to take advantage of negative news in both sectors by snapping up high-quality issues from these undervalued markets. While Colonial California Tax Exempt might not have the sizzle of more aggressive total-return-oriented funds, individual state tax-free investments don't get much better than what this fund is offering.

Suitability

Age 55 and under	*A-*
Age 55 to 70	*A-*
Age 70+	*A-*

Inception Date: 6/16/86

Manager Tenure: 1986

Telephone: (800) 248-2828

Minimum Initial Investment: $1,000.00

Direct Deposit: No

205

Dreyfus Intermediate Muni

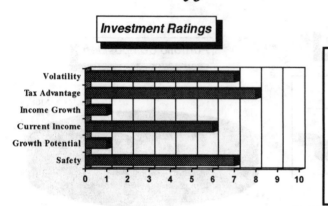

Investment Statistics

Initial Sales Charge:	**None**
Annual Cost per $1,000:	**$7.22**

Annualized Returns

3 Year	*10.18%*
5 Year	*9.11%*
Inception(8/11/83)	*9.30%*

Total Return on $10,000

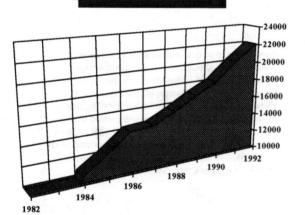

Income on $10,000 Investment

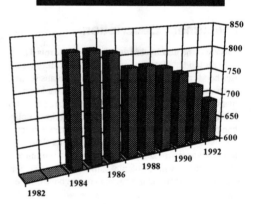

Historic Returns

	1982	1983	1984	1985	1986	1987	1988	1989	1990	1991	1992
Total Return (%)			7.46	16.06	15.43	1.15	8.04	8.72	6.75	11.14	8.72
Lehman Index (%)	31.30	8.00	15.00	21.30	15.60	2.30	7.60	14.20	8.30	16.10	7.60
Dividend Yield			8.21	8.31	7.67	6.87	7.29	7.18	6.94	6.68	6.09
Income on $10,000 ($)			821	821	813	780	780	772	756	724	688

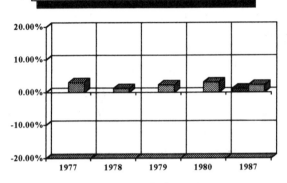

Annual Return During Bear Markets

20.00%
10.00%
0.00%
-10.00%
-20.00%

1977 1978 1979 1980 1987

☒ Dreyfus Intermediate Muni ☒ Lehman Corp/Govt Index

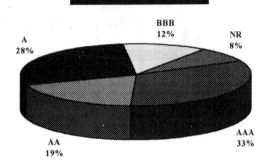

Portfolio Composition

BBB 12%
NR 8%
A 28%
AAA 33%
AA 19%

As of 6/30/93

Investment Description

Dreyfus Intermediate Muncipal fund looks and sounds like an intermediate fund but it really wants to be much more. Convinced that long-term rates are headed down, fund manager Monica Wieboldt has been a buyer of long-term muncipal bonds, bringing the fund's average maturity just under the 10-year maximum mandated by the prospectus. Wieboldt also sees opportunity in health care and education bonds, recently shunned by many other managers because of upcoming health-care reform and budget cuts. While loading up on AAA and AA issues, the fund also delves into less-secure nonrated bonds and BBB issues, although the prospectus only allows up to 20% of the portfolio to be rated BBB or less. By concentrating on high-yielding geographic locations, such as Texas and Florida, and by taking advantage of oversold issues in problem-plagued cities like Denver and New York, Dreyfus Intermediate Muncipal has racked up an enviable track record. Boasting the stability of an intermediate fund with the return of a longer-term municipal fund, Dreyfus Intermediate Municipal is an excellent choice for anyone wanting long-term returns without the NAV flucuation that usually follows.

Suitability

Age 55 and under	*B+*
Age 55 to 70	*B+*
Age 70+	*B+*

Inception Date: 8/11/83

Manager Tenure: 1985

Telephone: (800) 645-6561

Minimum Initial Investment: $2,500

Direct Deposit: No

Dreyfus NJ Muni Bond

Investment Ratings

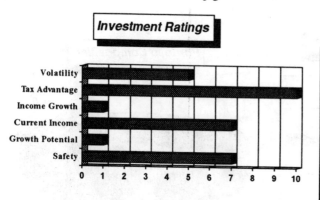

Investment Statistics

Initial Sales Charge:	**None**
Annual Cost per $1,000:	**$6.92**

Annualized Returns

3 Year	*11.28%*
5 Year	*10.39%*
Inception(11/6/87)	*10.80%*

Total Return on $10,000

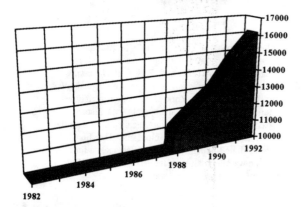

Income on $10,000 Investment

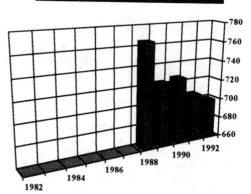

Historic Returns

	1982	1983	1984	1985	1986	1987	1988	1989	1990	1991	1992
Total Return (%)							12.59	9.11	7.94	11.95	8.78
Lehman Index (%)	31.30	8.00	15.00	21.30	15.60	2.30	7.60	14.20	8.30	16.10	7.60
Dividend Yield							7.57	6.83	6.72	6.50	6.13
Income on $10,000 ($)							765	723	726	707	699

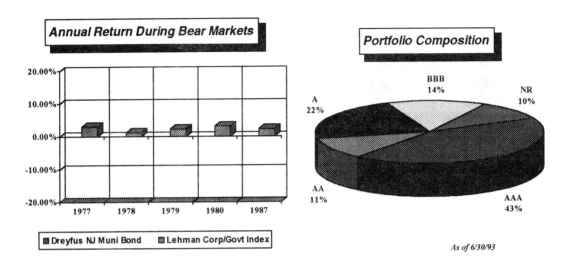

Annual Return During Bear Markets

■ Dreyfus NJ Muni Bond   ▨ Lehman Corp/Govt Index

Portfolio Composition

BBB 14%
NR 10%
A 22%
AA 11%
AAA 43%

As of 6/30/93

Investment Description

Dreyfus New Jersey Municipal Bond fund chooses neither the high nor low road, but rather the middle. The fund isn't completely focused on capital gains, yet neither is it obsessed with yield. Choosing a balanced approach to New Jersey's bond market has helped it take the best from both total return and income strategies, and pass it along to its shareholders. Since New Jersey's govern-ment finances are in order compared to many other states, little differentiation exists amongst New Jersey bonds in terms of quality. Most municipal bonds lean toward the higher end of the rating scale. In order to excel, a fund has to dredge the bottom for the few lower-rated issues that exist, extend maturities to ride the wave of falling interest rates, or rely on premium coupons to increase cash flow. Dreyfus New Jersey Muncipal Bond fund eschews lower-quality bonds but practices a combination of investing in premium coupons and longer maturities. The premium bonds protect the fund from interest-rate spikes while the longer average maturity allows it to earn capital gains as interest rates fall. Although a middle-of-the-road approach can often lead to mediocre returns, in the case of this fund, its performance has more than matched its rivals. For New Jersey residents looking for tax relief, this fund is certainly a contender.

Suitability

Age 55 and under	*A*
Age 55 to 70	*A*
Age 70+	*A*

Inception Date: 11/6/87

Manager Tenure: 1988

Telephone: (800) 645-6561

Minimum Initial Investment: $2,500

Direct Deposit: No

Essential Service Municipal Bonds

Investment Ratings

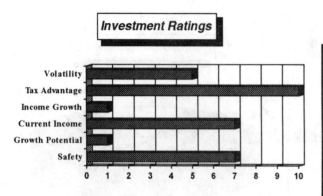

Investment Statistics

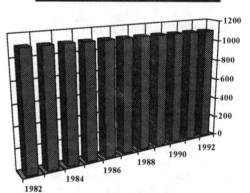

Initial Sales Charge: **Varies**
Markups vary, between 1% and 3%

Annual Cost per $1,000: **$0.00**

Annualized Returns

3 Year	*10.30%*
5 Year	*11.27%*
10 Year	*11.82%*

Total Return on $10,000

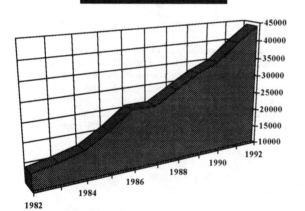

Income on $10,000 Investment

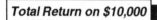

Historic Returns

	1982	1983	1984	1985	1986	1987	1988	1989	1990	1991	1992
Total Return (%)	43.90	8.70	11.00	22.80	21.00	0.00	13.50	12.00	7.20	13.60	10.20
Lehman Index (%)	31.30	8.00	15.00	21.30	15.60	2.30	7.60	14.20	8.30	16.10	7.60
Dividend Yield	11.60	9.50	10.20	9.20	7.40	7.70	7.80	7.20	7.30	6.90	6.40
Income on $10,000 ($)	1,103	1,103	1,103	1,103	1,103	1,103	1,103	1,103	1,103	1,103	1,103

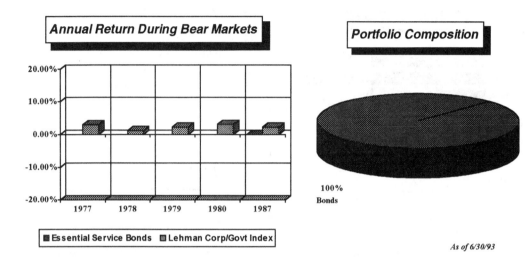

Annual Return During Bear Markets

	1977	1978	1979	1980	1987

☒ Essential Service Bonds   ☒ Lehman Corp/Govt Index

Portfolio Composition

100%
Bonds

As of 6/30/93

Investment Description

Muncipal revenue bonds have unjustly gotten a bad rap for years. General obligations bonds, backed by the full taxing power of a state or municipal government, are much safer, so the theory goes, than their revenue-backed counterparts. As city hall, county offices and state capitals are faced with serious budget shortfalls, many investors have begun to question this putative wisdom. Taxpayer revolts, similar to Proposition 13 in California, may limit the ability of municipal governments to raise taxes to cover shortfalls. The exodus of businesses, followed by residents, to low-tax states has also led to muncipal governments in some states giving a second thought to raising taxes. While general obligation bonds are falling from favor, revenue bonds have never looked better. Considered stepchildren for years, essential services revenue bonds offer the safety and security of income-producing collateral. Water, sewer and electrical facilities can all be considered recession-proof, since each is a very basic need. Not every bond with "water, sewer, or electric" in its name is necessarily safe, but a good rating from a major credit rating agency should ease the selection process. As taxes continue to rise, essential service revenue bonds are probably one of the best values in fixed income

Suitability

Age 55 and under	*A-*
Age 55 to 70	*A-*
Age 70+	*A-*

Inception Date:

Manager Tenure:

Telephone:

Minimum Initial Investment:

Direct Deposit:

Fidelity CA Tax-Free High-Yield

Investment Ratings

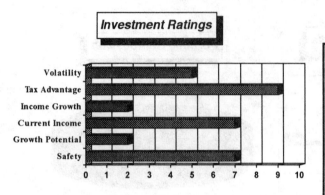

Investment Statistics

Initial Sales Charge:	**None**
Annual Cost per $1,000:	**$6.79**

Annualized Returns

3 Year	*10.39%*
5 Year	*9.98%*
Inception(7/7/84)	*10.06%*

Total Return on $10,000

Income on $10,000 Investment

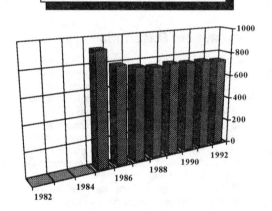

Historic Returns

	1982	1983	1984	1985	1986	1987	1988	1989	1990	1991	1992
Total Return (%)				16.56	17.54	-3.67	11.77	9.67	6.96	10.16	8.70
Lehman Index (%)	31.30	8.00	15.00	21.30	15.60	2.30	7.60	14.20	8.30	16.10	7.60
Dividend Yield				9.19	7.40	6.53	7.12	6.92	6.66	6.66	7.28
Income on $10,000 ($)				918	789	763	747	757	747	747	737

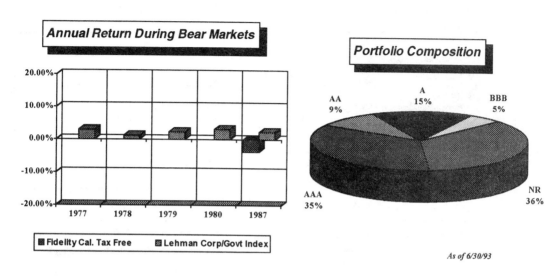

Annual Return During Bear Markets

20.00%
10.00%
0.00%
-10.00%
-20.00%

1977   1978   1979   1980   1987

■ Fidelity Cal. Tax Free   ▨ Lehman Corp/Govt Index

Portfolio Composition

AA 9%
A 15%
BBB 5%
AAA 35%
NR 36%

As of 6/30/93

Investment Description

Fidelity California Tax-Free High-Yield fund is high yield in name only. While the term high yield usually denotes low quality, this fund has one of the highest concentrations of AAA-rated bonds of any tax-free fund surveyed. Fund manager John Haley simply isn't comfortable with California's continuing budget deficits and is avoiding any issue dependent on state funding. Not that the fund has totally abandoned its original charter. A healthy mix of nonrated bonds, such as Mello Roos, add a bit of yield boost to an otherwise staid mixture. A quick glance at the portfolio reveals a penchant for water, health and redevelopment bonds with a noticeable lack of general obligation and certificate of participation issues. A stake in zero coupons and derivative securities adds a moderate amount of risk but has probably also contributed to the California Tax-Free's steadily rising NAV. A relatively short duration and lack of premium bonds make Fidelity California Tax-Free High-Yield a superior choice for Californians looking for tax relief without a lot of risk.

Suitability

Age 55 and under	*A-*
Age 55 to 70	*A-*
Age 70+	*A-*

Inception Date: 7/7/84

Manager Tenure: 1985

Telephone: (800) 544-8888

Minimum Initial Investment: $2,500.00

Direct Deposit: No

213

Fidelity NY Tax-Free Insured

Investment Ratings

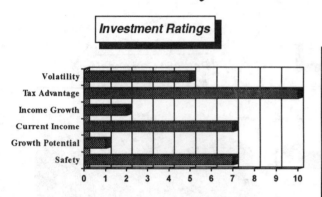

Investment Statistics

Initial Sales Charge:	**None**
Annual Cost per $1,000:	**$6.33**

Annualized Returns

3 Year	*10.88%*
5 Year	*10.07%*
Inception(10/11/85)	*9.44%*

Total Return on $10,000

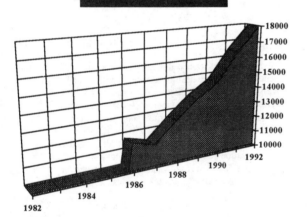

Income on $10,000 Investment

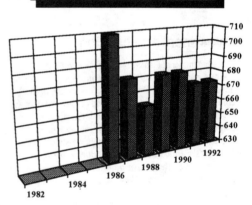

Historic Returns

	1982	1983	1984	1985	1986	1987	1988	1989	1990	1991	1992
Total Return (%)					17.51	-3.22	11.23	9.07	6.19	12.47	8.69
Lehman Index (%)	31.30	8.00	15.00	21.30	15.60	2.30	7.60	14.20	8.30	16.10	7.60
Dividend Yield					7.02	6.21	6.65	6.57	6.43	6.37	6.02
Income on $10,000 ($)					710	682	663	682	682	673	673

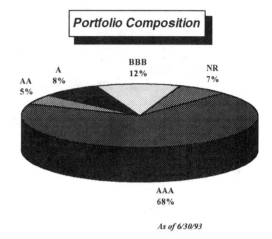

BBB 12%

A 8%

NR 7%

AA 5%

AAA 68%

As of 6/30/93

20.00%
10.00%
0.00%
-10.00%
-20.00%

1977   1978   1979   1980   1987

◼ Fidelity NY Tax Free   ◪ Lehman Corp/Govt Index

Investment Description

Managing a New York Muncipal fund during the last decade probably isn't what most portfolio managers dream about. New York has never really recovered from fiscal woes that began in the '70s and has been a treacherous market at best even for professional bond managers. New manager David Murphy has taken the reins of Fidelity New York Tax-Free Insured with a bit of an advantage over many New York municipal managers. First, the fund buys mostly insured bonds that usually rate AAA. Although Murphy has been increasing exposure to lower-grade bonds to boost yield, at least

65% must be in insured issues by charter. Secondly, the fund has a good track record to build upon. Fidelity's research resources and pool of talented managers usually produces at least competent (sometimes even extraordinary) performance. Murphy' is not only looking for better yields but also better total returns as 1994 approaches. Highly taxed New Yorkers should be attracted by the tax advantage but persuaded by the outstanding quality Fidelity New York Tax-Free Insured offers.

Suitability

Age 55 and under	*A*
Age 55 to 70	*A*
Age 70+	*A*

Inception Date: 10/11/85

Manager Tenure: 1992

Telephone: (800) 544-8888

Minimum Initial Investment: $2,500.00

Direct Deposit: No

215

Franklin California Insured Tax-Free Income

Investment Ratings

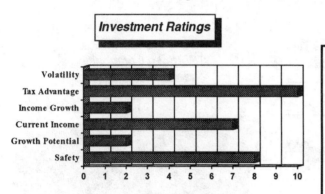

Investment Statistics

Initial Sales Charge:	**4.00%**
Annual Cost per $1,000:	**$11.92**

Annualized Returns

3 Year	*8.18%*
5 Year	*8.79%*
Inception(9/3/85)	*8.65%*

Total Return on $10,000

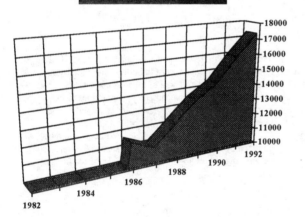

Income on $10,000 Investment

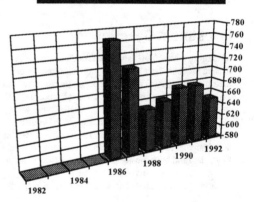

Historic Returns

	1982	1983	1984	1985	1986	1987	1988	1989	1990	1991	1992
Total Return (%)					20.61	-5.17	12.12	10.06	6.33	10.80	8.60
Lehman Index (%)	31.30	8.00	15.00	21.30	15.60	2.30	7.60	14.20	8.30	16.10	7.60
Dividend Yield					7.98	6.70	6.85	6.63	6.61	6.64	6.14
Income on $10,000 ($)					766	720	650	659	677	677	650

Annual Return During Bear Markets

| | 1977 | 1978 | 1979 | 1980 | 1987 |

■ Franklin Cal. Insured   ▨ Lehman Corp/Govt Index

Portfolio Composition

100%
AAA

As of 6/30/93

Investment Description

Franklin California Insured Tax-Free income fund's bond quality is second to none. Every bond in the portfolio carries an AAA-rating and is insured. As California's debt crisis has shaken the state's municipal bond market, investors have been flocking to this safe haven, boosting assets in the fund from $356 million in 1990 to over $1.2 billion in 1992. It's no surprise. Franklin Insured fund is the only game in town. Fund manager Donald Duerson invests in a variety of issues, each carrying private insurance, which guarantees the repayment of principal. Even riskier issues, such as COPs (Certificates of Participation), which may come under pressure as state subsidies to city and county issuers come under pressure, become relatively secure when backed by insurance. A few private-activity bonds might subject part of the income to alternative minimum tax but, otherwise, California Insured Tax-Free fund is long on safety without giving up much in return. The recent popularity of insured California issues has helped total return, allowing the fund to outperform many of its uninsured rivals. As the California economy continues to flounder, Franklin California Insured Tax-Free should continue to offer rock-solid safety with a more than competitive return.

Suitability

Age 55 and under	*A-*
Age 55 to 70	*A-*
Age 70+	*A-*

Inception Date: 9/3/85

Manager Tenure: 1986

Telephone: (800) 342-5236

Minimum Initial Investment: $100.00

Direct Deposit: Yes

217

Franklin California Tax-Free Fund

Investment Ratings

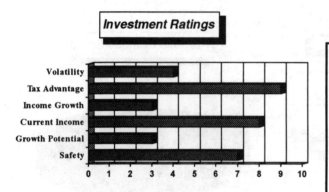

Investment Statistics

Initial Sales Charge:	**4.00%**
Annual Cost per $1,000:	**$11.37**

Annualized Returns

3 Year	*7.81%*
5 Year	*8.36%*
10 Year	*8.98%*

Total Return on $10,000

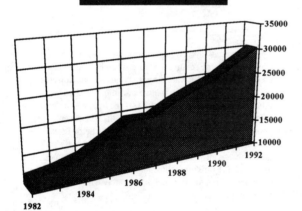

Income on $10,000 Investment

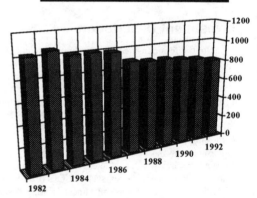

Historic Returns

	1982	1983	1984	1985	1986	1987	1988	1989	1990	1991	1992
Total Return (%)	26.39	6.23	9.95	17.04	16.47	-0.50	11.95	8.67	6.58	10.97	9.28
Lehman Index (%)	31.30	8.00	15.00	21.30	15.60	2.30	7.60	14.20	8.30	16.10	7.60
Dividend Yield	10.66	9.62	9.49	9.51	8.75	7.34	7.82	7.54	7.33	6.97	6.74
Income on $10,000 ($)	1,023	1,057	1,006	1,006	990	889	872	872	855	839	805

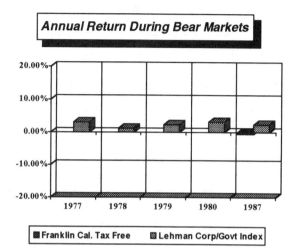

Annual Return During Bear Markets

20.00%					
10.00%					
0.00%					
-10.00%					
-20.00%	1977	1978	1979	1980	1987

■ Franklin Cal. Tax Free   ▨ Lehman Corp/Govt Index

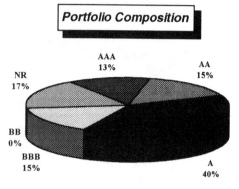

Portfolio Composition

AAA 13%
AA 15%
NR 17%
BB 0%
BBB 15%
A 40%

As of 6/30/93

Investment Description

Who said bigger isn't better? Franklin California Tax-Free Fund's $13 billion in assets is more than all other California tax-free funds combined. Mutual fund pundits assert that a fund this size can only aspire to perform no better than average, especially when investing in as limited a market as California tax-free bonds. Yet Franklin continues to defy its critics. One of the highest-yielding California tax-free funds, it has also been one of the most stable, steadily climbing in price in the past decades while other funds have zigged and zagged. While bond quality has declined in past years, fund manager Bernie Schroer has moderated risk with selectivity. Boasting a large percentage of essential service bonds, and high-quality real estate backed bonds, Schroer looks for value in often overlooked places. An excellent in-house research department and a California presence helps Franklin gain an edge on many of its smaller rivals. The income-oriented strategy also prevents surprises at tax time, since the fund hasn't paid a taxable gain in more than 10 years. An unbeatable yield and quality management make this fund an excellent choice for the conservative investor.

Suitability

Age 55 and under	*A*
Age 55 to 70	*A*
Age 70+	*B+*

Inception Date: 3/14/77

Manager Tenure: 1987

Telephone: (800) 342-5236

Minimum Initial Investment: $100.00

Direct Deposit: Yes

Franklin Valuemark Utilities

Investment Ratings

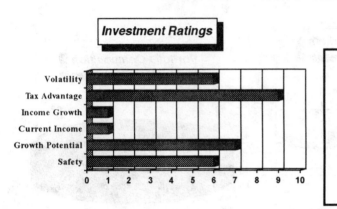

Volatility
Tax Advantage
Income Growth
Current Income
Growth Potential
Safety

0 1 2 3 4 5 6 7 8 9 10

Investment Statistics

Initial Sales Charge: **None**
Back end charges apply for early withdrawal

Annual Cost per $1,000: **$20.30**

Annualized Returns

3 Year *18.68%*

5 Year

Inception(1/24/89) *13.88%*

Total Return on $10,000

Income on $10,000 Investment

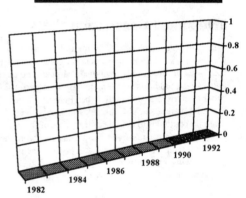

Historic Returns

	1982	1983	1984	1985	1986	1987	1988	1989	1990	1991	1992
Total Return (%)									0.42	22.89	7.22
S and P 500 (%)	21.47	22.46	6.13	31.64	18.68	5.26	17.50	31.68	-3.20	30.40	7.92
Dividend Yield											
Income on $10,000 ($)									0	0	0

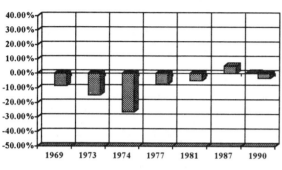

Annual Return During Bear Markets

| | 1969 | 1973 | 1974 | 1977 | 1981 | 1987 | 1990 |

■ Franklin Valuemark Utilities ⊠ S & P 500

Portfolio Composition

Cash
18%

Stocks
82%

As of 6/30/93

Investment Description

Franklin Valuemark Utilities shares almost everything with its twin sibling, Franklin Utilities fund. They're both managed by the same managers, both share a common conservative approach, and each has an excellent track record, even though Valuemark has only been in existance since 1989. The major difference lies in structure and taxability. Since Valuemark is part of the Franklin Variable annuity offering, no income tax is paid until funds are withdrawn, a major advantage for investors who reinvest dividends. Since penalities apply

to withdrawals made before investors are 59 1/2 and expenses are substantially higher because of annuity costs, Valuemark isn't as well-suited to income-oriented investors who need regular checks. Franklin's annuity does offer a guarantee of the original investment upon death and a 15% annual cummulative withdrawal (with no penalties) for those willing to let their earnings accumulate. For equity investors looking for tax relief, Franklin Valuemark Utilities is an attractive alternative to conventional mutual funds.

Suitability

Age 55 and under	*B+*
Age 55 to 70	*A-*
Age 70+	*A-*

Inception Date: 1/24/89

Manager Tenure: 1989

Telephone: (800) 342-5236

Minimum Initial Investment: $2,000.00

Direct Deposit: No

221

Hartford PCM Voyager

Investment Ratings

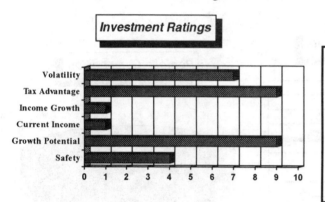

Volatility
Tax Advantage
Income Growth
Current Income
Growth Potential
Safety

0 1 2 3 4 5 6 7 8 9 10

Investment Statistics

Initial Sales Charge: **None**
Back end charges apply for early withdrawal

Annual Cost per $1,000: **$21.50**

Annualized Returns

3 Year **26.60%**
5 Year **17.55%**
Inception(1/2/88) **15.40%**

Total Return on $10,000

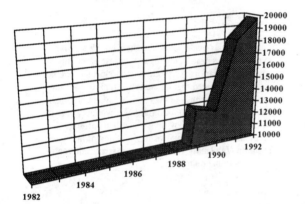

Income on $10,000 Investment

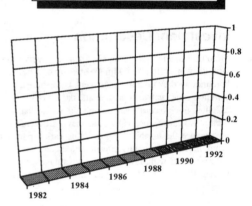

Historic Returns

	1982	1983	1984	1985	1986	1987	1988	1989	1990	1991	1992
Total Return (%)								30.51	-3.39	44.06	8.83
S and P 500 (%)	21.47	22.46	6.13	31.64	18.68	5.26	17.50	31.68	-3.20	30.40	7.92
Dividend Yield											
Income on $10,000 ($)								0	0	0	0

Annual Return During Bear Markets

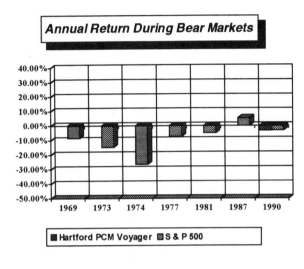

| | 1969 | 1973 | 1974 | 1977 | 1981 | 1987 | 1990 |

40.00%
30.00%
20.00%
10.00%
0.00%
-10.00%
-20.00%
-30.00%
-40.00%
-50.00%

☒ Hartford PCM Voyager ☒ S & P 500

Portfolio Composition

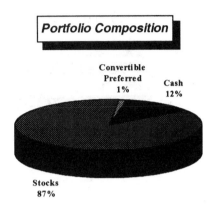

Convertible Preferred 1%

Cash 12%

Stocks 87%

As of 6/30/93

Investment Description

As with all variable annuity clones of successful funds, Hartford Life's Putnam Capital Manager Voyager fund has advantages and disadvantages over its mutual fund namesake. On the positive side, all earnings and growth are tax-deferred until withdrawal, a big plus with rising tax rates. The original investment is also guaranteed to heirs in the event of death, something that market-wary share-holders should appreciate. On the other hand, fund expenses are also substanially higher and IRS penalties apply to withdrawals made before age 59 1/2. Putnam, as with most variable annuity companies, allows 10% withdrawals yearly and switching between funds without penalty or tax consequence. Otherwise this fund mimics the Voyager fund and investors can expect the same above-average returns and safety levels found in that fund.

Suitability

Age 55 and under	*A*
Age 55 to 70	*B+*
Age 70+	*B-*

Inception Date: 1/2/88

Manager Tenure: 1988

Telephone: (800) 862-6668

Minimum Initial Investment: $1,000.00

Direct Deposit: No

Mid Coupon Callable Municipals

Investment Ratings

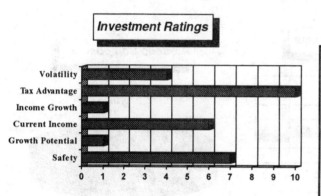

Investment Statistics

Initial Sales Charge: **Varies**
Markups vary, usually 1% to 3%

Annual Cost per $1,000: **$0.00**

Annualized Returns

3 Year	*10.30%*
5 Year	*11.27%*
10 Year	*11.82%*

Total Return on $10,000

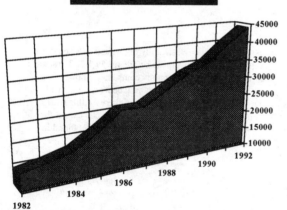

Income on $10,000 Investment

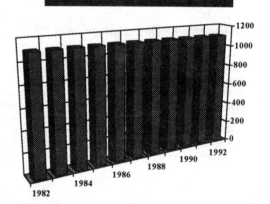

Historic Returns

	1982	1983	1984	1985	1986	1987	1988	1989	1990	1991	1992
Total Return (%)	43.90	8.70	11.00	22.80	21.00	0.00	13.50	12.00	7.20	13.60	10.20
Lehman Index (%)	31.30	8.00	15.00	21.30	15.60	2.30	7.60	14.20	8.30	16.10	7.60
Dividend Yield	11.60	9.50	10.20	9.20	7.40	7.70	7.80	7.20	7.30	6.90	6.40
Income on $10,000 ($)	1,103	1,103	1,103	1,103	1,103	1,103	1,103	1,103	1,103	1,103	1,103

Annual Return During Bear Markets

```
20.00%
10.00%
 0.00%
-10.00%
-20.00%
        1977    1978    1979    1980    1987
```

■ Mid |Coupon Bonds   ▨ Lehman Corp/Govt Index

Portfolio Composition

100%
Bonds

As of 6/30/93

Investment Description

While falling interest rates have left many municipal bond investors shell shocked, a few enterprising individuals have found opportunity in the surge of bond calls. While many bonds have been called in recent months, an even larger number have been pre-refunded. Municipalities with high coupon bonds that are callabel in the next few years issue new bonds and use the proceeds to buy U.S. government securities or other securities to be put into an escrow account to pay off the higher-yielding bonds. Regardless of what the bonds

previous rating was, the rating is often raised to AAA because of the escrowed cash. The opportunity lies in lower-grade bonds, say BBB or A, which are about to be refunded. This usually bumps up the price without affecting the yield that was locked in by an early investor. Since most of these pre-refunding candidates have higher coupons, investors need to be cautious and look at yield-to-call rather than the normal yield-to-maturity. Otherwise, this strategy offers above-average total returns without a lot of risk.

Suitability

Age 55 and under	*A*
Age 55 to 70	*A*
Age 70+	*A*

Inception Date:

Manager Tenure:

Telephone:

Minimum Initial Investment: $5,000.00

Direct Deposit:

225

MFS California Municipal Bond Fund

Investment Ratings

Investment Statistics

Initial Sales Charge: **4.75%**
B shares available with no initial sales charge

Annual Cost per $1,000: **$11.31**

Annualized Returns

3 Year	*11.20%*
5 Year	*10.30%*
Inception(6/19/85)	*9.30%*

Total Return on $10,000

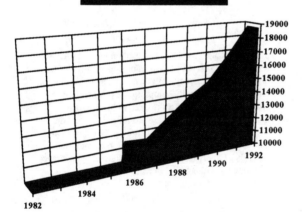

Income on $10,000 Investment

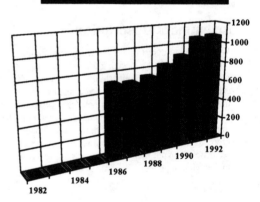

Historic Returns

	1982	1983	1984	1985	1986	1987	1988	1989	1990	1991	1992
Total Return (%)					21.20	-1.00	10.90	9.80	6.40	12.30	9.10
Lehman Index (%)	31.30	8.00	15.00	21.30	15.60	2.30	7.60	14.20	8.30	16.10	7.60
Dividend Yield					6.46	6.35	6.69	6.11	6.31	6.76	6.25
Income on $10,000 ($)					712	696	731	825	901	1,063	1,075

Annual Return During Bear Markets

	1977	1978	1979	1980	1987

(y-axis: 20.00%, 10.00%, 0.00%, -10.00%, -20.00%)

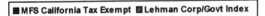
■ MFS California Tax Exempt ⊞ Lehman Corp/Govt Index

Portfolio Composition

A 41%
BBB 4%
NR 3%
AAA 34%
AA 18%

As of 6/30/93

Investment Description

MFS California Municipal Bond can't seem to get any respect. In spite of a top-notch track record (up 11.2% for three years), fund assets still hover around the $300 million mark, a relatively small amount in the huge California market. Most major mutual fund rating services and financial publications have yet to discover the fund, which boasts an excellent track record given the low-risk approach fund management espouses. The bulk of the portfolio rests firmly in the A to AAA range, with almost a third of the portfolio rated AAA. While safety usually comes at the expense of performance, MFS California Municipal Bond fund takes a back seat to no one. The fund exploits the advantage of its relatively small size by taking positions in smaller, more attractively priced bond issues that larger funds often ignore. Manager David Smith favors revenue issues and maintains a good mix of traditional water, power and waste bonds, along with a healthy dose of out-of-favor COPs and hospital bonds. Most of the over 140 issues have current coupons, or slightly higher, eliminating the risk of imminent bond calls that older, larger funds are facing. Given its low risk level and excellent performance, MFS California Municipal Bond fund offers one of the best values in the California tax-free mutual fund market.

Suitability

Age 55 and under	*A-*
Age 55 to 70	*A-*
Age 70+	*A-*

Inception Date: 6/19/85

Manager Tenure: 1992

Telephone: (800) 225-2606

Minimum Initial Investment: $1,000.00

Direct Deposit: Yes

227

MFS VA Muni Bond

Investment Ratings

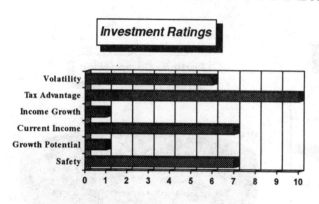

	0 1 2 3 4 5 6 7 8 9 10
Volatility	
Tax Advantage	
Income Growth	
Current Income	
Growth Potential	
Safety	

Investment Statistics

Initial Sales Charge: **4.75%**

Annual Cost per $1,000: **$17.64**

Annualized Returns

3 Year	*9.80%*
5 Year	*8.40%*
Inception(11/01/84)	*9.41%*

Total Return on $10,000

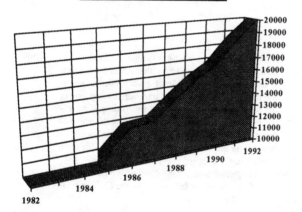

Income on $10,000 Investment

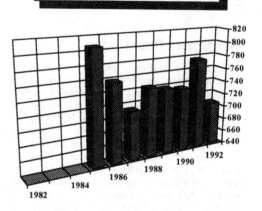

Historic Returns

	1982	1983	1984	1985	1986	1987	1988	1989	1990	1991	1992
Total Return (%)				16.58	15.41	1.25	11.17	9.39	6.79	10.40	7.40
Lehman Index (%)	31.30	8.00	15.00	21.30	15.60	2.30	7.60	14.20	8.30	16.10	7.60
Dividend Yield				8.41	7.35	6.38	7.07	6.72	6.57	6.40	6.09
Income on $10,000 ($)				807	758	713	743	738	735	776	706

Annual Return During Bear Markets

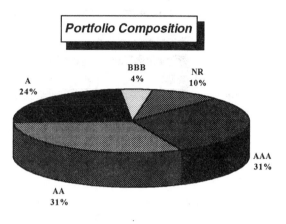

20.00%
10.00%
0.00%
-10.00%
-20.00%

1977   1978   1979   1980   1987

▣ MFS VA Muni Bond   ▩ Lehman Corp/Govt Index

Portfolio Composition

A
24%

BBB
4%

NR
10%

AAA
31%

AA
31%

As of 6/30/93

Investment Description

The MFS Virginia Municipal Bond fund suffers from the same problem that plagues other funds in states with well-managed state finances and well-heeled, highly taxed inhabitants: bonds are hard to come by. Virginia's lack of short-term municipal paper has even led manager Cynthia Brown to go out of state, buying North Carolina and Wyoming paper even though it's state taxable (under 5% of the portfolio, so there's little taxable effect on shareholders). Her endless search for double tax-free issues oftens takes her to the District of Columbia and Peurto Rico (both are state and federal tax free in every state), which make up over 10% of the fund's holdings.

In spite of MFS Virginia Muncipal's diversions into out-of-the-ordinary bonds, it still remains a solidly conservative fund. Turnover remains low, mostly because of a lack of replacement issues, and the average bond quality far exceeds most national funds. A small stake in zero coupon bonds is about the only flyer Brown has taken, and with falling interest rates, it has paid off handsomely. Considering the few alternatives available to high-income Virginia taxpayers, choosing MFS Virginia Muncipal Bond fund shouldn't be a difficult decision at all.

Suitability

Age 55 and under	*A-*
Age 55 to 70	*A-*
Age 70+	*A-*

Inception Date: 11/1/84

Manager Tenure: 1987

Telephone: (800) 225-2606

Minimum Initial Investment: $1,000.00

Direct Deposit: Yes

229

Municipal Bond Unit Trusts

Investment Ratings

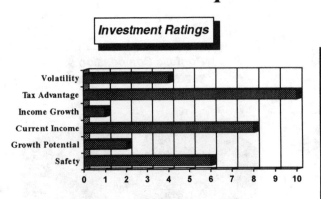

Investment Statistics

Initial Sales Charge: **Varies**
Charges vary, usually 4%-5%

Annual Cost per $1,000: **$7.93**

Annualized Returns

3 Year   *10.30%*

5 Year   *11.27%*

10 Year   *11.82%*

Total Return on $10,000

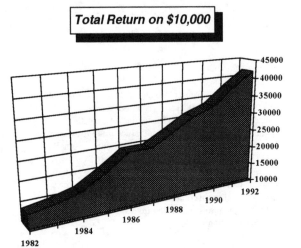

Income on $10,000 Investment

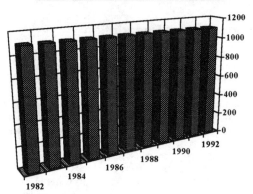

Historic Returns

	1982	1983	1984	1985	1986	1987	1988	1989	1990	1991	1992
Total Return (%)	43.90	8.70	11.00	22.80	21.00	0.00	13.50	12.00	7.20	13.60	10.20
Lehman Index (%)	31.30	8.00	15.00	21.30	15.60	2.30	7.60	14.20	8.30	16.10	7.60
Dividend Yield	11.60	9.50	10.20	9.20	7.40	7.70	7.80	7.20	7.30	6.90	6.40
Income on $10,000 ($)	1,103	1,103	1,103	1,103	1,103	1,103	1,103	1,103	1,103	1,103	1,103

Annual Return During Bear Markets

```
20.00%
10.00%
 0.00%
-10.00%
-20.00%
        1977   1978   1979   1980   1987
```

■ Municipal Bond Unit Trusts ▨ Lehman Corp/Govt Index

Portfolio Composition

100%
Bonds

As of 6/30/93

Investment Description

Muncipal bond units trusts have been around longer than mutual funds, yet investors continue to confuse the two tax-free investments. A unit trust is unmanaged, and usually divided between 10 to 20 different municipal bond issues. The trust almost always has a sales charge up front and simply passes on pro rata bond interest to shareholders. The advantage over a regular mutual fund lies in the interest. Unlike an open-ended mutual fund, where new shareholders constantly add new dollars,

diluting earnings and dividend yields, a unit trust's income remains constant, until bonds either are called or mature. Most fixed-income mutual fund holders have seen dividends fall dramatically in their funds while unit trust investors still get the same check they've received the past few years, in many cases. Of course, professional management does have its merits, but for the do-it-yourself type of investor, a unit trust offers a low cost, fixed-income alternative to mutual funds.

Suitability

Age 55 and under	*A-*
Age 55 to 70	*A-*
Age 70+	*A-*

Inception Date:

Manager Tenure:

Telephone:

Minimum Initial Investment: $100.00

Direct Deposit:

New England Zenith Life Managed

Investment Ratings

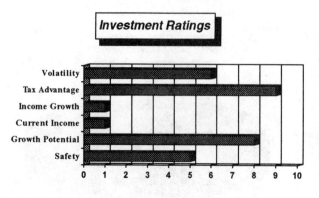

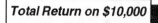

Investment Statistics

Initial Sales Charge:	**None**
Penalty for early withdrawals	
Annual Cost per $1,000:	**$0.00**

Annualized Returns

3 Year	*9.76%*
5 Year	*20.43%*
Inception(5/31/87)	*18.12%*

Total Return on $10,000

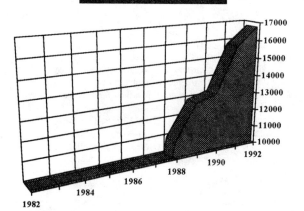

Income on $10,000 Investment

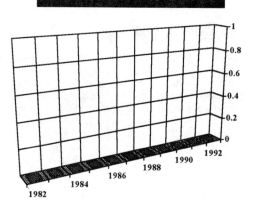

Historic Returns

	1982	1983	1984	1985	1986	1987	1988	1989	1990	1991	1992
Total Return (%)							8.83	18.37	2.59	19.45	6.06
S and P 500 (%)	21.47	22.46	6.13	31.64	18.68	5.26	17.50	31.68	-3.20	30.40	7.92
Dividend Yield											
Income on $10,000 ($)											

Annual Return During Bear Markets

	40.00%							
	30.00%							
	20.00%							
	10.00%							
	0.00%							
	-10.00%							
	-20.00%							
	-30.00%							
	-40.00%							
	-50.00%	1969	1973	1974	1977	1981	1987	1990

■ New England Zenith ▨ S & P 500

Portfolio Composition

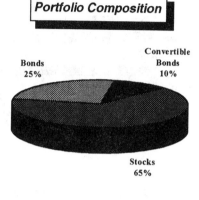

Bonds 25%

Convertible Bonds 10%

Stocks 65%

As of 6/30/93

Investment Description

Mention life insurance and most investors shudder. Almost everyone, at one time or another, has been approached by a life insurance salesman selling his or her wares. While insurance provides an essential component to most financial plans, traditional life insurance, with its low yields and lack of flexibility, has been ignored as an investment. New England Zenith Managed Life gives insurance buyers the best of both worlds. While providing life insurance coverage for family needs and special situtations, this variable life policy has returned double-digit growth from a conservatively managed mutual fund. Loading up on blue chips, manager Micheal Martino isn't taking any chances with quality. A large U.S. Treasury position (almost 25%) helps anchor the fund in case of an unexpected market turnaround. While the fund's peformance is reduced by the insurance cost of the policy its attached to, its returns have more than match most non-insurance mutual funds, quite a feat since many variable insurance funds' performances are hampered by hefty expense ratios. For insurance buyers finding life insurance interest rates unpalatable, New England Life's Zenith Managed serves up an attractive alternative.

Suitability

Age 55 and under	*A-*
Age 55 to 70	*B*
Age 70+	*C*

Inception Date: 5/31/87

Manager Tenure: 1987

Telephone: (617) 578-2000

Minimum Initial Investment: None

Direct Deposit: No

233

Nuveen Municipal Bond

Investment Ratings

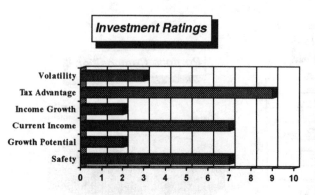

Investment Statistics

Initial Sales Charge: **4.75%**

Annual Cost per $1,000: **$13.66**

Annualized Returns

3 Year	*9.60%*
5 Year	*8.49%*
10 Year	*9.93%*

Total Return on $10,000

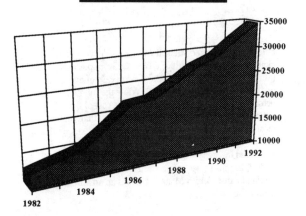

Income on $10,000 Investment

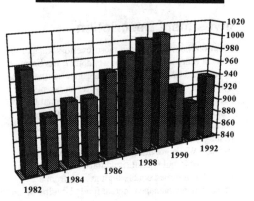

Historic Returns

	1982	1983	1984	1985	1986	1987	1988	1989	1990	1991	1992
Total Return (%)	32.39	9.90	8.75	21.41	19.19	2.13	10.40	10.88	5.69	10.71	8.48
Lehman Index (%)	31.30	8.00	15.00	21.30	15.60	2.30	7.60	14.20	8.30	16.10	7.60
Dividend Yield	10.29	7.97	7.97	7.93	7.28	6.70	7.16	6.96	6.20	6.04	6.04
Income on $10,000 ($)	979	915	931	931	963	986	1,003	1,008	928	899	937

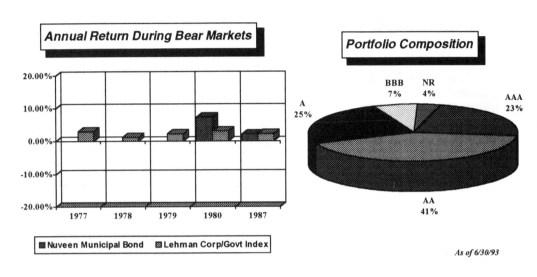

Annual Return During Bear Markets

| | 1977 | 1978 | 1979 | 1980 | 1987 |

■ Nuveen Municipal Bond   ▨ Lehman Corp/Govt Index

Portfolio Composition

- BBB 7%
- NR 4%
- AAA 23%
- A 25%
- AA 41%

As of 6/30/93

Investment Description

Nuveen Municipal Bond fund is a victim of its own success. While keeping its duration low compared to other funds has given it a reputation as a stable fund offering, most of its competitors have soundly trounced the fund with higher total returns, a result of the municipal rally of the past few months. Investors take heart: The fund has proven its mettle time and again in the past and remains one of this group's most conservative components. Manager Thomas Spalding seems to be sticking to his guns as the average duration of the fund still remains relatively short. The fund's

yield, while not spectacular compared to rivals with much longer durations, remains competitive, as does longer-term total return. Nuveen Municipal Bond fund should truly shine in a bear market, when the shorter maturities and high bond quality could help shore up the share price. While the short-term investor may find the fund temporarily lacking, long-term returns, bond quality and price stability make the Nuveen Municipal Bond fund an ideal choice for anyone who values safety first and short-term gains second.

Suitability

Age 55 and under	*A-*
Age 55 to 70	*A-*
Age 70+	*A-*

Inception Date: 11/29/76

Manager Tenure: 1978

Telephone: (800) 351-4100

Minimum Initial Investment: $1,000.00

Direct Deposit: No

235

Oppenheimer Tax-Free Bond Fund

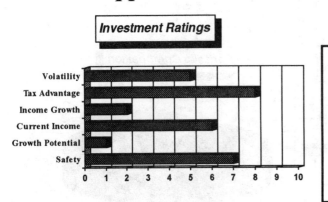

Investment Ratings

- Volatility
- Tax Advantage
- Income Growth
- Current Income
- Growth Potential
- Safety

(scale: 0 1 2 3 4 5 6 7 8 9 10)

Investment Statistics

Initial Sales Charge: **4.75%**

Annual Cost per $1,000: **$16.07**

Annualized Returns

3 Year	*11.01%*
5 Year	*8.47%*
10 Year	*10.42%*

Total Return on $10,000

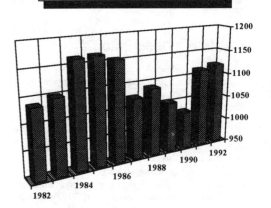

Income on $10,000 Investment

Historic Returns

	1982	1983	1984	1985	1986	1987	1988	1989	1990	1991	1992
Total Return (%)	43.75	16.92	10.60	21.38	19.75	0.00	9.51	9.46	5.87	12.14	9.70
Lehman Index (%)	31.30	8.00	15.00	21.30	15.60	2.30	7.60	14.20	8.30	16.10	7.60
Dividend Yield	11.33	8.85	8.75	8.64	7.61	6.93	7.57	7.23	6.88	6.97	6.35
Income on $10,000 ($)	1,087	1,099	1,164	1,166	1,154	1,074	1,089	1,053	1,027	1,113	1,120

Annual Return During Bear Markets

Year	
20.00%	
10.00%	
0.00%	
-10.00%	
-20.00%	1977 1978 1979 1980 1987

■ Oppenheimer Tax Free   ▨ Lehman Corp/Govt Index

Portfolio Composition

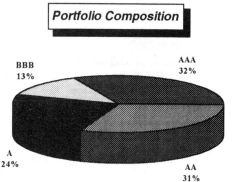

BBB 13%

AAA 32%

A 24%

AA 31%

As of 6/30/93

Investment Description

Oppenheimer Tax-Free fund manager Robert Petterson believes in very calculated risk. Not that he often takes a gamble. The bulk of the fund's assets rest in solidly conservative AAA and AA bonds. Rather, if he's going to take a chance, he wants to be compensated for it. The avoidance of middle-tier bonds is a case in point. Why take the added risk when the extra return benefits shareholders only marginally? The extent of the fund's high-flyers are a few inverse floaters and a fair number of discounted bonds. Since Patterson looks for yet lower interest rates, both positions should add capital gains to

Oppenheimer Tax-Free's somewhat average dividend yield. The more aggressive positions are balanced by premium bonds to counteract any hiccups in the bond markets, as interest rates continue their presumed decent. In spite of a few small bets, the fund is, by and large, a very conservative offering with a relatively short average maturity (making the portfolio more stable) and a high-quality portfolio (averaging AA). Conservative investors looking for a tax-advantaged bond fund should find their every wish fufilled by this sterling fund.

Suitability

Age 55 and under	*A-*
Age 55 to 70	*A-*
Age 70+	*A-*

Inception Date: 10/27/76

Manager Tenure: 1985

Telephone: (800) 525-7048

Minimum Initial Investment: $1,000.00

Direct Deposit: Yes

Scudder Medium Term Tax-Free

Investment Ratings

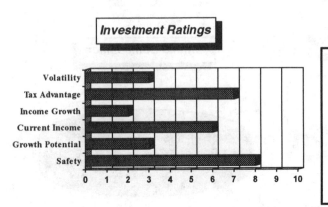

Investment Statistics

Initial Sales Charge:	**None**
Annual Cost per $1,000:	**$5.90**

Annualized Returns

3 Year	*10.23%*
5 Year	*8.19%*
Inception(4/12/83)	*7.96%*

Total Return on $10,000

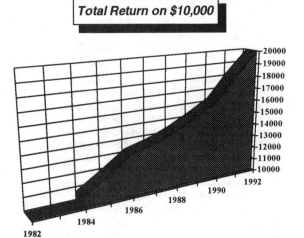

Income on $10,000 Investment

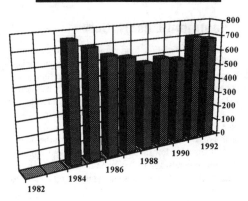

Historic Returns

	1982	1983	1984	1985	1986	1987	1988	1989	1990	1991	1992
Total Return (%)			8.11	11.10	10.61	3.73	4.92	6.00	6.29	12.13	8.93
Lehman Index (%)	31.30	8.00	15.00	21.30	15.60	2.30	7.60	14.20	8.30	16.10	7.60
Dividend Yield			7.56	7.03	6.18	5.71	5.36	5.59	5.38	6.63	6.12
Income on $10,000 ($)			756	704	642	617	567	588	567	704	684

Annual Return During Bear Markets

20.00%
10.00%
0.00%
-10.00%
-20.00%

1977 1978 1979 1980 1987

■ Scudder Medium Term Tax ▩ Lehman Corp/Govt Index
Free

Portfolio Composition

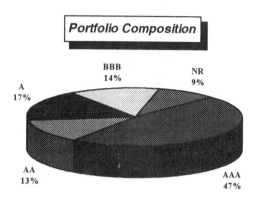

BBB
14%

NR
9%

A
17%

AA
13%

AAA
47%

As of 6/30/93

Investment Description

Scudder Medium Term Tax-Free fund is a fund in transition. Originally Scudder Tax-Free Target of 1990, the fund converted to its current charter in that year. By subsidizing management fees, the fund has produced above-average returns. The expenses, currently capped at .25%, could rise at the beginning of 1994 when management will again review the pricing structure. Still, in spite of a possible rise in expenses, the Medium Term Tax Free has a lot to offer. A barbell investment strategy, popular in U.S. government funds allows the fund to participate in the downward interest rate trend (it holds a large stake in zero coupon muni's) and yet hedge against rising rates (another large stake in premium coupon muni's). A high average bond quality (averaging AA) and a short average maturity (6.7 years) make Medium Term Tax Free attractive for gun-shy investors who want to cut their tax bill but don't want to get run over by rising interest rates.

Suitability

Age 55 and under	*B*
Age 55 to 70	*B*+
Age 70+	*B*

Inception Date: 4/12/83

Manager Tenure: 1986;1990

Telephone: (800) 225-2470

Minimum Initial Investment: $1,000.00

Direct Deposit: No

239

SunAmerica Tax-Exempt Insured

Investment Ratings

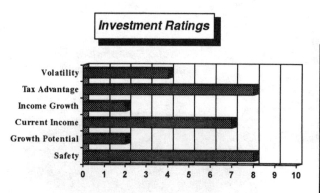

Investment Statistics

Initial Sales Charge:	**4.75%**
Annual Cost per $1,000:	**$18.63**

Annualized Returns

3 Year	**8.44%**
5 Year	**6.91%**
Inception(11/22/85)	**7.08%**

Total Return on $10,000

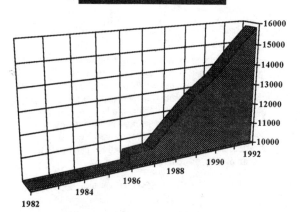

Income on $10,000 Investment

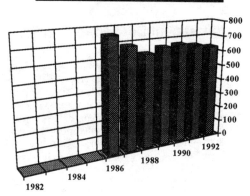

Historic Returns

	1982	1983	1984	1985	1986	1987	1988	1989	1990	1991	1992
Total Return (%)					11.28	0.65	10.67	8.70	6.17	8.45	6.81
Lehman Index (%)	31.30	8.00	15.00	21.30	15.60	2.30	7.60	14.20	8.30	16.10	7.60
Dividend Yield					7.83	6.87	6.99	6.68	7.05	6.39	6.52
Income on $10,000 ($)					757	684	623	656	665	650	631

Annual Return During Bear Markets

20.00%
10.00%
0.00%
-10.00%
-20.00%

1977   1978   1979   1980   1987

☒ SunAmerica Tax Exempt ☒ Lehman Corp/Govt Index

Portfolio Composition

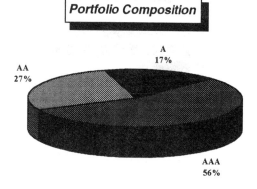

AA
27%

A
17%

AAA
56%

As of 6/30/93

Investment Description

SunAmerica Tax-Exempt Insured fund abhors risk. Like many insured municipal funds, it invests the majority of its money in insured municipal bonds to avoid the credit risk that often accompanies uninsured bonds. But that's where the similarities end between SunAmerica and its insured rivals. The addition of insurance usually drags down yields in insured funds, well below uninsured averages. SunAmerica Tax-Exempt's yield is almost half a percent better than its average uninsured counterpart. While insured funds often fluctuate widely because of increased sensitivity to interest-rate changes, Sunamerica is one of the least volatile funds in the entire municipal bond fund universe. The success is owed, in part, to

fund manager John Keogh's strategy of buying tax-free housing bonds. These premium bonds tend to have higher yields than other bonds because of their predisposition to being called, due to refinancing as interest rates tumble. Keogh has found that those who borrow through low-income housing programs, though, have a tendency not to prepay as fast, because of borrowers' limited opportunities to refinance. The high coupons protect against interest-rate spikes, and the propensity for prepayment results in a shorter average duration in the portfolio. The result is a low-risk, high-yielding insured fund that should make the choosiest of tax-free investors content.

Suitability

Age 55 and under	*A-*
Age 55 to 70	*A-*
Age 70+	*A-*

Inception Date: 11/22/85

Manager Tenure: 1985

Telephone: (800) 858-8850

Minimum Initial Investment: $500.00

Direct Deposit: No

Transamerica California Tax-Free Fund

Investment Ratings

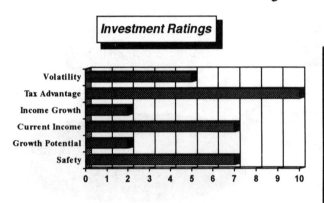

Investment Statistics

Initial Sales Charge: **4.75%**
B shares with no initial sales charge available

Annual Cost per $1,000: **$12.72**

Annualized Returns

3 Year *9.66%*

5 Year

Inception(12/31/89) *8.75%*

Total Return on $10,000

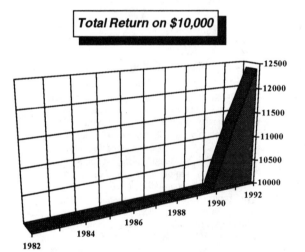

Income on $10,000 Investment

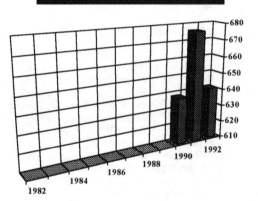

Historic Returns

	1982	1983	1984	1985	1986	1987	1988	1989	1990	1991	1992
Total Return (%)									6.14	12.26	9.14
Lehman Index (%)	31.30	8.00	15.00	21.30	15.60	2.30	7.60	14.20	8.30	16.10	7.60
Dividend Yield									6.70	7.16	6.49
Income on $10,000 ($)									638	676	641

Annual Return During Bear Markets

	1977	1978	1979	1980	1987

(Y-axis: 20.00%, 10.00%, 0.00%, -10.00%, -20.00%)

■ Transamerica Cal. Tax Free ▥ Lehman Corp/Govt Index

Portfolio Composition

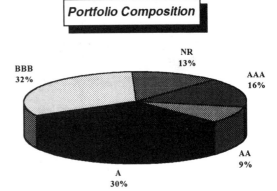

BBB 32%
NR 13%
AAA 16%
AA 9%
A 30%

As of 6/30/93

Investment Description

Transamerica California Tax-Free Fund might be one of the newest funds on the block, but if its debut indicates what the future holds, it certainly won't be one of the smaller California tax-free funds for long. Managed in Los Angeles by the same management team that selects muncipal bonds for insurance giant Transamerica's own portfolio, the fund's eclectic style has already carved out a unique niche in the over-crowded California tax-free marketplace. Practicing what might be called a contrarian management style, fund managers look for out-of-favor sectors and individual bonds that have been unfairly abandoned by the marketplace. The fund has been focusing on revenue bonds as state credit agency ratings continue to fall, but the lack of interest in general obligation bonds has more to do with value than with safety. Fund managers have demonstrated their undaunted attitude toward risk in the past and a willingness to move into lower-rated sectors, if sufficient value exists. A large percentage of often-maligned certificates of participation and nonrated bonds demonstrates the fund willingness to go where others fear to tread. While Transamerica California Tax-Free's bond quality might not be as high as a few other funds, its management and returns are second to none in this highly competitive environment.

Suitability

Age 55 and under	*A-*
Age 55 to 70	*A-*
Age 70+	*A-*

Inception Date: 12/31/89

Manager Tenure: 1989

Telephone: (800) 343-6840

Minimum Initial Investment: $1,000.00

Direct Deposit: No

243

T. Rowe Price MD Tax-Free Bond

Investment Ratings

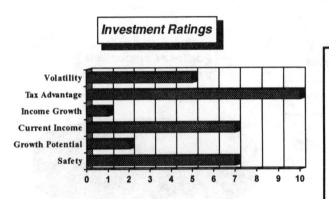

Investment Statistics

Initial Sales Charge:	**None**
Annual Cost per $1,000:	**$7.88**

Annualized Returns

3 Year	*10.65%*
5 Year	*9.60%*
Inception(3/31/87)	*7.12%*

Total Return on $10,000

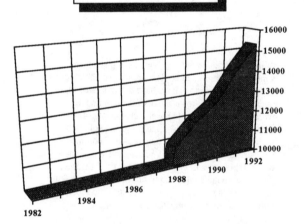

Income on $10,000 Investment

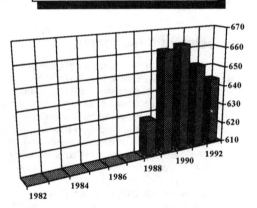

Historic Returns

	1982	1983	1984	1985	1986	1987	1988	1989	1990	1991	1992
Total Return (%)							8.88	9.58	6.23	11.21	8.55
Lehman Index (%)	31.30	8.00	15.00	21.30	15.60	2.30	7.60	14.20	8.30	16.10	7.60
Dividend Yield							6.28	6.46	6.30	6.21	5.86
Income on $10,000 ($)							628	661	663	652	644

Annual Return During Bear Markets

	1977	1978	1979	1980	1987

20.00%
10.00%
0.00%
-10.00%
-20.00%

■ T. Rowe Price MD Tax Free ▨ Lehman Corp/Govt Index

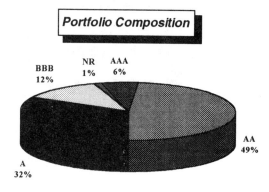

Portfolio Composition

BBB 12%
NR 1%
AAA 6%
AA 49%
A 32%

As of 6/30/93

Investment Description

T Rowe Price Maryland Tax-Free Bond fund's biggest problem isn't which bonds to choose but rather how to get them. High income levels and taxes in the state, combined with budget constraints, have made Maryland municipals difficult to come by, and demand still grows. Manager Mary Miller faces the choice of digging deeper among lower-quality bonds or waiting for old issues to get called and new ones to take their place. She's been able to do a bit of both. As interest rates have fallen and many higher-coupon bonds have been called, new lower-yielding issues have replaced them. A larger supply of yielding issues have replaced them. A larger supply of higher-quality bonds has allowed the fund to replenish its supply. Miller has also found value in some overlooked sectors, such as hospital and health care bonds, adding a bit of yield at the expense of bond rating. The average credit rating has declined but T. Rowe seems to have a "lock on" its home state; it has never had a default yet in any bond owned. While higher yields can be found, T. Rowe Price Maryland Tax-Free Bond fund can't be beat on quality or reliability.

Suitability

Age 55 and under	*A-*
Age 55 to 70	*A-*
Age 70+	*A-*

Inception Date: 3/31/87

Manager Tenure: 1990

Telephone: (800) 638-5660

Minimum Initial Investment: $2,500.00

Direct Deposit: No

USAA Tax-Exempt Intermediate Term

Investment Ratings

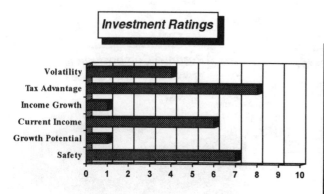

Investment Statistics

Initial Sales Charge:	**None**
Annual Cost per $1,000:	**$6.67**

Annualized Returns

3 Year	*10.05%*
5 Year	*9.04%*
10 Year	*9.27%*

Total Return on $10,000

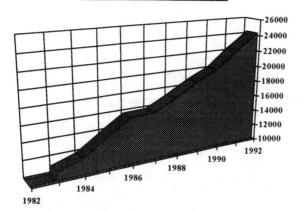

Income on $10,000 Investment

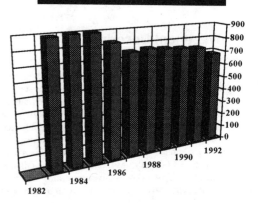

Historic Returns

	1982	1983	1984	1985	1986	1987	1988	1989	1990	1991	1992
Total Return (%)		9.67	8.86	16.40	13.24	0.95	8.72	9.24	6.72	11.14	8.49
Lehman Index (%)	31.30	8.00	15.00	21.30	15.60	2.30	7.60	14.20	8.30	16.10	7.60
Dividend Yield		8.91	8.95	9.00	7.74	6.72	7.24	7.06	6.84	6.79	6.04
Income on $10,000 ($)		890	900	900	827	754	764	755	746	737	683

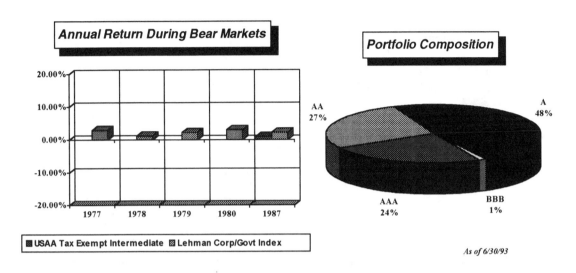

Annual Return During Bear Markets

Legend: ■ USAA Tax Exempt Intermediate ▧ Lehman Corp/Govt Index

Portfolio Composition

AA 27%
A 48%
AAA 24%
BBB 1%

As of 6/30/93

Investment Description

USAA Tax-Exempt Intermediate fund has being investing on autopilot for a few years now. Even though Kenneth Willman, who had managed the fund since 1981, stepped down earlier this year, his replacement, Cliff Gladstone, probably won't change very much. The fund's prospectus is quite specific as to what can and cannot be purchased. For example, maturities over 12 years are not allowed and the weighted average must fall under 10 years. In addition, 95% of the bonds must be rated A or better. Although other funds follow this formula approach to intermediate-term muncipal investing, USAA does have an edge because of its low expense ratio. This allows it to pay out more while taking less risk than comparable funds. Even though it maintains a conservative core, the fund does venture into less predictable areas at times, if the yield warrants it. Housing bonds and hospital bonds do have larger-than-average weighting although only higher-quality issues are purchased. The fund might seem uninspired, but USAA Tax-Exempt Intermediate delivers in both yield and quality.

Suitability

Age 55 and under	*A-*
Age 55 to 70	*A*
Age 70+	*A-*

Inception Date: 12/7/81

Manager Tenure: 1993

Telephone: (800) 382-8722

Minimum Initial Investment: $3,000.00

Direct Deposit: No

Vanguard Muni Limited-Term

Investment Ratings

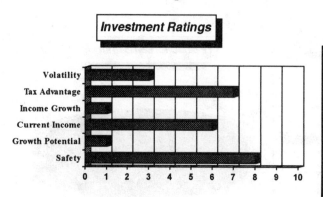

Investment Statistics

Initial Sales Charge: **None**

Annual Cost per $1,000: **$2.58**

Annualized Returns

3 Year	*7.83%*
5 Year	*7.37%*
Inception(8/31/87)	*7.49%*

Total Return on $10,000

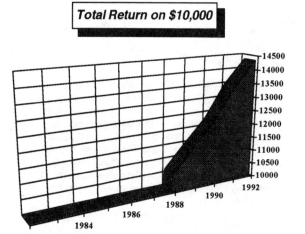

Income on $10,000 Investment

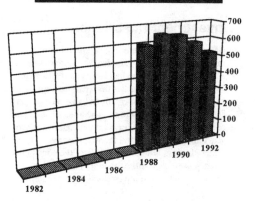

Historic Returns

	1982	1983	1984	1985	1986	1987	1988	1989	1990	1991	1992
Total Return (%)							6.40	8.07	7.04	9.47	6.38
Lehman Index (%)	31.30	8.00	15.00	21.30	15.60	2.30	7.60	14.20	8.30	16.10	7.60
Dividend Yield							5.96	6.44	6.26	5.74	4.92
Income on $10,000 ($)							595	646	636	587	520

Annual Return During Bear Markets

| | 1977 | 1978 | 1979 | 1980 | 1987 |

- Vanguard Muni
- Lehman Corp/Govt Index

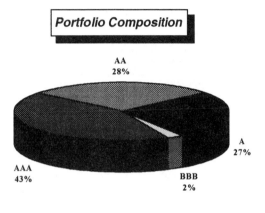

Portfolio Composition

AA
28%

A
27%

BBB
2%

AAA
43%

As of 6/30/93

Investment Description

Vanguard Municipal Limited-Term doesn't aspire to greatness. Fund managers Ian MacKinnon and Chris Ryon don't seem to be shooting for anyone's top 10 municipal bond fund list or for first prize in a total return contest of any type. The fund has stuck to its objective bravely, considering that almost everyone else has jumped on the total return band wagon. Paying out a yield higher than a money market with much less risk than a longer-term fund has been the fund's objective since inception. It's accomplished that task handily. An extremely low expense ratio, typical of all Vanguard funds, has helped accomplish the high-yield part of the fund's objective. Risk is contained by a short average maturity (2 to 5 years only by prospectus) and a high-quality portfolio. The fund's average rating is AA, with the bulk of the portfolio residing in AAA and AA bonds. While lagging in total return because of competitors' use of lower-quality bonds and longer maturities, Vanguard Municipal Income should show its worth in a bear market in bonds, which it has yet to experience. While it may not turn heads with eye-catching total returns, the Vanguard Municipal Limited-Term fund deserves a second look by anyone looking for unparalleled stability with a competitive tax-free return.

Suitability

Age 55 and under	*A-*
Age 55 to 70	*A-*
Age 70+	*A*

Inception Date: 8/31/87

Manager Tenure: 1987/1988

Telephone: (800) 662-7447

Minimum Initial Investment: $3,000.00

Direct Deposit: No

249

Chapter 14

Turnaround and Special Situation Investments

AIM Value Fund

Investment Ratings

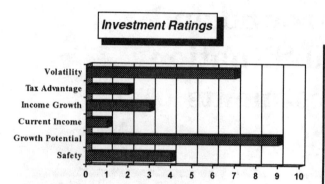

Investment Statistics

Initial Sales Charge: **5.50%**
B shares available with no initial sales charge

Annual Cost per $1,000: **$24.57**

Annualized Returns

3 Year	*9.76%*
5 Year	*10.30%*
Inception(5/1/84)	*18.12%*

Total Return on $10,000

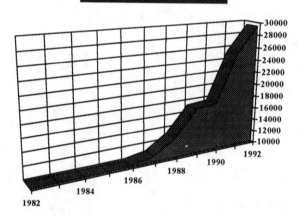

Income on $10,000 Investment

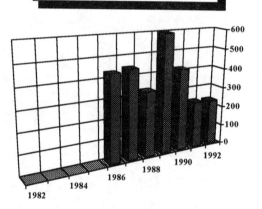

Historic Returns

	1982	1983	1984	1985	1986	1987	1988	1989	1990	1991	1992
Total Return (%)					8.79	5.96	20.61	31.54	1.89	43.45	16.39
S and P 500 (%)	21.47	22.46	6.13	31.64	18.68	5.26	17.50	31.68	-3.20	30.40	7.92
Dividend Yield					3.33	3.18	2.27	3.36	1.79	1.02	0.68
Income on $10,000 ($)				328	433	446	327	596	417	237	233

Annual Return During Bear Markets

| | 40.00% |
| 30.00% |
| 20.00% |
| 10.00% |
| 0.00% |
| -10.00% |
| -20.00% |
| -30.00% |
| -40.00% |
| -50.00% |

1969 1973 1974 1977 1981 1987 1990

■ AIM Value Fund ▨ S & P 500

Portfolio Composition

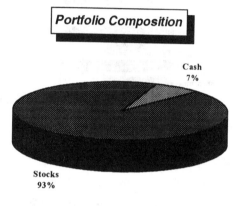

Cash
7%

Stocks
93%

As of 6/30/93

Investment Description

AIM Value Fund is a value offering in name only. While most funds in the same class buy undervalued stocks and turnaround situation, AIM brings its unique earning growth philosphy to this newly acquired fund. Managers Claude Cody and Joel Dobberpuhl view value as stocks with impressive earnings growth currently selling at a discount. Since the company took over the fund in July 1992, many of its utilities and other low-growth holdings have been ejected in favor of higher growth alternatives, such as technology and financial stocks. In typical AIM fashion, the fund searches every nook and cranny of the investment markets for stocks meeting their high-growth, low-price criteria. Diverse holdings like Texas Instruments, Circus Circus, and Banc One illustrate the breadth of holdings and the fund's lack of predisposition toward one particular group of stocks. AIM Value Fund is poised to take advantage of an inevitable rebound in growth-oriented issues, and in typical AIM fashion, will probably see above-average returns with a lower-than-average risk level.

Suitability

Age 55 and under	*A-*
Age 55 to 70	*B*
Age 70+	*B-*

Inception Date: 5/1/84

Manager Tenure: 1992

Telephone: (800) 347-1919

Minimum Initial Investment: $500.00

Direct Deposit: No

253

Boeing

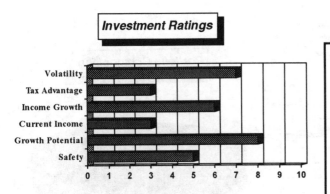

Investment Ratings

Volatility
Tax Advantage
Income Growth
Current Income
Growth Potential
Safety

0 1 2 3 4 5 6 7 8 9 10

Investment Statistics

Initial Sales Charge:	**NA**

Individual stock, brokerage commissions may apply

Annual Cost per $1,000:   **$0.00**

Annualized Returns

3 Year	*2.70%*
5 Year	*22.22%*
10 Year	*17.73%*

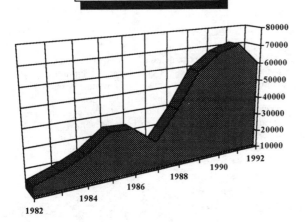

Total Return on $10,000

80000
70000
60000
50000
40000
30000
20000
10000

1982 1984 1986 1988 1990 1992

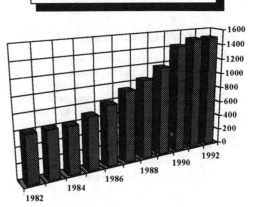

Income on $10,000 Investment

1600
1400
1200
1000
800
600
400
200
0

1982 1984 1986 1988 1990 1992

Historic Returns

	1982	1983	1984	1985	1986	1987	1988	1989	1990	1991	1992
Total Return (%)	50.35	29.28	29.40	38.36	-2.15	-27.65	63.88	46.93	14.65	5.23	-15.97
S and P 500 (%)	21.47	22.46	6.13	31.64	18.68	5.26	17.50	31.68	-3.20	30.40	7.92
Dividend Yield	6.15	4.09	3.16	2.74	2.28	2.73	4.20	2.90	2.40	2.20	2.09
Income on $10,000 ($)	614	614	614	689	794	929	1,034	1,169	1,423	1,498	1,498

Annual Return During Bear Markets

40.00%	
30.00%	
20.00%	
10.00%	
0.00%	
-10.00%	
-20.00%	
-30.00%	
-40.00%	
-50.00%	

1969 1973 1974 1977 1981 1987 1990

■ Boeing   ▨ S & P 500

Portfolio Composition

100%
Stocks

As of 6/30/93

Investment Description

Boeing's stock has been grounded again in recent months. Airline price wars and low passenger traffic have slowed down orders to the passenger airline giant. Investor fears of a continuing airline recession, growing competition from Airbus, the European consortium and a seemingly revitalized McDonnell Douglas have kept the stock hovering below 40. Still, Boeing remains the market leader (well over 50% of the market) and its research and development is second to none. An eventual rebound in airline sales should push the stock considerably higher in the next few years. Meanwhile, the company continues to be profitable, based on current orders, and expects an upturn in sales when its new 777 Jet is ready for delivery in 1995. The company's blue-chip finances and rock-solid credit rating enable it to weather just about any economic storm. Profits are off slightly over past years but the stock remains an ideal turnaround candidate with a decent dividend as a bonus for patient, long-term investors.

Suitability

Age 55 and under	*A-*
Age 55 to 70	*B+*
Age 70+	*B*

Inception Date:

Manager Tenure:

Telephone:

Minimum Initial Investment:

Direct Deposit:

255

Fidelity Contrafund

Investment Ratings

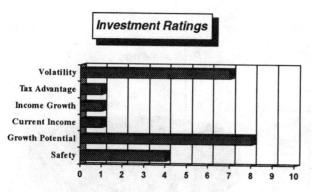

Investment Statistics

Initial Sales Charge: **3.00%**

Annual Cost per $1,000: **$15.60**

Annualized Returns

3 Year   *23.92%*

5 Year   *24.90%*

10 Year   *16.42%*

Total Return on $10,000

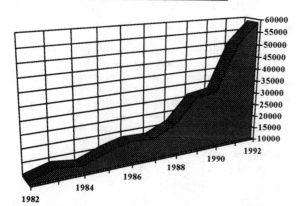

Income on $10,000 Investment

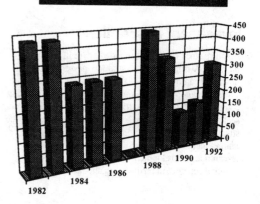

Historic Returns

	1982	1983	1984	1985	1986	1987	1988	1989	1990	1991	1992
Total Return (%)	17.18	23.28	-8.27	27.06	13.32	-1.90	20.93	43.27	3.94	54.92	15.89
S and P 500 (%)	21.47	22.46	6.13	31.64	18.68	5.26	17.50	31.68	-3.20	30.40	7.92
Dividend Yield	4.48	4.07	2.28	2.56	2.06	0.00	2.99	1.98	0.54	0.63	0.78
Income on $10,000 ($)	434	434	288	291	291	0	444	346	132	162	307

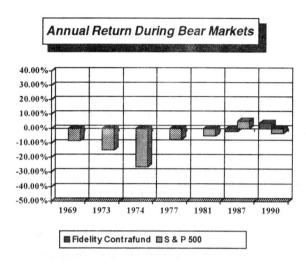

Annual Return During Bear Markets

Legend: ■ Fidelity Contrafund ▨ S & P 500

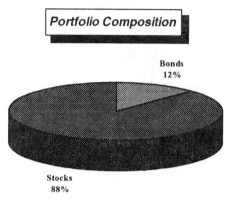

Portfolio Composition

Bonds 12%

Stocks 88%

As of 6/30/93

Investment Description

Fidelity Contrafund is aptly named. Fund manager Will Danoff is a consummate opportunist, usually positioning the fund in out-of-favor industries with rapidly improving prospects. Danoff's forays into oils, precious metals and overseas stocks all paid off rather well during the first half of 1993, pushing up Contra's price 20.7% through 9/8/93. In typical Fidelity fashion, Contrafund lacks a clear investment style, leaving most of the decision-making process with the fund manager. While investment anarchy would seem to be the most likely result of this type of hands-off management, Danoff's astute judgement and flexibility has earned the fund a reputation as a top-notch growth vehicle. This success has caused Danoff more anxiety than the markets. More than tripling in size since 1991, Contrafund would seem to be a bit unwieldly as rapid movement between sectors has become more difficult. In spite of the problems success brings, Contrafund remains a premier growth fund and should continue to outperform the averages for some years to come.

Suitability

Age 55 and under	*A*
Age 55 to 70	*A-*
Age 70+	*B*

Inception Date: 5/17/67

Manager Tenure: 1990

Telephone: (800) 544-8888

Minimum Initial Investment: $2,500.00

Direct Deposit: No

France Growth

Investment Ratings

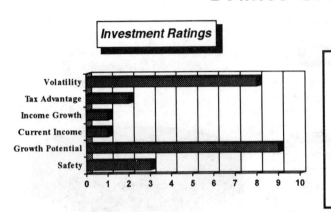

Investment Statistics

Initial Sales Charge:	**None**
Closed end fund	
Annual Cost per $1,000:	**$20.20**

Annualized Returns

3 Year	
5 Year	
Inception(5/18/90)	*7.98%*

Total Return on $10,000

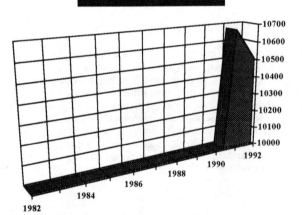

Income on $10,000 Investment

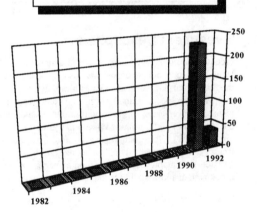

Historic Returns

	1982	1983	1984	1985	1986	1987	1988	1989	1990	1991	1992
Total Return (%)										6.77	-1.60
S and P 500 (%)	21.47	22.46	6.13	31.64	18.68	5.26	17.50	31.68	-3.20	30.40	7.92
Dividend Yield										2.32	0.37
Income on $10,000 ($)										229	38

Annual Return During Bear Markets

| 40.00% |
| 30.00% |
| 20.00% |
| 10.00% |
| 0.00% |
| -10.00% |
| -20.00% |
| -30.00% |
| -40.00% |
| -50.00% |

1969 1973 1974 1977 1981 1987 1990

■ France Growth ■ S & P 500

Portfolio Composition

100%
Stocks

As of 6/30/93

Investment Description

Investors in France Growth fund have cause to break out the brie and champagne. Falling German interest rates have sparked a long overdue rally in the French market this year, pushing returns on this specialty fund into the double digits. The best may be yet to come. A radical swing to the right in French politics coupled with lower interest rates may mark the begining of a French bull market. As the sale of government-owned companies picks up and French government takes on a more pro-business stance, French companies may see profit trends reverse in the near future. For now, manager Phillip Cartier is looking toward interest rate sensitive stocks to continue to propel France Growth fund's returns through 1994. Politcal turmoil and the inevitable displacement of workers and capital as France painfully changes its economic and social policies could signal a short-term decline in profits in some cyclical French companies. Long-term, France looks extremely attractive and the France Growth fund, selling at a slight discount to net asset value, is an excellent way to participate in the country's and region's future economic recovery.

Suitability

Age 55 and under	A-
Age 55 to 70	B
Age 70+	C

Inception Date: 5/18/90

Manager Tenure: 1990

Telephone: (212) 713-2421

Minimum Initial Investment:

Direct Deposit: No

International Business Machines

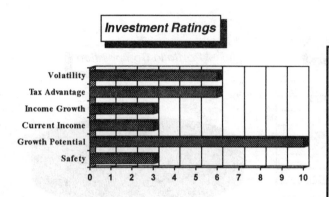

Initial Sales Charge: **NA**
Individual stock, brokerage commissions may apply

Annual Cost per $1,000:   **$0.00**

Annualized Returns

3 Year   *-13.60%*

5 Year   *-16.21%*

10 Year   *-2.20%*

Total Return on $10,000

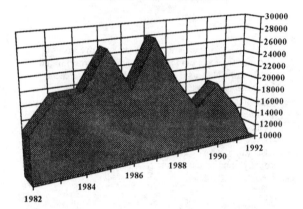

Income on $10,000 Investment

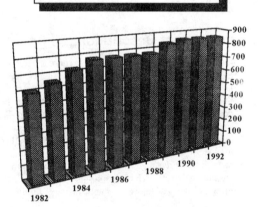

Historic Returns

	1982	1983	1984	1985	1986	1987	1988	1989	1990	1991	1992
Total Return (%)	69.23	26.75	0.92	26.29	-22.83	33.33	-23.83	-22.77	20.05	-21.24	-43.40
S and P 500 (%)	21.47	22.46	6.13	31.64	18.68	5.26	17.50	31.68	-3.20	30.40	7.92
Dividend Yield	6.05	3.85	3.36	3.57	2.83	3.67	2.75	3.88	5.14	4.28	5.44
Income on $10,000 ($)	604	652	720	773	773	773	773	831	850	850	850

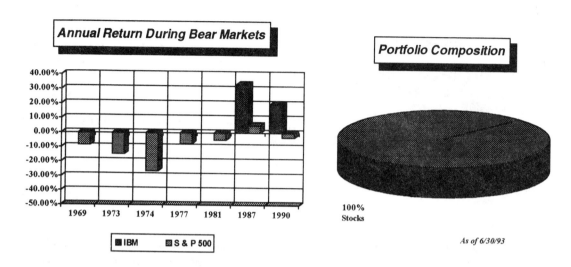

Annual Return During Bear Markets

40.00%	
30.00%	
20.00%	
10.00%	
0.00%	
-10.00%	
-20.00%	
-30.00%	
-40.00%	
-50.00%	

1969 1973 1974 1977 1981 1987 1990

■ IBM   ■ S & P 500

Portfolio Composition

100%
Stocks

As of 6/30/93

Investment Description

IBM has taken a lot of heat in the past year, much of it deserved and some of it not. The company has been in decline for several years, as its technological edge in large computers has been whittled away by smaller, more aggressive personal computer makers, and its marketing prowess has been non-existent since the early 1980s. A lot can be learned from the decline of IBM. Investors hung on to the bitter end, even though the writing was on the wall while the price remained relatively high. While much could be written about what IBM has done wrong, little is being said about what its doing right. Its laptop computer, the Think Pad, is a huge hit. Its computer outservicing, networking and other select businesses are growing by leaps and bounds, each unit's success coming after breaking out of the company's stifling bureaucracy as management slowly completes a 180-degree turn. The most favorable sign of all is the fact that no one has a good thing to say about IBM in spite of some of the good news that's been coming out. This contrarian appeal and the genuine change becoming apparent in some of its businesses reminds me of Chrysler in 1990. Need I say more?

Suitability

Age 55 and under	*A-*
Age 55 to 70	*B*
Age 70+	*C*

Inception Date:

Manager Tenure:

Telephone:

Minimum Initial Investment:

Direct Deposit:

Oppenheimer Global Biotech Fund

Investment Ratings

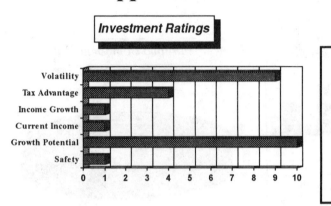

Investment Statistics

Initial Sales Charge: **5.75%**
B shares available with no initial charge

Annual Cost per $1,000: **$29.34**

Annualized Returns

3 Year *13.18%*

5 Year *13.67%*

Inception(12/30/87) *14.22%*

Total Return on $10,000

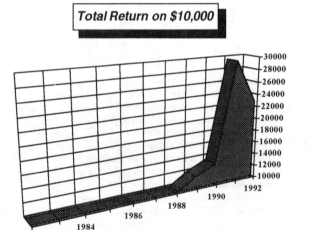

Income on $10,000 Investment

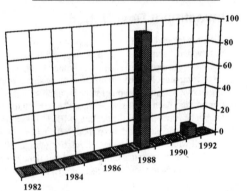

Historic Returns

	1982	1983	1984	1985	1986	1987	1988	1989	1990	1991	1992
Total Return (%)						0.80	1.29	23.41	12.62	121.13	-22.88
S and P 500 (%)	21.47	22.46	6.13	31.64	18.68	5.26	17.50	31.68	-3.20	30.40	7.92
Dividend Yield						0.00	0.01	0.00	0.00	0.00	0.00
Income on $10,000 ($)						0	94	0	0	9	0

Annual Return During Bear Markets

40.00%
30.00%
20.00%
10.00%
0.00%
-10.00%
-20.00%
-30.00%
-40.00%
-50.00%

1969   1973   1974   1977   1981   1987   1990

■ Oppenheimer Global Biotech ⊠ S & P 500

Portfolio Composition

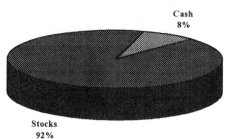

Cash
8%

Stocks
92%

As of 6/30/93

Investment Description

Oppenheimer Global Biotech has had an exciting, albeit short, history. Its spectacularly volatile returns have ranged from a dismal -22.88% return in 1992 (it would have been a lot worse if not for a fourth-quarter rally in biotech stocks) to an incredible 121.13% return in 1991. While not for the faint-of-heart, Oppenheimer has the only game in town when it comes to a biotechnology fund. It's the only pure biotech mutual fund there is. No large drug companies, no health care companies, only biotechnology companies that tend to be start-up ventures by nature. Therein lies this fund's appeal. As biotechnology moves from laboratories to living rooms, no investment is better-suited to take advantage of what could very well be a key growth industry in the next several decades. If you can stomach the ride, this could be the opportunity of a lifetime.

Suitability

Age 55 and under	*A*
Age 55 to 70	*B-*
Age 70+	*C*

Inception Date: 12/30/87

Manager Tenure: 1992

Telephone: (800) 525-7048

Minimum Initial Investment: $1,000.00

Direct Deposit: Yes

Putnam Dividend Income

Investment Ratings

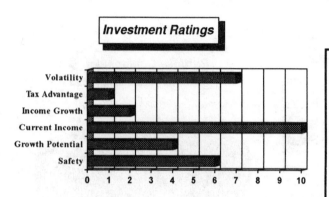

Investment Statistics

Initial Sales Charge: **None**
Closed end fund

Annual Cost per $1,000: **$20.20**

Annualized Returns

3 Year **14.51%**

5 Year

Inception(9/28/89) **9.74%**

Total Return on $10,000

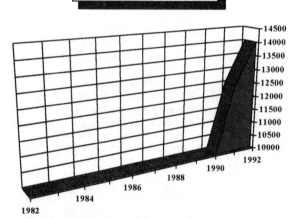

Income on $10,000 Investment

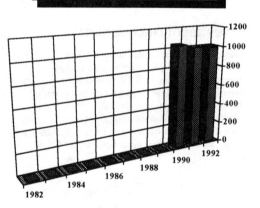

Historic Returns

	1982	1983	1984	1985	1986	1987	1988	1989	1990	1991	1992
Total Return (%)									-3.44	29.23	12.20
S and P 500 (%)	21.47	22.46	6.13	31.64	18.68	5.26	17.50	31.68	-3.20	30.40	7.92
Dividend Yield									10.53	11.90	10.22
Income on $10,000 ($)									1,042	1,008	999

Annual Return During Bear Markets

40.00%	
30.00%	
20.00%	
10.00%	
0.00%	
-10.00%	
-20.00%	
-30.00%	
-40.00%	
-50.00%	

1969   1973   1974   1977   1981   1987   1990

■ Putnam Dividend Income   ▨ S & P 500

Portfolio Composition

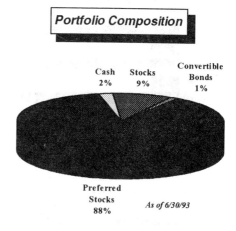

Cash 2%   Stocks 9%   Convertible Bonds 1%

Preferred Stocks 88%   *As of 6/30/93*

Investment Description

Putnam Dividend Income has battened down the hatches and is preparing for a storm in the financial markets. Fund manager Jeanne Mockard has begun to shorten average maturities and switch to variable-rate preferred issues. In spite of the perceived threat of rising rates, Putnam Dividend Income still manages to turn heads when it comes to yield and total return. The fund's unique strategy of purchasing high-yielding, yet relatively safe, preferred issues has enabled it to produce a remarkable mix of growth and income. While yielding over 8%, the fund has also managed to post double-digit total returns for the past three years. In theory, the preferred stocks that make up the portfolio should be interest-rate sensitive but also participate in stock market rallies to a limited degree. So far, theory has coalesced into reality, as the fund has posted a 14.51% three year annualized total return. The only warning flag in sight is the use of short-term debt to enhance income. While contributing greatly to total returns in good markets, this leveraging strategy could add to losses if interest rates should rise. Nevertheless, it's hard to find an 8% return anywhere and Putnam Dividend Income fund seems to be managing it without betting the farm.

Suitability

Age 55 and under	*A-*
Age 55 to 70	*A-*
Age 70+	*B+*

Inception Date: 9/28/89

Manager Tenure: 1993

Telephone: (800) 634-1587

Minimum Initial Investment:

Direct Deposit: No

Putnam Global Growth

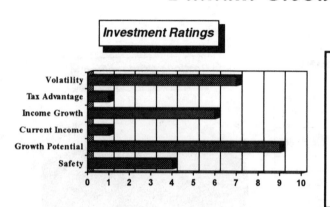

Investment Statistics

Initial Sales Charge: **5.75%**
B shares with no initial sales charge available

Annual Cost per $1,000: **$24.87**

Annualized Returns

3 Year	*4.76%*
5 Year	*9.47%*
10 Year	*15.70%*

Total Return on $10,000

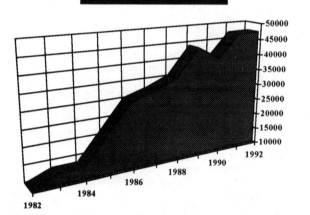

Income on $10,000 Investment

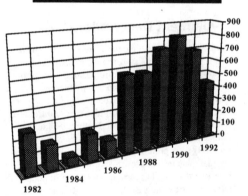

Historic Returns

	1982	1983	1984	1985	1986	1987	1988	1989	1990	1991	1992
Total Return (%)	9.66	27.93	0.74	65.04	37.69	7.23	9.00	24.58	-9.20	17.97	0.24
S and P 500 (%)	21.47	22.46	6.13	31.64	18.68	5.26	17.50	31.68	-3.20	30.40	7.92
Dividend Yield	3.32	1.79	0.41	1.52	0.51	1.71	1.81	2.15	0.19	1.82	0.93
Income on $10,000 ($)	286	178	60	199	122	576	572	735	812	699	435

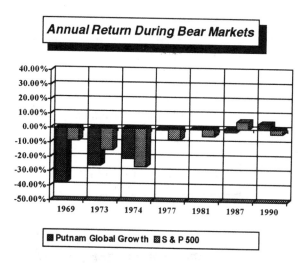

Annual Return During Bear Markets

40.00%
30.00%
20.00%
10.00%
0.00%
-10.00%
-20.00%
-30.00%
-40.00%
-50.00%

1969   1973   1974   1977   1981   1987   1990

■ Putnam Global Growth ▨ S & P 500

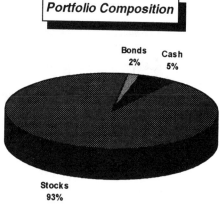

Portfolio Composition

Bonds 2%   Cash 5%

Stocks 93%

As of 6/30/93

Investment Description

For Putnam Global Growth fund, diversification has paid off well in the past few years. Unlike other international portfolios, it seeks a wide exposure to international markets, seldom concentrating its holdings. The strategy has served shareholders well, cushioning the blow from the 1992 European currency crash and boosting returns when markets like Japan's unexpectingly turn around. While the fund might be diversified regionally, it will never be confused with an index fund. After choosing which world markets to emphasis, fund managers Tony Regan and Robert Beck carefully select their stocks, focusing on undervalued and overlooked equities. Diverse issues such as Bangkok Bank, Unilever and Pfizer are a trademark of this often varied offering, as are above-average returns. Putnam Global Growth fund's balanced approach to the sometimes volatile world markets should allow the most cautious investor to rest easy.

Suitability

Age 55 and under	*A*
Age 55 to 70	*B*
Age 70+	*B-*

Inception Date: 9/1/67

Manager Tenure: 1988

Telephone: (800) 225-1581

Minimum Initial Investment: $250.00

Direct Deposit: Yes

267

Putnam New Opportunities

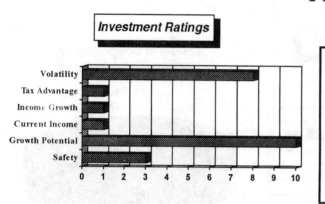

Investment Ratings

- Volatility
- Tax Advantage
- Income Growth
- Current Income
- Growth Potential
- Safety

0 1 2 3 4 5 6 7 8 9 10

Investment Statistics

Initial Sales Charge: **5.75%**
B shares with no initial sales charge available

Annual Cost per $1,000: **$27.53**

Annualized Returns

3 Year

5 Year

Inception(8/31/90) *39.33%*

Total Return on $10,000

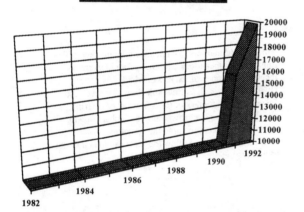

Income on $10,000 Investment

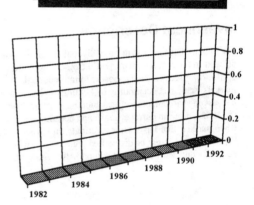

Historic Returns

	1982	1983	1984	1985	1986	1987	1988	1989	1990	1991	1992
Total Return (%)										67.64	25.52
S and P 500 (%)	21.47	22.46	6.13	31.64	18.68	5.26	17.50	31.68	-3.20	30.40	7.92
Dividend Yield											
Income on $10,000 ($)										0	0

Annual Return During Bear Markets

	1969	1973	1974	1977	1981	1987	1990

40.00%
30.00%
20.00%
10.00%
0.00%
-10.00%
-20.00%
-30.00%
-40.00%
-50.00%

■ Putnam New Opportunities ▨ S & P 500

Portfolio Composition

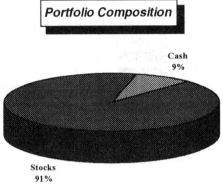

Cash
9%

Stocks
91%

As of 6/30/93

Investment Description

Putnam New Opportunities is not a big proponent of diversification. Fund manager Dan Miller prefers to focus his attention on five sectors of the market where he sees the most growth in the next decade. Currently, five sectors make up the bulk of the portfolio: media/entertainment, medical technology/cost containment, applied advanced technology, value-oriented consumer services and personal communications. Each area has experienced high growth in the past year and should continue an upward trend for the next few years. The fund's path to new highs has not been a smooth one. Miller's concentrated approach is accompanied by exaggerated ebbs and flows in price, which should only be expected of a high-performance fund such as this. Overall, however, the trend has been up, way up. After returning an astonishing 67.64% in 1991, Putnam New Opportunities came back with an encore of 25.52% in 1992, a mediocre year for most growth funds. While not designed for the timid, Putnam delivers performance unlike any other fund on the market, and for those willing to tolerate an occasional sharp dip, aggressive-growth investing doesn't get much better.

Suitability

Age 55 and under	*A*
Age 55 to 70	*B*
Age 70+	*C*

Inception Date: 8/31/90

Manager Tenure: 1990

Telephone: (800) 225-1581

Minimum Initial Investment: $500.00

Direct Deposit: Yes

269

Scudder New Europe Fund

Investment Ratings

Investment Statistics

Initial Sales Charge:	**None**
Closed end fund	
Annual Cost per $1,000:	**$18.16**

Annualized Returns

3 Year	*-3.32%*
5 Year	*0.00%*
Inception(2/9/90)	*-1.40%*

Total Return on $10,000

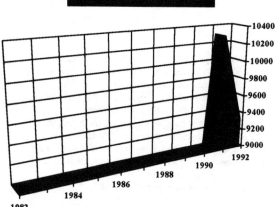

Income on $10,000 Investment

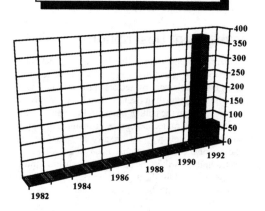

Historic Returns

	1982	1983	1984	1985	1986	1987	1988	1989	1990	1991	1992
Total Return (%)										3.05	-9.59
S and P 500 (%)	21.47	22.46	6.13	31.64	18.68	5.26	17.50	31.68	-3.20	30.40	7.92
Dividend Yield										3.98	0.79
Income on $10,000 ($)										381	72

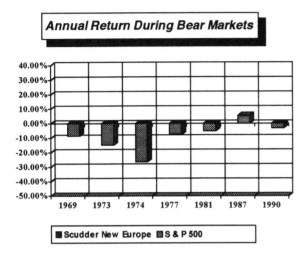

Annual Return During Bear Markets

■ Scudder New Europe ▨ S & P 500

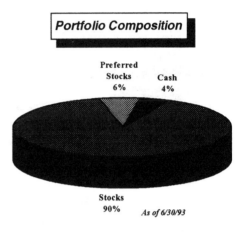

Portfolio Composition

Preferred Stocks 6%   Cash 4%

Stocks 90%   *As of 6/30/93*

Investment Description

Scudder New Europe fund has the wind to its back. The fund is sailing, as small cap European stocks begin to soar. Falling European interest rates have finally ignited the market, after a long-awaited and financially painful hibernation. While the fund's three-year total return is less than spectacular, year-to-date it's been an exceptional performer. And the best is yet to come. Small cap stocks have been strong in other countries, including the United States, and European issues should be playing catch-up in the months and years to come. Fundamentally, Europe itself is poised for a bull market as interest rates decline and pro-business sentiment

grows in a region slowly abandoning large government social programs and state-owned corporations. Privatization, lower borrowing costs and potentially large Eastern markets should fuel a long-term bull market in Europe in the years to come. Scudder's large bet on French and Germany stocks should continue to fare well, along with its exposure to weaker, more market-sensitive economies like Greece and Spain. A healthy discount to NAV is the icing on the cake, making Scudder New Europe fund one of the best buys in the overseas fund category.

Suitability

Age 55 and under	*A-*
Age 55 to 70	*B*
Age 70+	*C*

Inception Date: 2/9/90

Manager Tenure: 1990

Telephone: (800) 225-2470

Minimum Intial Investment: None

Direct Deposit: No

SunAmerica Balanced Assets

Investment Ratings

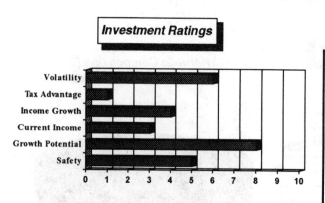

Investment Statistics

Initial Sales Charge: **None**
5% declining deferred charge

Annual Cost per $1,000:   **$18.59**

Annualized Returns

3 Year	*11.68%*	
5 Year	*10.31%*	
Inception(1/29/85)	*12.27%*	

Total Return on $10,000

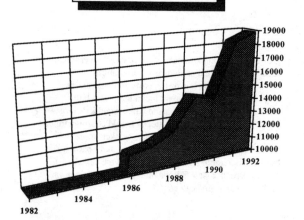

Income on $10,000 Investment

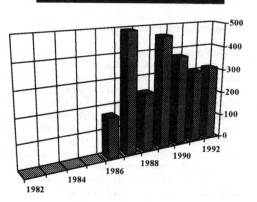

Historic Returns

	1982	1983	1984	1985	1986	1987	1988	1989	1990	1991	1992
Total Return (%)					13.15	2.79	6.51	18.44	-2.34	27.32	3.46
S and P 500 (%)	21.47	22.46	6.13	31.64	18.68	5.26	17.50	31.68	-3.20	30.40	7.92
Dividend Yield					1.67	4.43	2.18	4.02	2.84	2.42	0.02
Income on $10,000 ($)					167	493	239	462	373	302	311

Annual Return During Bear Markets

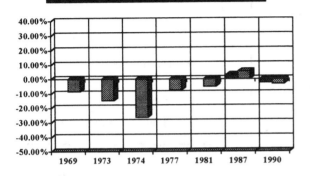

1969	1973	1974	1977	1981	1987	1990

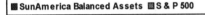

■ SunAmerica Balanced Assets ▨ S & P 500

Portfolio Composition

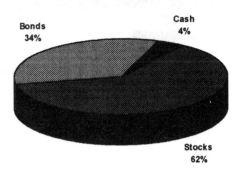

Bonds
34%

Cash
4%

Stocks
62%

As of 6/30/93

Investment Description

There's a new sheriff in town at SunAmerica Balanced Assets fund. Stan Feeley, chief investment officer at SunAmerica, now heads up the group's flagship conservative equity fund. Gone is the consistent underperformance and hodge-podge of investment strategies that led the fund into mutual fund purgatory for the past few years. Feeley has proven his ability at Delaware fund (1998 through 1991), using his top-down approach to investing to churn out superior returns during his tenure there. Focusing on economic themes, Feeley selects sectors that he feels will outperform the market for a variety of fundamental reasons and then chooses stocks with the best appreciation potential from the group. His shift from consumer stocks to cyclicals, for example, helped Balanced Assets return top-notch gains to shareholders during the first three-quarters of 1993. The bond portion of the fund also fared well as interest rates declined during the year. The jury may be out on the fund's reliability because of the lack of a long-term track record. With Feeley at the helm, given his performance at Delaware and returns so far from his new charge, critics should give the SunAmerica Balanced Assets two thumbs up when the dust has finally cleared.

Suitability

Age 55 and under	*A-*
Age 55 to 70	*A-*
Age 70+	*B+*

Inception Date: 1/29/85

Manager Tenure: 1992

Telephone: (800) 858-8850

Minimum Initial Investment: $500.00

Direct Deposit: No

Templeton Developing Markets

Investment Ratings

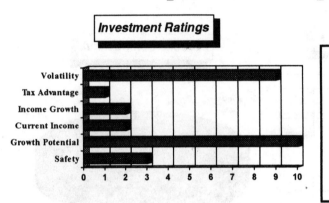

Investment Statistics

Initial Sales Charge:	**5.75%**
Annual Cost per $1,000:	**$33.01**

Annualized Returns
3 Year
5 Year
Inception(10/17/91)   *5.15%*

Total Return on $10,000

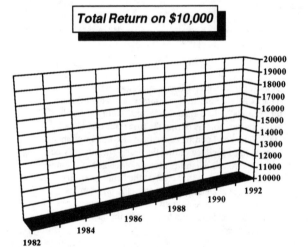

Income on $10,000 Investment

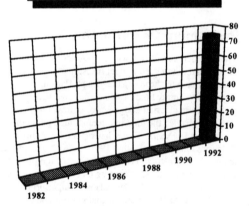

Historic Returns

	1982	1983	1984	1985	1986	1987	1988	1989	1990	1991	1992
Total Return (%)											-9.75
S and P 500 (%)	21.47	22.46	6.13	31.64	18.68	5.26	17.50	31.68	-3.20	30.40	7.92
Dividend Yield											0.08
Income on $10,000 ($)											75

Annual Return During Bear Markets

| | 40.00% |
| 30.00% |
| 20.00% |
| 10.00% |
| 0.00% |
| -10.00% |
| -20.00% |
| -30.00% |
| -40.00% |
| -50.00% |

1969   1973   1974   1977   1981   1987   1990

■ Templeton Emerging Markets   ▧ S & P 500

Portfolio Composition

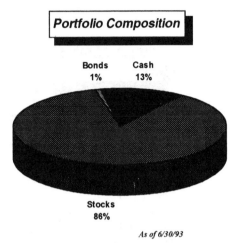

Bonds 1%   Cash 13%

Stocks 86%

As of 6/30/93

Investment Description

Templeton Developing Markets fund is an iconoclast amongst international funds. While most overseas mutual funds extol the virtues of international diversification, Developing Markets focuses solely on an often overlooked and extremely lucrative niche-- developing countries. You won't find any Japanese or British blue chips in this portfolio. Some of the largest holdings include Philippine Long Distance Telephone, Telefonos de Mexico and Malaysian International Shipping, hardly household names. The fund also tends to focus its energies where it sees value. The charter

specifically states that geographic diversification is not a primary goal. Concentrating on a few select groups resulted in its up and downs. A large position in Turkey hurt it in 1992 but fueled a recovery in 1993, along with Brazilian holdings. If Templeton's closed-end fund is any indicator of this sister fund's potential, investors should be well-rewarded in future years. While Templeton Developing Markets may not be for everyone, patient investors should be rewarded as global growth shifts to nimbler, developing economies.

Suitability

Age 55 and under	*A*
Age 55 to 70	*B+*
Age 70+	*B-*

Inception Date: 10/17/91

Manager Tenure: 1991

Telephone: (800) 237-0738

Minimum Initial Investment: $100.00

Direct Deposit: Yes

Templeton Foreign

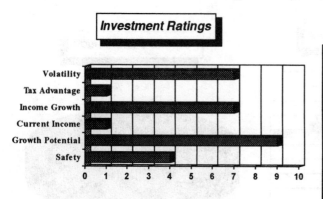

Investment Ratings

Investment Statistics

Initial Sales Charge:	**5.75%**
Annual Cost per $1,000:	**$20.39**

Annualized Returns

3 Year	**3.09%**
5 Year	**11.59%**
10 Year	**15.90%**

Total Return on $10,000

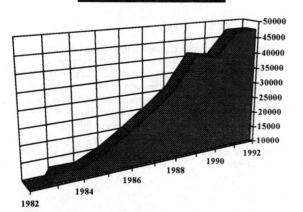

Income on $10,000 Investment

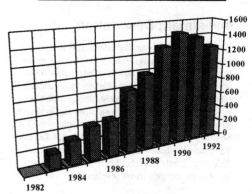

Historic Returns

	1982	1983	1984	1985	1986	1987	1988	1989	1990	1991	1992
Total Return (%)		36.51	-1.19	26.89	28.77	24.75	22.00	30.54	-3.01	18.25	0.16
S and P 500 (%)	21.47	22.46	6.13	31.64	18.68	5.26	17.50	31.68	-3.20	30.40	7.92
Dividend Yield		1.91	2.24	3.27	2.74	3.76	3.57	3.90	3.34	3.29	0.66
Income on $10,000 ($)		188	300	433	460	815	978	1,306	1,462	1,391	1,255

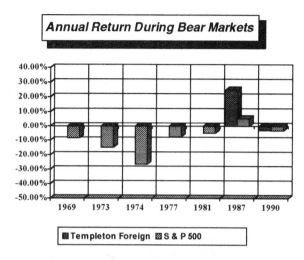

Annual Return During Bear Markets

Templeton Foreign ⬛ S & P 500

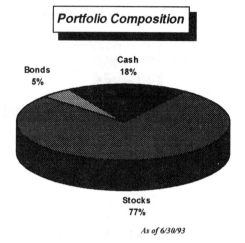

Portfolio Composition

Cash 18%

Bonds 5%

Stocks 77%

As of 6/30/93

Investment Description

Sometimes caution has a price, the Templeton Foreign fund learned during 1992. Staunchly value-driven, as are all Templeton offerings, this fund missed the big rally in Japan and took a beating in Europe. Fortunately for the fund, most shareholders aren't concerned. Templeton has returned almost 16% a year for the past 10 years, one of the best performance records of any foreign fund. Manager Mark Holowesko seems to be riding out the storm in hopes of a better 1993. Most of the positons in Europe, for example, are intact, as are non-Japanese Pacific Rim holdings. Unlike its Developing Markets sibling, Templeton Foreign favors large cap stocks in established countries. Nestle, British Airways and Bayer are among the household names held by Holowesko. While the fund might not have the sizzle of some its go-go competitors, Templeton investors are almost always happier and wealthier, when bear markets hit. A low turnover and expense ratio add to its attractiveness. Overseas investing couldn't be easier, safer or more lucrative.

Suitability

Age 55 and under	*A*
Age 55 to 70	*B+*
Age 70+	*B-*

Inception Date: 10/5/82

Manager Tenure: 1987

Telephone: (800) 237-0738

Minimum Initial Investment: $100.00

Direct Deposit: Yes

Vanguard World International Growth

Investment Ratings

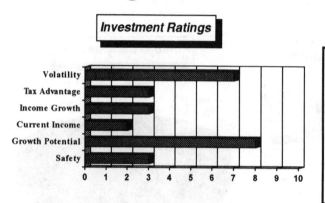

Investment Statistics

Initial Sales Charge:	**None**
Annual Cost per $1,000:	**$8.08**

Annualized Returns

3 Year	*-0.23%*
5 Year	*5.93%*
10 Year	*15.45%*

Total Return on $10,000

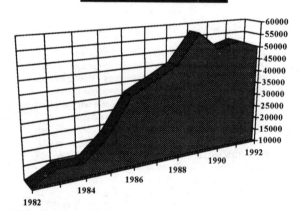

Income on $10,000 Investment

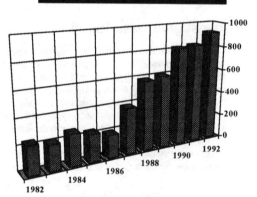

Historic Returns

	1982	1983	1984	1985	1986	1987	1988	1989	1990	1991	1992
Total Return (%)	5.25	43.06	-1.02	56.96	56.71	12.48	11.61	24.76	-12.05	4.74	-5.79
S and P 500 (%)	21.47	22.46	6.13	31.64	18.68	5.26	17.50	31.68	-3.20	30.40	7.92
Dividend Yield	2.31	2.03	1.80	1.61	0.90	1.15	1.55	1.46	1.61	1.89	2.06
Income on $10,000 ($)	231	208	259	226	191	380	578	598	815	827	925

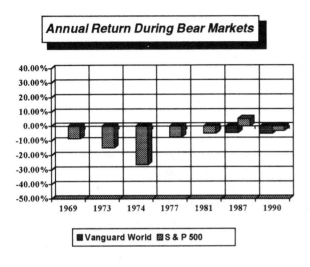

Annual Return During Bear Markets

40.00%
30.00%
20.00%
10.00%
0.00%
-10.00%
-20.00%
-30.00%
-40.00%
-50.00%

1969   1973   1974   1977   1981   1987   1990

■ Vanguard World ▨ S & P 500

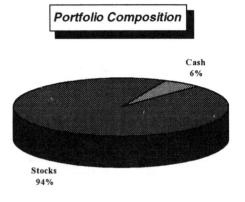

Portfolio Composition

Cash
6%

Stocks
94%

As of 6/30/93

Investment Description

Vanguard World International fund seems to have been hibernating the past few years. After returning astonishing returns in the mid-1980s, the fund slipped into a slumber for the rest of the decade. Its success and failure mimic that of the Japanese market, which powered the ascent in the 1980s and contributed to the fund's near collapse more recently. But things are changing. Manager Richard Foulkes has been looking to Europe and non-Japanese Pacific Rim countries more recently, looking for value difficult to come by in Japan lately. While retaining a decent exposure to Japan, and

participating in its recent rally, Foulkes hopes to benefit from falling European interest rates by investing in interest-sensitive and small cap stocks, and from double-digit growth rates in Pacific countries other than Japan. So far, the strategy looks promising, as both markets continue to perform well. Vanguard's low expense ratios should help this fund gain back some of the ground lost during the early part of the decade. A longer-term investor should fare quite well in this fund as it continues to scour the globe for opportunity.

Suitability

Age 55 and under	*B+*
Age 55 to 70	*B*
Age 70+	*B-*

Inception Date: 9/30/81

Manager Tenure: 1981

Telephone: (800) 662-7447

Minimum Initial Investment: $3,000.00

Direct Deposit: No

279

Chapter 15

Estate Planning in the '90s

"Stop probate!" the fliers read. They had been distributed in mailboxes in the retirement community Aunt Mary had moved to last winter. A slick slide presentation and more than a few cute anecdotes convinced Aunt Mary and about half of the audience of their need for the $1,200 trust package. True, the leather-bound black binder was rather nice, and it did smell like genuine leather. But was such an expensive trust package enough? Or too much?

How estates are passed on

When someone dies and leaves his or her estate, or collection of worldly goods and assets, it must go through some legal process by which the title transfers from the deceased owner into someone else's name.

A whole industry has been built on facilitating this process. Judges, lawyers, probate clerks, county offices and a variety of other people earn a living solely from transferring property as a result of settling an estate. The process may vary, depending on how carefully the person leaving the property planned for his or her death.

First, for those who die intestate—not leaving a will or any other record of how they would like their possessions divided—their property is taken care of according to a series of rules laid down

over the years. Usually a spouse, and then family have first claim. But the ultimate decision is left up to a judge.

If a will is involved, the process is quite different. A will is a document an individual draws up, identifying how his or her property should be disposed of upon death. The will is not a binding document. It only expresses the person's wishes. A court makes the final determination through a process called *probate*. Assets pass through probate to be transferred from the deceased person's estate into someone else's name. Again, a judge makes the final determination.

Although most judges will accede to the wishes expressed in the will, this may not always be the case. Wills can be contested. Someone can claim that the person writing the will was not competent at the time the will was written, or they may contend that the deceased was coerced into writing it. Contesting a will can tie up an estate for years.

The third way of transferring assets is through *joint tenancy* or *community property*. By adding the name of a person to an asset, it can be specified that upon death of one individual, the other owns the property. This is called the *right of survivorship*. While anybody can be added in a joint tenancy agreement, only spouses can be listed as holding community property. Another problem with joint tenancy is that the individual added to the asset could then claim half the property before the other person dies. Or his or her creditors could attach half of the property.

The fourth and final method of transferring property is through a *living trust*. A living trust allows the beneficiaries to take title of the property without going through probate. But, unlike joint tenancy, it doesn't give them title to the assets until the *trustor*, the person making the trust, is deceased.

The avoidance of probate is important because of the fees involved. Probate attorneys charge a percentage of assets to settle an estate. Court costs and other administrative fees add more to the bill. In short, probate can be expensive. And if the assets are illiquid, like real estate, they may have to be sold at fire sale prices to raise money for fees.

No matter what, estate taxes can add additional expense to larger estates. Often running as high as 55 percent on very large estates, these taxes can take a large chunk out of a bequest. Since estate size is determined by value not including any debt, real estate and business holdings are especially susceptible. For example, if a person with $1 million worth of property owes $800,000 worth of mortgages on that property, he would pay estate taxes on the full $1 million. The cost of settling an estate could be the largest one-time tax a person will ever pay.

Fortunately, there are several methods of reducing the cost of passing on an estate.

Estate planning tools

From the simple to the sophisticated, following are several strategies that can insure a smooth transition from you to your heirs.

A simple will. It's surprising how many people don't have even the simplest of estate planning tools, the will. A will written in your own handwriting or drawn up by an attorney suffices in most states. Most attorneys charge only a nominal fee, $50 or so. Wills not only divide your estate but also convey any other wishes, such as disposition of personal property and rearing of children. A will should be an essential part of even the most complicated estate, and should accompany even the most sophisticated trusts.

All assets solely in the owner's name will pass through probate and be disposed of according to the instructions in the will, assuming the court approves. If the assets total less than a given amount, usually around $60,000, many states allow a simplified procedure that bypasses probate, avoiding many of the fees associated with it. Often called "poor man's probate," it only applies to smaller, simpler estates where no one is contesting the will. Real property, such as real estate, must always be probated.

Joint tenancy. The most common, but often ill-advised, method of estate planning is the use of joint tenancy with rights of survivorship. By adding a name of a spouse, child or relative, the owner of the asset hopes to avoid probate costs on those assets. While it does avoid probate, it creates a host of other problems. For example:

- Adding a name to an account as a joint tenant is a gift. If the estate is subject to gift tax, this gift could reduce the size of the estate tax credit upon death.

- Since another party now owns half of the property legally, creditors can attach that property in the event of a loan default or lawsuit.

- When adding a spouse as a joint tenant, only half of the property's cost basis is adjusted upon death of one of the spouses. The other half remains at the original cost.

While better than single ownership, and sometimes essential for the sake of cost, there are better ways to protect assets from probate and estate taxes, not to mention capital gains taxes.

Community property. In those states that allow it, community property is an excellent way for married couples to hold assets. When someone dies, his or her assets adjust up in cost for tax purposes as of the day of death. In other words, if Uncle Harry bought IBM at $5 a share in 1951 and it's worth $50 a share the day he dies, his beneficiary records his cost as $50 a share. If his nephew sells the stock for $50 a share, he pays no capital gains. On the other hand, if Uncle Harry put his nephew's name on the stock when it was at $25 a share, he would in effect be giving his nephew half of the stock at $25 a share. When his nephew sold the stock after he inherited it, half would have a cost of $50 a share and the other half $25 a share, so he'd pay capital gains on half of it.

The same is true of spouses. With a community property agreement, all the assets would adjust up when one spouse dies, regardless of the date acquired. Community property agreements can be found at stationery stores or drawn up by an attorney. They're also present in most living trusts.

Living trusts. At one time only a tool of the wealthy, intense marketing by attorneys has made *living trust* a household word. A trust avoids probate and the fees involved. But it doesn't avoid all fees—attorneys may charge for administering the trust. Most trusts also include *powers of attorney, pour over wills* (in case some property is not included in the trust), and community property agreements.

A living trust also offers tremendous benefits while the trustor (person making the trust) is alive, as well. If the trustor is incapacitated, the trust provides for the smooth transition to another trustee, chosen by the trustor in advance, to take over affairs. For a smaller estate, a living trust may not be necessary, especially if there's only one beneficiary and no real estate involved. A married couple, for example, who does not own a home, has no immediate relatives and relatively few assets, most of which are liquid, may not need a trust. Powers of attorney and a community property agreement may suffice.

Anyone with a larger estate and more beneficiaries should consider a living trust. But trusts can differ greatly, depending on your needs.

Advanced estate planning tools

For anyone with over $600,000 in assets, more advanced versions of the living trust, along with other strategies, might be worth looking at. For example:

The A-B trust. Married couples have an unlimited estate tax exemption. In other words, one spouse can pass an unlimited amount of assets to another spouse without estate tax. The same spouse can only pass $600,000 worth of assets to a child or other heir without paying estate taxes. So if a husband leaves a $1.2 million estate to his wife, who then leaves it to their child, the child will pay estate taxes on about $600,000—roughly $192,000 in taxes. If the husband and wife set up an A-B trust, the child will pay no estate taxes after the second spouse's death. A savings of $192,000.

Here's how it works: The couples' assets are split upon the first death. So when the husband dies, $600,000 goes into the A trust, which is the wife's property, and $600,000 goes into the B trust, which was the husband's property. The B trust is somewhat restricted in that usually only interest and up to 5 percent of the principal can be taken out annually. Anything more than that can be withdrawn for living expenses, housing or education. Adding a C trust raises the credit even higher.

Charitable trusts. More charities are promoting this type of trust aggressively, for obvious reasons. A charitable trust is a gift to charity from which you get to keep income during a certain period of time. After that, the money reverts to the charity named.

There are two big differences between the living trust and the charitable trust. First, the living trust is *revocable*. It can be changed, modified or canceled at any time before death without tax ramifications. The charitable trust is *irrevocable*. It can never be changed. Secondly, because of the irrevocable nature, charitable trust contributors lose control of their assets in the trust. The management of the trust is limited.

There are two types of charitable trusts: the *charitable remainder trust* and the *charitable income trust*. The first pays a fixed rate of income to those

who donate for a fixed period. The second gives the income to a charity for a fixed period of time with the remainder reverting to a beneficiary at the end of that time. The donor gets to take a write-off for the donation, based on an annuity table. The longer the income is paid, the smaller the write-off.

One big advantage of the charitable trust is that appreciated property can be donated and capital gains avoided. For example, a couple has an estate of $2 million, $800,000 of it in raw land they purchased 20 years ago for $100,000. They want to sell the land to a developer and convert the proceeds into tax-free bonds to raise their retirement income. They sell, pay $196,000 in taxes and invest the rest in tax-free bonds earning $27,720 a year. When they die in 20 years, they leave $1,704,000 to their nephew, on which he pays $157,280 in estate taxes, leaving $1,546,720.

Had the couple put the land in a charitable trust, it would have generated no capital gains. The $800,000 could then be converted to municipal bonds, producing $44,000 a year in income, or $16,280 more a year in tax-free income. If the couple were 60 years old at the time of the donation, they would have received an immediate tax deduction of $204,072 based on the value of their remainder estate. And their nephew would pay no estate taxes and would receive $1.2 million. Besides the deduction of $204,072 received immediately, the couple would earn $325,600 more income over a 20-year period.

As you can see, charitable trusts can save thousands of dollars at little expense to heirs in the right situations.

Gifting programs. Any individual can give any other person $10,000 a year and not be subject to gift-tax consequences. A father can give a son $10,000, a daughter-in-law $10,000, and the grandchildren each $10,000. It can be a direct gift, or a gift to a trust for their benefit. His wife can also give $10,000 to each.

As you can see, a person can give away a lot of money. Why would they? To avoid estate taxes, if the estate is large enough. Money given away no longer belongs to an estate. And the gift doesn't have to be money.

For example, an illiquid asset can be given away in portions. Let's say a father owns a business that's the bulk of his estate. The business is worth $3 million and he already has an A-B trust. If he dies, the business would have to be sold at a fire sale price to raise the money to pay the estate taxes. The son, who wants to take over the business, could not raise that kind of money. The father wants to transfer the business to his only son before he passes away. Breaking up the company into shares, the father gives to his son, $10,000 worth of shares a year. He also gives $10,000 worth of shares to his daughter-in-law and each of the two grandchildren. Over the course of a few years, he reduces his ownership enough to avoid estate taxes. Gifting offers powerful alternative to individuals who face high estate taxes.

Life insurance. After exhausting or passing over all other strategies, life insurance offers a way of paying pennies on the dollar for your estate taxes. For example, if estate taxes are estimated to be approximately $400,000, purchase a life insurance policy with a face value of $400,000. If you're under 60, the cost will be low compared to paying the

taxes. So if the premiums amount to a total of $60,000 over seven years, with the policy being "paid up" then, you will have paid $60,000 in advance for what would amount to $400,000 in estate taxes in the future.

Remember to account for growth in your estate. There's also another catch. The ownership of the policy can't be in your own name. If it is, the value of the policy upon death counts as part of the estate, defeating the whole purpose in setting it up. There are two options. The first is to have a beneficiary buy the policy and gift them the premiums to pay for it. The only drawback is that the beneficiary could cash the policy in and spend the money.

The second alternative is to use an irrevocable life insurance trust. Then, the trust purchases the insurance with premiums you put in it as a gift. The proceeds can only be used to pay estate taxes, with any amount left over going to other beneficiaries. Like the charitable remainder trust, you can never have access to the money or else the trust could be disallowed after your death, and estate taxes assessed against the proceeds. Either way, life insurance can save thousands of dollars in unavoidable taxes.

Estate taxes are constantly changing. If you anticipate a large estate upon your death, you really need to consult a competent estate attorney. There are several even more complicated strategies, such as family limited partnerships and private foundations that may be applicable to your particular situation. If you're single with more than $600,000 in your estate or married with more than $1.2 million, seek out a competent, estate planning specialist.

Chapter 16

Safeguarding Against Catastrophic Risk

Becoming disabled is one of the greatest fears of growing older. Dehabilitating diseases, such as Alzheimer's, can devastate families both emotionally and financially in a very short time. A lifetime's worth of savings can be used up in a matter of months by soaring health care costs.

While this fear haunts anyone who faces retirement, surprisingly few people take any precautions against this risk. Improved medical techniques drastically increase the odds of current retirees spending at least some time in a convalescent home or other care facility. No one can afford to overlook planning for this type of emergency.

What happens when you're disabled?

It might begin with forgetfulness or a temporary loss of memory. Or a sudden catastrophe, like a stroke. Regardless of the cause, hundreds of thousands of retired Americans discover they are unable to care for themselves every year. Some are fortunate enough to have family members to help out, but others are forced to find alternative care and to pay for it out of personal savings or other sources.

But the other sources can be limited. Medicare applies only to medical-related treatment, not custodial care. Medicaid, which covers custodial care, is needs-based. In other words, to qualify, you must only have a minimal amount of money, usually around $2,000, before Medicaid will pay the bills. Anything above that must be spent before Medicaid picks up the tab.

With nursing home bills often topping $5,000 a month or more for advanced care, exhausting a life savings can take only a few years—or even months. A spouse can be left destitute and children without an inheritance. Medicaid allows a spouse to keep up to $60,000 while children aren't allow anything. Overall, the effect of a catastrophic illness not only affects the persons afflicted, but their families as well.

- Any assets above $66,480 left to one spouse, or $2,000 for a single person, must be spent down to qualify for Medicaid.

- Medicaid will look back 30 months and count any gift made to children or relatives as assets, which must be used for nursing home care. Even if the gift was legitimate, until that amount is spent, Medicaid won't pay any expenses.

- Although a home is exempt initially for the spouse and minor, disabled or blind child, a lien can be placed against it after the second spouse's death, leaving nothing for heirs. However, in certain cases, adult children and siblings may live in the house, keeping it exempt.

- Jointly held assets are considered owned by the Medicaid recipient unless the other party can prove they contributed to the asset.

Avoiding these catastrophes requires careful planning in the early years of retirement.

Medicaid planning

The only way to prevent a serious illness from becoming a financial catastrophe as well is through good long-term planning. The goal is to position your assets in a way that minimizes out-of-pocket costs for care, if the need should ever arise.

Medicaid is not based on age at all, unlike Medicare, but it does demand certain requirements be met. All Medicaid applications consider age, disability, assets and income. The applicant must be either over 65 *or* physically or mentally disabled or blind. Assets and income requirements vary from state to state. Typically, applicants may only have a maximum of $2,000 in assets and $900 in income. If married, the spouse is allowed to keep up to $66,480 in assets and $1,662 per year in spousal income. Several assets are also exempt from being counted:

- A home
- One automobile
- Insurance cash value up to $1,500
- Burial contracts and plots
- Household belongings
- Inaccessible funds such as immediate annuities or certain trusts

Basically, Medicaid planning involves moving as much as possible into the exempt assets. Financially speaking, this may not be wise until it is obvious that someone will need special care. Strategies that might immediately precede an application for Medicaid are:

- Paying off a home loan or doing home renovation
- Purchasing a new car
- Purchasing burial plots or contracts
- Converting assets into income with an annuity

Some long-term planning, however, can be started at any time:

- Gifting assets to children or grandchildren (*must* be done 30 months before applying for Medicaid).
- Setting up a durable power of attorney, allowing others to conduct business for you. Spouses should have one for each other and perhaps elect a third person in case both are incapacitated. Be careful: Powers of attorney can be used even if you're *not* incapacitated.
- Setting up a Medicaid trust.
- Setting up an additional trust provision in your living trust—coming into effect in the event of incapacity.
- Purchasing long-term health care insurance.

The first three strategies are relatively straightforward. The last three deserve further explanation.

The Medicaid trust

Assets are exempt for Medicaid purposes *if they're not accessible.* This is the whole purpose of the Medicaid trust. By taking assets and putting them into a trust, and only allowing income to be drawn, the assets can become exempt. The trust must meet several requirements.

- It must be irrevocable. It can never be changed once in place. If it is revocable, it would not qualify.

- The person establishing the trust or benefiting from it can't have access to the principal. If he or she does, the amount will count in calculating Medicaid eligibility.

- The trustee or spouse can't be the individual setting up the trust, nor can either be able to withdraw funds for their own use.

Medicaid trusts are extremely complicated and should not be attempted without legal advice.

Modifying a living trust

Rather than creating a separate trust, many people opt for modifying a revocable living trust by adding a clause that causes the trust to become irrevocable and only pay interest in the event of incompetence of either spouse.

Medicaid would not begin paying until 30 months after the trust became irrevocable, but at least the amount paid would be limited to 30 months of care, saving some of the assets for heirs. The trust would provide for principal payments during those 30 months only.

Long-term health care insurance

Insurance companies have only recently begun to offer long-term care insurance. While the first policies were riddled with exclusions and fine print, many newer versions offer a good degree of protection, although the premiums can be quite high, especially if you're older. Limiting coverage to 30 months or until Medicaid cuts in can be one way to reduce the premiums paid. Whether you are shopping for a stop-gap measure or a permanent solution, here's what to look for:

What's covered and what's not? Does it cover home care? Is only skilled care covered or does intermediate care qualify also? Does it exclude certain conditions such as Alzheimer's (the number-one cause of nursing home confinement), Parkinson's disease and other nervous disorders? Are pre-existing conditions excluded? Look for a policy that covers all levels of care, including home care, and does not include a time limitation on pre-existing conditions.

Is there a benefit limit? Most policies will limit benefits, but in different ways. Some not only have a cap on total spending but also pay only part of costs, usually 80 percent to 90 percent. Most cover only a limited length of stay. The longer the benefit period, the larger the premium. As a stop-gap measure used in conjunction with a trust, 30 months is the longest benefit period needed. Most nursing home stays are shorter. Some policies raise benefit levels to keep up with inflation, an important feature for younger buyers.

Is there a waiting period? A waiting period of 10 days to 100 days is not uncommon. This period of time must pass before benefits begin. Since Medicare only covers skilled care and medical-related care, you can't count on it to pay for the initial period not covered by insurance. Shorter waiting periods are better, but also raise premiums.

Does the policy require prior hospitalization? Some companies require prior hospitalization before paying benefits. Since most people enter nursing homes without going to a hospital first, policies requiring this should be avoided. Some will waive this requirement for a higher premium, while others have no requirement at all.

Is the policy cancelable, and can premiums be raises? If the policy can be canceled at any time by the insurance company, it may not be worth the paper it's written on or the premiums paid. The same is true if the premiums increase as sickness develops. If increases are allowed, the amount should be limited and the increases applied to everyone holding policies, rather than individuals who become ill. Some even offer a waiver of premiums when the benefits begin being paid, eliminating additional premiums while the policyholder is in a nursing home.

How safe is the insurance company? Look at an insurance company's rating and portfolio just as you would for any other insurance investment. Review Chapter 7 for details.

Many annuities and life insurance products now offer features designed especially for emergencies such as nursing home confinements. Some life insurance policies allow the owner to dip into the value of the policy if confined to a nursing home. Several annuities allow the withdrawal of money without penalty in the case of disability. Look for these features when you're shopping for annuities and life insurance.

This chapter provides a mere outline of information about catastrophic care, and should in no way be used as the sole basis of planning. An attorney specializing in estate planning or long-term health care matters should be consulted, since laws often change. Specific planning with the help of an expert may not eliminate all the risks of long-term confinement, but can ease the transition both financially and emotionally.

We all hope we never have to deal with a catastrophic illness, but you really can't afford *not* to include long-term health care planning in your overall retirement plan.

Chapter 17

And What About Uncle Sam?

"The income tax has made more liars out of the American people than golf has."

—Will Rogers

It is an American habit to complain about taxes. We grimace around April, promise devoutly never to elect an incumbent again, and then go about our business.

This attitude is especially true after retirement. After all, why bother taking action when taxes go down after retirement anyway? Americans are retiring younger and wealthier than ever before, and, accordingly, are bearing an increasingly larger percentage of the tax burden. The combination of federal, state and local taxes can take up to 50 percent of retirement income in some states. All this on a fixed-income.

Tax planning has become an important part of any retirement plan. Retirees have some of the greatest flexibility in lowering their taxes. Yet, they're also least likely to take such tax planning seriously.

How much is too much?

Most people, if asked how much their tax rate is, make a face and say that it's high, regardless of the percentage it might be. Tax planning can help individuals in any tax bracket, but many strategies apply only to those in higher brackets. It's not very hard to be in a high bracket, however. For 1992 federal taxes only, the following rates apply to taxable income (income after deductions have been taken out, or line 37 on your tax return).

Single:

$0 to $21,450	15%
$21,450 to $51,900	28%
$51,900+	31%

Married filing jointly:

$0 - $35,800	15%
$35,800 - $86,500	28%
$86,500+	31%

One-half of Social Security benefits are taxable if you're single and earning over $25,000, or married and filing jointly, and earning more than $32,000. And 85 percent of benefits are taxed if you're earning $34,000, or $44,000 if married and filing jointly.

These rates are likely to rise dramatically in the next few years. Almost everyone in the 28-percent or higher bracket can benefit from tax planning. Those in lower brackets have less to gain, but should have a tax plan in place, especially if there are pending capital gains from the sale of assets. The following are some strategies that may help reduce your tax bill.

1. Convert taxable income
to tax-free

Tax-free bonds and funds are one of the few truly tax-free investments left after the numerous tax reform bills passed during the 1980s. These municipal bonds benefit most of those paying 28 percent or more in tax, but can also make sense to investors in lower brackets, if rates are high enough compared to taxable investment equivalents.

Bonds are available in almost any term from six months to 40 years, some offering state tax exemptions in the state of issue. A municipal bond paying 5.5 percent has a taxable equivalent yield of 7.64 percent to someone in a 28-percent bracket. An investor would have to earn 7.64 percent on a taxable investment to put as much money in their pocket as 5.5-percent tax-free. This doesn't take into account the advantage of state tax exemption on some bonds.

The best strategy, in most cases, is to allow your taxable income to come close to the top end of the 15-percent bracket and then convert the remaining income to tax-free. For example, a married couple has annual income of $20,000 from pensions, $12,000 in Social Security, $16,000 from CDs and $5,000 from T-bills. Their taxable income, after deductions, is $40,000. Since they only pay taxes of 28 percent on the amount over $35,800 (in other words the tax rate is not retroactive to every dollar earned), they would do best to earn $35,800 in taxable income and the remainder in tax-free income. By converting $4,200 of their CD income to tax-free bonds, this is accomplished.

2. Tax deferral

Another strategy for reducing your tax bills is to use annuities to defer taxes. Although the interest on annuity income is eventually taxed, controlling the timing of declaring the taxes is an advantage to the investor.

For example, if a tax-deferred annuity is purchased a few years before retirement, the income tax won't be paid during the last few income-earning years. If, after retirement, the investor's income level drops, the money can be withdrawn in small enough amounts to avoid additional taxation. The investor can control the amount withdrawn, creating a tax-planning advantage.

Mutual funds purchased within an annuity produces benefits unavailable in regular taxable funds. These variable annuities defer all income and capital gains payments from funds until they're withdrawn. Since bond funds and conservative stock funds often surprise shareholders with large capital gains in good years, deferring these gains helps eliminate unexpected income.

Tax-deferred annuities are the only investments in this book that do not generate 1099s. The income isn't reported. Unrecorded income isn't counted when calculating Social Security tax. While even tax-free municipal income counts as income toward the $25,000 or $32,000 mark where Social Security is taxed, annuity interest doesn't.

3. Real estate

While many retired homeowners are proud to say that their home is completely paid off, from a tax standpoint, they may have nothing to boast about. Consider this: A fixed-rate home loan (15-year loan) found in many parts of the country costs 6.75 percent. All the interest can be deducted from income tax. A person paying 42 percent in combined taxes, in a high-tax state like

California, really only pays 3.92 percent to borrow that money after considering the taxes saved. If he or she can earn more than 3.92 percent tax-free, having the mortgage is better than having the house paid off. With taxes rising, the advantage is even greater.

4. *Maximizing your write-offs*

It's amazing how few people take full advantage of all the deductions they can claim on income tax. Here are a few examples:

- **Amortization of premium on taxable bonds.** A bond bought at more than par value can be written off, a portion each year, as it nears maturity.

- **Gifts of appreciated assets.** Rather than writing a check to your favorite charity, give an appreciated asset, such as a stock. Not only do you get to deduct the full market value, but there is no long-term capital gains, a double benefit.

- **Fees for safe deposit boxes.** These are considered part of investment-related expenses

- **Retirement trustee fees.** Rather than having them taken from your IRA account, pay them separately and it's fully deductible.

- **Penalties on early withdrawals of CDs.** These are netted against the interest income.

- **Losses in worthless securities.** Remember the sure thing your neighbor convinced you to buy into 10 years ago? If it can be shown to have no recognizable value, it could be deemed worthless.

5. *Retirement plans*

Many people continue to work after retirement, as consultants or in part-time businesses. Any income produced from being self-employed is eligible for retirement plan deductions. A combined business retirement plan can allow you to deduct up to 25 percent of your income. The tax break isn't the only benefit—the earnings also grow tax-deferred, much like an IRA. A SEP IRA allows a self-employed individual to deduct up to 15 percent of his or her income for the retirement plan, as does a profit-sharing plan. A profit-sharing plan combined with a pension plan (or money purchase plan) allows up to 25-percent deductions. Each has certain rules and limitations worth examining before investing.

6. *Deferring income*

Choosing to take income at a later time may not sound like much of a strategy, but it does keep more money in you hands for a longer period. A CD, for example, set up to pay interest in January rather than December, gives the investor an extra year before taxes on that interest are due. The same is true of income from a job. Many companies offer salary deferral plans, especially to those close to retirement. A dollar deferred may not be a dollar saved, but it sure feels good to keep that dollar out of Uncle Sam's hands for an extra year.

7. *Lumping expenses and income*

Rather than taking profits one year on a stock, and losses on another the following year, lump them together to offset one another. Another example is custodial fees: Pay last year's and this year's in January, maximizing your deduction. This strategy is especially

100 Safest Investments for Retirement

useful for deductions only allowed on a certain percentage of your income, which is just about anything appearing on your Schedule A.

8. Gifting

Giving a gift is not only good for the heart, but also for the pocketbook. Several charitable strategies have already been discussed.

Family gifts are another area that can benefit taxpayers. Rather than promising to pay for a child's or grandchild's college education, *gift* them the money. A Uniform Transfer to Minors Act account (also known as UGMA, or Uniform Gift to Minors Act) cannot only be used to accumulate college tuition, but to avoid taxes, too. The first $500 of income from this type of account is tax-free at any age. The next $700 is taxed at the child's rate.

Using stocks or stock funds for younger children is often wisest, while zero coupon bonds and balanced funds work best for older children. When the child turns 14, the income is taxed at the ordinary income levels. So if the assets accumulate, they can then be sold and taxed at the child's lower rate after

he or she is 14. Taxes on the gains can be minimized or eliminated, depending on how much income the child has.

Remember that donors should not make themselves custodians on such accounts, since upon their death the assets will increase the value of their estate for estate tax purposes. Place a spouse, other relative or trusted friend as the custodian, unless estate taxes are not anticipated to be a problem.

9. Advanced tax planning

Other options, such as family limited partnerships, charitable trusts and private foundations, can all reduce taxes for those of you fortunate enough to have the income to warrant such planning. Find a good tax attorney or better yet, a tax attorney who also has a CPA credential. Use Chapter 3 as a start. Most advanced strategies require upfront investments but pay for themselves in the appropriate situations.

Tax planning is just as important as choosing a good investment. As the old adage goes, "a penny saved is a penny earned." Choose your advisors carefully and the results could be as lucrative as the year's best performing mutual fund.

Putting it all together

At one time, investing was relatively easy. Bank accounts were the choice for most savers, while stocks and bonds were relegated to wealthier investors. Today, investors choose from thousands of mutual funds, stocks and specialty investments that can perplex the most knowledgable investor. Add an equally bewildering tax code and probate system, and most of us are at a loss. Choosing good advisors is a good start. Having

enough knowledge to understand the advice you're being given is an important second step. This book provides a basic blueprint for a successful retirement. Now the rest is up to you.

Every investor's needs are different and individualized advice is essential. Consult a reputable advisor or feel free to contact me if you have any questions regarding this book or the topics discussed. My number is 714-240-6417.

100 Safest Investments for Retirement

100 Safest Investments for Retirement

Index

Get retirement investment advice year-round

"*Money Over 50,*" a newsletter written specifically for retired investors, offers a free six-month trial subscription to anyone purchasing a copy of *100 Safest Investments for Retirement*. Just return the coupon below to subscribe. After receiving two quarterly issues, you can choose to continue your subscription or cancel with no further obligation.

Mail the coupon below to: Phoenix Associates
                              638 Camino De Los Mares
                              Suite C-240-113
                              San Clemente, CA 92673

✂-----------------✂------------------------✂---------------------✂------------------✂----

Please begin my trial subscription to "*Money Over 50*" today!

Name: _____

Address: _____

City: _____ State_____ Zip _____